Cowboy Logic
Family Style

By Ryan M. Taylor

Author of "A Collection of Cowboy Logic"
and "Cowboy Logic Continues"

Sandhill Communications

The publisher:
Sandhill Communications
5435 13th Ave. NE
Towner, ND 58788

Illustrations by Steve Stark
Back cover and inside front cover photos by Corinne Frey Photography
Edited by Kim Deats
Designed & Printed in the United States of America
    United Printing, Bismarck, ND
First Printing, 2012
Library of Congress Control Number: 2012906985
ISBN 0-9667756-2-7

Dedication: In memory of Bud Taylor (1921-2010) and Liz Taylor (1932-2009), a rancher and a writer who made me who I am. Their good humor, love for the life they were given and commitment to family and community are a legacy for us all.

Table of Contents

Introduction .... **IX**

Chapter 1: Family Friendly **1**

Toddler tornado
Priorities
A couple days off
Sidekick
Family roadster
Proud as punch
Diet of a dad
Sleeping babies
Early exposure
The working school
Sickness and health
It's a girl!
Upfront child rearing
Rough weeks
Well dressed
The wheels on the bus
Dress for the elements
Full time father
Little ranchhands
Horsepower or human power
Daddy the draft horse
Dangerous jobs
Follow the directions
Team ranchers
Keeping up with the Jones (kids)
Climbing the walls
Big screen entertainment
Life's a circus
Color the eggs
Finding appreciation
Small concessions
This day
Roughing it
Road trip
Child's play
Nothing nice anymore
Where'd that go?
Pay it forward

Chapter 2: Generations.. **47**
Hand-me-downs
Paintings from the prairie
Treasured obstacles
Executive skills
Putting things in perspective
Life without Mom
Saving the trees
Generation motivation
Historical perspective
Words out loud
Godspeed gentle father
Hall of fame moments
Pass it on
Losing Liz Taylor
Intimate knowledge
What makes you, you

Chapter 3: Ranch Realities.. **73**
Keep or cull
Tagmanship
Gated community
Tying up
Memory missed
Haying help
Fleet prognosis fails
Calving surprises
Dead and dying wood
Turn 'em out
Let the wind blow
Stomachs of steel
Green grass sensors
Independence Day sale
Llamas on the loose
I walk the line
Hauling for home
Simple tools
PG time
A full freezer
Land man
High speed ID
Haying etiquette
Sink or swim
In crisis
Improbable situation

The hay maze
Ravages of ranch time
Rodeo ranch style
Tough fencing
Cow pie patrol
King of hay
Getting late
Planting posts
At a loss
That one paycheck

Chapter 4: Grease and Grime **117**
Monster trucks
Learning to share
Diggin' it
Plugging leaks
Demo day
Winter white
Chillin' and gellin'
Cashing in the reserves
Out of order
Four wheels or four legs
Saving gas
Waging war in the wind
Trade in value
Avoiding the mechanic
Cars in crisis
Equipped for borrowing
Cashed in clunker
Zerks in hiding
Guilty pleasures
Warranty woes
Loose rocks
Dragging chain
Giving season

Chapter 5: Community Cowboy **145**
The phone tree
Promoted to protégé
In the cards
Cowboy cameo
Super, mega, giganza shopping
Nice and neighborly
Queen for a year
Everything you need

When the going gets tough
Our sense of place
Love that lutefisk
March madness
Going to court
Water, water everywhere

Chapter 6: Going Domestic 163

Pesky varmints
Roughing it
Oh Christmas tree
Big, heavy gifts
Half finished
Don't try this at home
Unwanted guests
Heated comfort
Conservation to consumption
In the doghouse
Taylor taters
Up, up, up
Big Backyards
Oh, Tannenbaum!

Chapter 7: Taylored Technology 181

Cow chips
On the paper trail
Who am I, anyway?
Out of range
Wireless and clueless
Button bidding
Going digital
Always lost
Socially networked
The new West
Packin' the berry
Texting while tractoring
Driving with confidence

Chapter 8: All The Rest 199

Left-handed living
Poor pen pal
Wine snob
Going to the dogs
Idle time
Speed bumps
Cash, credit or crap?

Nesting season
Polo, anyone?
Poco bilingual
No-show Taylor
Daylight lost
On the ice
North to Alaska
Leisure time
Rain dancing
Cowboy Yogi
Sunday smash
The road home
Tall, skinny cowboys
Staying put
Mass transit
Let them eat steak
Mail time
Repainting the prairie
Yard pets
Vacation weather
Pairing wine and beef
Lanky Labrador
Hot sales incentives
Behold the biathlon
Puddle problems
Historical weather
Christmastime thoughts
Running
The will to endure

Post Script Tributes **243**
Meanwhile back at the ranch
Everybody's Bud
Fathers, sons and North Dakota

Introduction

It's been quite a ride, Cowboy Logic readers. Some of you have hung with me since I started this journey as a 24-year-old rancher with a penchant for writing my thoughts down and finding a few magazine editors who were willing to actually pay me a little to set those words down in type. I published my first book of those writings at the age of 28, and the second book at the age of 34. Now, at the age of 42, I can mark my life's timeline by those books and these columns as we publish No. 3, "Cowboy Logic Family Style."

I think we can all look back and realize who we are and what we've become is shaped by a lot of different factors. I've been more than fortunate with the circumstances I've been given. We never had family fortune, but we have been fortunate in family. I wouldn't have picked them any different. Dad was 48 when I was born and Mom was 37. I missed out on grandparents, three of the four had passed away before I was even born, but I had loving parents of "grandparent age" who gave me their most valuable gift - time.

I was raised by a World War II combat veteran father. He was raised by his mother and grandmother after the tragic loss of his father, grandfather and uncle in a short span of time. He was less than 2 years old when his dad died, but his father's cousin, a horse rancher from Culbertson, Mont., stepped in to become his fatherly role model. Dad was fashioned by him and by two strong independent pioneer women, as well as a Depression, a war, a hardscrabble homestead ranch and a landscape that was not very forgiving. And all the experiences that shaped Dad, in turn, shaped me. I guess that helped to make me what some would call "an old soul." You'll get a sense of that in these stories.

My mother was born to an immigrant Norwegian father and a mother who was a first-generation American. Her first language as a child was Norwegian, and English fluency came later at a one-room country school. Born in 1932, she was one of seven children raised on a quarter section of land in the midst of the Depression with an admiration for America and Franklin Roosevelt. Her family valued books, newspapers, reading, music, art, animals, humor and conversation. She was raised to show compassion for those down on their luck, maybe because they never were far from that reality themselves. And if she saw anyone being picked on, bullied or put upon by another unjustly, she would rise to their defense and let the offender know they had a smart, savvy, 6-foot-tall Scandinavian to contend with if they didn't back off. She married Dad, and I had the good fortune of being born to these two. They made me who I am, and their lessons will be passed on to my children. You'll learn about them in a few of these stories.

I called this book "Cowboy Logic Family Style" because these are the stories written around some life-changing events. My wife and I were blessed by the birth of our two little boys and our baby girl. Raising them is a joy, a challenge and an adventure that we're just beginning. Tempering the joy of those new lives was the loss of both my parents and my wife's father. We were part of the sandwich generation trying to balance caring for both our children and our parents. Lots of introspection and thought comes when you are both a new father and a mourning son. I was lucky to have writing as an outlet through the glad times and the sad times. I always said writing was good therapy and cheaper than a psychiatrist. If you've been through similar experiences, maybe there's a little therapy in the reading.

Like the books before, you'll get a good dose of columns about small-town culture, rural and ranch life, good neighbors, bad weather and a place on earth that always is loved, but sometimes disliked if the cows are out and the wind is blowing. We've seen cattle markets make a turn for the better, a good thing when you're raising a family and paying your bills. I've had the pleasure of meeting people across the prairie who thought enough of my writing to invite me to speak and entertain at their organization's annual banquet or community gathering. I sometimes bring my Will Roger's spinning ropes to make my point. And I've enjoyed the 10 years I've served in the North Dakota Senate. Like the ranch, it's sometimes gratifying and sometimes frustrating. As I write this, I'm in the race to be the next governor of North Dakota. All the people I've met in all my travels have added to who I am and what I've written.

Quotes I have framed on my wall come from Will Rogers and Theodore Roosevelt. Like Will Rogers, I like people, and like Theodore Roosevelt, I have a deep affection for places. Will Rogers said he "never met a man he didn't like." I don't know if I'd go that far. I have met a few I probably could do without complimenting, but I am intrigued by and interested in the people I've been lucky enough to meet in my travels, the audiences I've encountered on the roast beef dinner speaking circuit and the hands I've shook on the campaign trail. Like Will Rogers, I appreciate people more for their qualities and their character than how they're labeled or look. "They may call me a rube and a hick," he said, "but I'd a lot rather be the man who bought the Brooklyn Bridge than the man who sold it." I'll take the honest, trusting man over the unscrupulous swindler, too.

And, like Theodore Roosevelt, I feel affected by and attached to the places in my life. The ranch I was raised on, the state I've called home, the country I was fortunate to have been born a citizen. Teddy Roosevelt, who became our country's president when he was 42 years old, said, "I would not have been president if it hadn't been for my experience in North Dakota." Here he found a "land of vast silent spaces, a place of grim beauty." My family found that in this land, too, for four generations past, and, hopefully, for at least four generations more to come. Our love for this place we call home is so great that I not only write about it, I will do all I can to protect it and make sure that the generations to follow are given the same chances I've had to be moved and motivated by its special qualities.

The people who've raised me, the people I've met, the place where I've grown and worked and played - it's all wrapped up in these stories I sit down to write every other week, 26 times a year. Some of my favorites are in this third publication. I hope you enjoy reading them. I've sure enjoyed writing them and living them.

Chapter 1
Family Friendly

Toddler tornado
Living in the wake

They say fatherhood changes a man's outlook. I can testify that it not only changes your outlook on things, it'll also have you out looking for most of your things.

Fact is, I've been looking for things that I never used to have to search for since our precocious little boy reared up on his hind legs and started walking five months ago. It's hard to say where you'll find the remote control for the television after he's grabbed it. He's also partial to phones and any other piece of small electronic equipment he can wrap his little hands around.

Kitchen helper

He spends a lot of time in the kitchen with his mother helping her rearrange her cupboards. We put the little locks on the cupboard that held our assorted everyday poisons, but the rest of the cabinets are fair game.

If she's looking for anything in the bottom cabinets, she doesn't even have to open the door. Everything's scattered out nicely on the floor in front of it in plain view.

She knows exactly what she has on hand for baking and cooking supplies because she picks it up and puts it back on the shelf several times a day.

She knows she's a little short on Bisquick baking mix because a little white, powdery mouth was smiling from coated ear to coated ear after he shook the bag of powder a little too vigorously once he got it out of its box.

She also knows she's a little short on rhubarb cake. When Mom left the room for split second, Lil' Bud spotted an opportunity to climb up a box, onto some furniture and onto the kitchen counter to grab a couple of fistfuls right out of the middle of the cake. When Mommy came around the corner and saw her little boy sitting up on the counter smearing cake all over himself and everything around him, she was so mad she laughed out loud.

Not many 14-month-olds have that kind of determination and climbing ability. There's a fine line between talent and terror — or pride and panic, for that matter.

Book boy

Like Mom's cabinets, my book shelves usually are empty. First, it was the bottom shelf, then the second shelf, now he's going three high and we're wondering if even the top shelf is safe.

I'm a book guy. I like books and I own quite a few. Most I've read, some I plan to read, a few I just like to own for reference or to simply admire on the shelf. The way Lil' Bud pulls a book off the shelf, flips through the pages, tosses it aside and grabs another one may indicate that he's got the makings of a burgeoning book guy.

I now know why hardcover books that still have the book jacket in good shape are worth more in collector circles. It's because anyone who has children probably doesn't have the jackets for their books anymore, and, if they do, they're surely torn and tattered. I know the books on my bottom three shelves no longer will bring top dollar from book collectors.

On the positive side, if you're having trouble getting rid of any old magazines or newspapers, Bud can destroy them to the point where you'll have no desire to keep them any longer.

I guess that's why some parents and grandparents tell me my column is the first thing they read. I reckon if they don't read it right away, a tornado toddler will leave my column in his wake.

Priorities
Changing with the times   February 6, 2006

It's tough to accept, but I'm beginning to realize that it's not about me anymore.

I guess I should've started learning that lesson after I got married, but when you and your spouse like doing a lot of the same things, "us" isn't really that much different than "me." And when you don't like doing the same things, two people can do their "me" things, then get back together and still be an "us."

Throw a baby into the mix, though, and everything changes. Mostly for the better, but it takes some getting used to.

Attention getter

Being the baby of my own family, I've grown used to getting plenty of attention. My wife is the last born in her family, too, and the only girl. We both need to take turns acting like first born or middle children just to keep our partnership cheery.

So with my wife and I both being "babies," adding our own little creation to the mix made for three babies under one roof. He, however, has quickly ascended to the role of No. 1 baby in the house, and he knows it.

He's pretty lucky as far as little boys go. There's always a parent within reach, 24/7. My wife ranches with me, and that allows her to be what today's lexicon would call a stay-at-home mom. And, for the most part, I guess you could call me a stay-at-home dad.

That's a luxury in today's world that we don't take for granted. I guess it's a big reason why those of us in agriculture choose to stay in agriculture. You know, poor pay but good benefits.

The good thing about ranching is you get to be home with your family. And, sometimes, the bad thing about ranching is you get be home with your family.

Some days, we wish we had a day care center in the neighborhood to give us a break from our busy boy toddler, but we know we'd miss out on a lot that you just can't recreate when the moment has passed.

Adjusting

I've made a few adjustments in my old self-centered routine since our baby came along.

I used to be real productive in the mornings and get a lot of work done. Now, before I pour my second cup of coffee, the little 3-foot guy in the house comes shuffling out of his room, dragging his blankets and looking for Daddy's lap to crawl up into.

I used to watch the morning news. Now I watch "Sesame Street." I traded my morning news anchors for Big Bird and Elmo. I can't tell you what the day's headlines are, but I can tell you what the letter and number of the day is.

I used to enjoy good, thick tomes of hardbound nonfiction. Our little guy's a voracious reader, too. But he pulls my book out of my hands, replaces it with "Moo, Baa, La La La" or "The Very Hungry Caterpillar" and settles in for a good read.

Our DVD player hasn't seen a good movie for awhile, but it has played and replayed a couple of Veggie Tales and Baby Einstein discs many times over.

I'm good at holding puzzle boards for our little puzzler, can assist in the placement of the triangular wooden block into its appropriate hole, and, together we can imitate the sounds of a whole barnyard full of farm animals.

In some areas, I am a lot less productive than I used to be. But I'm probably a lot more productive in another area that's infinitely more valuable.

And I've got a lot less time to be selfish. I think that's OK because it isn't really about me anymore.

A couple days off
And a lifetime ahead   August 7, 2006

"Darn poor timing." That's what my ranching neighbors said when I told them my wife and I were expecting a baby in early August.

Right in the middle of our haying season. If we did any crop farming, it'd have really messed up the harvest schedule. But, in our aging prairie community, I figure any time is a good time to bring a new life into the neighborhood.

So I shut down the haying crew in the middle of the afternoon, parked the hay baler for a little paternity leave and drove to the hospital with my wife to see what we could do about boosting the population of Gorman Township.

Since I was born in July and both my parents were born in August, this isn't the first time that haying had to take a break for childbirth.

Just after midnight, we added another summer birthday to the family and brought another healthy, strapping boy into the Taylor Ranch family.

We're truly blessed. Two big, strong boys to raise, a 2-year-old and a newborn, and two parents with the will to do it.

The future

Something about childbirth, "helping" your wife through labor and the sleep deprivation that comes with two nights in the hospital's torture cot for fathers makes a man pretty reflective.

Reading the newspaper the morning after a midnight birth and a few hours of sleep bent into the shape of a "C" is a sobering chore. Like so many others, I asked myself why we bring babies into this troubled world.

People killing each other in the name of gods professed to love peace. Grudges that last thousands of years and a list of wrongs tallied between factions across decades and centuries.

Bound to live in an economy tied to oil that's running short and costing society dollars we'd rather dedicate to better living or even basic living.

I wonder if my boys will be ranchers someday and if they'll have to deal with droughts that last longer and return quicker than they used to. Will normal weather be even more abnormal?

I wonder if we'll always have the intellect and the know-how to stop any potential virus or epidemic short of its destructive potential.

I hope my boys can inherit the advances of the generations passed before them free and clear. Will they know the satisfaction of a society that pays its bills as they go and puts self-restraint above instant gratification?

Heavy stuff

I guess the responsibilities of fatherhood make us think about pretty weighty topics. I doubt it was any different for my immigrant grandfather, who had my mother in the midst of the Great Depression. Or even for my dad, who had children in the turbulence of the 1960s and the Vietnam War.

All we can do is raise the children as best we can and be the kind of people we'd like them to grow up to be.

A friend of mine said the two best things you can do for your children is take them to church and teach them how to work. Pretty good advice.

I'll take my two boys to church and, if we all pay attention to the preacher when the sermon turns to talk about compassion and forgiveness and generosity, the world will find a way to live in peace.

The lessons of stewardship and responsibility for creation will allow us to keep the ranch and the planet intact for many more generations to use and enjoy.

And the ranch that shut down for a few days to bring them into this world will get back in motion and teach them not only how to work, but how to think and solve problems.

Sure there're problems in the world. We created most of 'em. That's why I know we can fix them.

I may have wondered why we bring babies into this world so laden with problems. But then I realize it's today's babies who'll help us solve those problems. The love of parents, the fresh start in our children — it can change the world for the better.

So, tonight as I read the paper, I look at my boys, and my worries turn to hope.

Sidekick
Daddy day care on the ranch   September 18, 2006

There's a new hired hand on the Taylor Ranch. He works cheap—three square meals, at least as many diapers and the occasional juice box. He's just over 2 years old, long on ambition but short on direction.

Since the new baby brother hit our house, big brother Bud has become my full-time sidekick. Like Matt Dillon and Festus, the Lone Ranger and Tonto, Bert and Ernie. We look out for each other.

He has all the qualities of a good sidekick. Faithful, helpful, ready to go at the drop of a hat.

He doesn't travel light, though. It used to be I could pull down my hat, head out the door and go to work. Not so now.

These days, I need to make sure I have a sippy cup, a blankie, a little container of raisins, a spare diaper and some wet wipes. The back of my pickup has about as many toys as it does tools.

You always can spot a daddy rancher. Just look in the back of his pickup and see if there's a toy dump truck and bulldozer back there with his fence stretcher and post hole digger.

We're still working on channeling his energy. Sometimes, the bulldozer fills up my post hole while I'm digging it. Most times I can stay ahead of him.

He's pretty good at bringing me stuff, even stuff I don't need. But it pleases him to bring me every tool out of the tool box or to empty a can of nails one by one, and it keeps him occupied. It doesn't take me long to put them back en masse.

He helps me appreciate my surroundings. "Windmill, windmill, windmill!" "Cows, cows, cows!" "Trees, trees, trees!" You can't slip anything by him. And he appreciates quick confirmation of everything he's identified.

Like barn cats

I guess you could say that my first born and I are spending a lot of quantity time together. There may be some quality to the quantity, but basically our relationship is blessed with sheer volume. It's a lucky father who has that opportunity.

It reminds me of the barn cat theory of parenting related to me by a reader who's a farm-raised family doctor.

He figures children are like the batch of kitties you find in the hay mow of your barn. You have to get out there and start petting and playing with them when they're little, before their eyes are open. Lots of love early on and you'll have cats that are tame and useful their whole life through.

If you wait too long to spend any time with them and their eyes open up without any taming and petting, you'll have a barn full of hissing, spitting cats that'll be wild the rest of their days.

When it comes to children, the time their eyes open up is teenaged adolescence and the time to be with them and tame them down is when they're infants and toddlers and little kids.

Everything I do on the ranch takes twice as long when my sidekick is helping me. But it's not wasted time.

I'm sure there will be days to come when his eyes open up and I won't be his idol and he won't be my sidekick. Right now, he's pretty sure I hung the moon. And I think life on the ranch without him would be pretty dull.

I wouldn't call him tame by any means, but we are putting in the time.

Family roadster
Minivan shopping takes a maximum effort   November 27, 2006

There comes a time in every man's life when he decides that it's time to get a minivan.

I've driven everything from an old gas guzzling four door road boat to a newer style gas guzzling SUV. My second vehicle for the ranch has been a big, diesel-guzzling pickup.

I really started thinking about a more fuel-efficient minivan when gas was 30 percent higher this summer. But, even at today's bargain-basement, price-gouging gas prices, 27 miles to the gallon in a minivan looks pretty good.

It's not all about the gas mileage, though. My family takes up a lot of space these days. Sure, the baby and the toddler aren't physical heavyweights, but their payload increases by a multiple of four when you add in their car seats and all the gear they require for a short road trip.

We don't pack very light for an overnighter with portable cribs, strollers, diaper bags, a few toys and a couple things for Mom and Dad. I wonder how my folks got us all down the road in the old Ford Galaxy. Maybe we just stayed home a little more.

At any rate, I started looking for a minivan after No. 2 was born this summer.

Van variables

There's a lot to consider when you're shopping for a minivan. It's really about the amenities, not the boring stuff like the motor. Sure, they have motors, but you can't see them or work on them or understand them, so you just hope your mechanic has the latest in computer diagnostics and you forget about it.

The real deciders in minivan shopping are things like cup holders, disappearing seats and entertainment systems.

I'm fine with an abundance of cup holders. I like my coffee when I'm driving down the road, and it's nice to have a place to put it where it won't spill on your lap.

Disappearing seats probably are a good thing. We may have to take the minivan on a parts run, and if the seats fold away to make room for sickles, tires or large chunks of steel, that's all the better.

I had to draw the line on having an "entertainment system" in any vehicle I'm going to own. I'll be darned if I'm going to cave in to the idea of having a DVD player, remote control and wireless headphones to entertain my kids on the open road.

I like to think that we drive through some pretty interesting country. Why, there are hay bales to count, cows to admire, farmers and ranchers in their fields and pastures to wave at. I see no need to have them zombied into a video game or some cartoon when there's all that out there to entertain them. At least that's what I say now.

Minivans are big on safety. They claim there's an air bag packed into every nook and cranny. There are lots of seat belts and latches for the car seats, computers that keep your vehicle on its "intended" path and some strategic steel placed to keep it from completely crumpling in a wreck.

It's hard to kick on that. I'm not so concerned about myself, but I've never hauled anything more valuable than my two boys and their mother.

So I finally did it. I'm now a full-fledged minivan man. I bought it used, of course, but there's enough head room for my cowboy hat, and the book says it has 18 cup holders. Just finding them all should keep me busy for a long time.

Proud as punch
Exercising a father's right to boast   April 30, 2007

Some things in life go hand in hand, like fatherhood and pride.

I've never considered myself a bragger, or excessively proud. I'm actually kind of modest; of course, like they say, I have a lot to be modest about.

But once I became a father, my sense of pride began to grow. My boys aren't old enough to have report cards, a trophy case or tales of competitive glory for me to recite, but I've found other ways to exercise my paternal pride.

Our oldest son is nearly 3 years old and smart as whip, among his many other fine attributes. To show off his intelligence, I put him through the paces like a trick pony whenever I find someone willing to spend a few minutes with the two of us.

I quiz him on his primary and secondary colors. He knows them all. Then I'll have him count to 10, assemble a 25-piece jigsaw puzzle, play a little tune on the piano and identify the animals of the world. We wrap up our routine with a high five and a hug.

He sometimes will suffer a little performance anxiety or get shy and hide behind me when I start throwing out the questions. When that happens, I just name the colors and count to 10 myself as a kind of proxy performance. That'll impress an audience nearly as well.

Above average baby

Our 9-month-old is a little young for that, so he has fewer tricks to please an audience. But he's baby cute, so he gets away with doing a lot less.

If I need to do a little bragging on him, I just pry open his mouth and show my friends his fine teeth. "See those two on the bottom? Got those when he was just 4 months old," I say, chest swelling with pride.

If that doesn't impress them, I take him out to the middle of a carpeted floor, stand him up and back away. "Look, see, he's standing! He'll be walking by 10 months, mark my words. His brother was walking by 10. Of course, you know, most children don't start until they're a year or more," I tell my listener as they began to realize just how impressive my boys are.

If I'm feeling especially proud, I whip out the statistics from hi six-month check up. They chart his height, weight, measurements and such.

The median of children nationally is the 50th percentile. Our guy, however, is nearly off the chart at the 95th percentile. If he were a bull, he'd be the highest index offering in the catalog.

He had a pretty good start, weighing in an ounce shy of 9 pounds, so you couldn't

8

call him a low-birth, high-growth "curve bender," as they say in the cattle catalogs. He's more of a high-birth, high-growth-performance type.

He has a hearty appetite that helps him lead the charts, and that makes me feel successful, too. When I get him to polish off a whole jar of vegetable beef baby mash and a container full of ground-up green beans, I call over my wife and report the news like we just climbed Mount Everest.

I suppose I should be careful not to become a bore and brag too much about my kids in public, but letting those boys know how proud I am of them shouldn't hurt them one bit.

I've seen a few statistics about the unfortunate problems and challenges facing some of the children in our society, but I've yet to see a column in the statistics of ill for children whose parents were too proud and loved them too much.

Diet of a dad
Waste not, want not   October 29, 2007

When I became a dad, I knew I was in for some changes in my life's routines.

I knew I'd sleep less, worry more, travel less and spend more money, but I didn't know my eating habits were in for such a drastic change.

Used to be, I'd sit down, give thanks, eat a hot meal and push my chair back until the next feeding.

Now, with a yearling and a 3-year-old to break bread with, it's not nearly as simple.

First, you have to get them to the table. At some point, you just pick them up and put them in their chair.

We let our 3-year-old pick the grace that we'll say. There's really no need to ask because we know he'll say "Super Man!" a little Bible camp prayer that has us all flying through the air like caped super heroes.

Then my wife and I commence to satisfying the needs of the two little eating machines. We spoon feed the little guy, cut things up for his big brother, make several trips to the fridge and smell the food we were hoping to eat.

We use a bib on the youngster, but probably should put rain coats on both of them and spread a drop sheet on the floor beneath them. I've considered bringing the dog in the house during supper to help with cleanup.

Eventually, my wife and I sit down to eat our once-hot food. The meal routine is harder on my wife than it is on me. She's been eating cold food since the first day of our first child I think.

When the kids are excused and unbuckled from the high chair, we dine together in peace like we still were dating. Sort of.

We still have the kids' dishes and tray and part of their food left for our grazing. We hate to waste good food, even if it is scattered about and partially masticated by our toothy sons.

Supper becomes a many-coursed affair. I reach for the partly eaten cob of corn with an abundance of good kernels scattered along its length by our aspiring eaters. My wife finds a piece of bread with the middle eaten out of it leaving a perfectly good crust.

We snack on tiny, cut-up pieces of meat; noodles adhering to the table top and chairs; maybe a slightly flattened banana lifted from the tray of the high chair.

Our clean up eating habits as parents continue out of the home, too. There's a lot of interesting food found in their car seats. Some I don't dare touch, but I will pick up an apple once in awhile that, although partly eaten and slightly brown and bruised, still has a lot of usable calories left in it.

At a recent campfire, I was trying to teach my toddler how to roast a hot dog on a stick. Steadiness and control were sorely lacking. That wiener spent more time being dipped in the ashes and drug through the sand than it did above the fire. It had a lot of grit and grind, but Daddy ate it and gave his son a clean one.

My used-food diet is nearly that of a Dumpster diver, except I know whose food and germs I'm exposing myself to. Food that would seem disgusting to people who've never parented has become part of my daily sustenance.

In the end, I'm just thankful that my family and I have so much food to sustain us. Even if it isn't always in the best of shape by the time it gets to my mouth.

Sleeping babies
The key to peace on earth   December 25, 2007

I try not to pay much attention to television ads, but every once in awhile, something in the advertising world reaches out and reels me in.

Such an ad has run for a couple of Christmas seasons now, but it still stops me in my tracks for its full 60-second duration.

The ad is from Pampers diapers, and for a full minute, all it does is show you pictures of sleeping babies from around the world with a single voice singing "Silent Night" in the background.

It ends with an image of the planet, the words "peace on earth" and a brief logo shot so you know who paid for the last precious minute.

In a season that's awash with crass consumerism, it calms us with a simple song and heartwarming pictures. And our hearts grow two times larger each time we see it.

I might still buy a cheaper diaper, but I have to thank Pampers for brightening my holiday.

Bedtime rituals

Maybe I connect with the commercial more than most because I have two diaper-clad lads. But I like to think that 99.9 percent of all humans can appreciate images of snoozing babies.

Life is pretty hectic in a house with two little ones just 27 months apart. There's plenty of crying and fighting and whining and playing and laughing and screams of joy and screams of frustration and other plain ol' noise.

Then, just before you lose all sanity, everyone winds down, the favorite books are read, and those two little people cuddle into their blankets, shut their eyes and are transformed into the earth's most perfect angels.

You have to love the sleeping baby. All the noise is forgotten, all the naughtiness is forgiven and you catch yourself smiling in deep satisfaction at the silence and whisper of their little lungs exchanging breath. If it weren't for moments like that, parenting as a practice would have disappeared from our culture and the human species would have become extinct long ago. I'm certain of that.

Bedtime's become a favorite part of my day. I check on one boy and then the other, stand by their crib or their bed, watch them for a moment, say a quick prayer for their future and call it a day myself.

Changing the world

I'm sure the underlying intent of the commercial is to sell diapers, and that's fine. I've changed an awful lot of diapers in the last three years and I can honestly say I'd much rather see them broadcast sleeping babies than show what I've seen in those dirty diapers.

But beyond the building of their brand, I think the commercial has real value in promoting the "peace on earth" it aspires to.

I haven't traveled a lot, but I've traveled some and I've met lots of people who I probably don't have an awful lot in common with. But if they've raised children or been a part of a loving family, we can establish a pretty quick bond.

We all love our children and we want a better life for them than we've had. If we can agree on that, we can tolerate a lot of differences of religion or politics or race or geography.

Not everyone in the world celebrates Christmas as we know it, but across every land, there are mothers and fathers standing by their sleeping child's bed smiling warmly at their snoozing angel and hoping for a better tomorrow.

If we realize that we all have that in common, then sleeping babies could truly bring peace on earth. Merry Christmas, everybody.

Early exposure
Long-term health   Jan. 21, 2008

We just finished a big trip across five states by train and car with our two kids in tow. It'll be awhile before I suggest we do something like that again.

Putting wheels under a set of parents, a 1-year-old and a 3-year-old for 32 hours straight is a real growing experience for a family.

Kids won't learn how to travel if you don't take them traveling, but we may have gone a little overboard with a 24-hour train trip followed by an eight-hour car drive in a blizzard for our first big outing.

Little boys love trains. It just comes natural. I'm convinced the first three obsessions for boy children are trains, tractors and guns. Even if they've never seen a gun, ridden a tractor or heard a train whistle, I guarantee you'll see them pointing stick guns, making tractor noises and yearning for a ride on the choo-choo.

You can't beat the expression on a boy's face when he sits in a train for the first time and it starts to move. It's hard to describe the expression on his mother's face after she's been riding the train with that same energetic boy for 24 hours.

Our somewhat-sheltered ranch kids saw a lot of new things on the trip. I'm pretty sure they saw more new germs than a protective parent can shake a disinfectant wipe at.

Hygiene hypothesis

I read a story once that said children who have high levels of exposure to germs and bacteria actually end up healthier than kids who live in too clean an environment. Farms were good sources of exposure, and farm kids proved a lower rate of allergies and asthma in the study.

Growing up around our place, surrounded by animals, dirt and manure, our kids are far from naïve. But I think they took their pathogenic inoculation to a whole new level on the trip.

Our boys seem to have an affinity for the floors in public places. I'm sure train depot floors are completely hygienic, at least I tried to convince my wife of that as the boys rolled around and laid down on them.

We practice the "three-second rule" for food at home that hits the floor as we retrieve it and keep on eating. The boys took that rule on the road with them at the restaurants, and I'm afraid they may have found other morsels down there that might have required a "three-month rule."

I caught our 17-month-old sticking his tongue on a mirror in a public restroom. His older brother touched every other surface in the bathrooms that he might have missed.

Water fountains provided hours of entertainment, and when they couldn't quite reach the spout before dad gave them a boost, germs probably made the crossover.

By the time they got to a playland at a fast-food joint, they'd already encountered every potential pathogen in their path on the train, in the depot, in the rental car and every other assorted public place. We just let them play and kept the disinfectant wipes packed away.

Time will tell us if that study on germ exposure was right. If exposure makes for better health, we may have the healthiest kids on the planet.

The working school
Resisting the urge to automate   March 17, 2008

If you want to know a rancher's age or family status, there's no need to ask, just take a look around their place.

Take two medium-sized ranches to compare. If you see a tractor hooked to an automated grinder/mixer wagon and a fenceline feeding system, they either don't have kids or the kids they had have all grown up and moved away.

If you see a bunch of feed bunks in the middle of the pens and a dozen plastic pails next to an old truck or grain bin, the rancher is in the prime of his child-rearing days. Kids and plastic pails go hand in handle.

The childless ranch with the feed wagon and fenceline feeding probably has a set of cone-shaped gravity bins to store their feed grains, too. The place with the kids running around probably has a bunch of flat-bottomed bins or wooden granaries and a collection of well-worn scoop shovels.

Blistered lessons

I got to thinking about this point of differentiation while I was bent over a scoop shovel in an old, wooden granary filling a set of 5- gallon plastic pails.

I was thinking how nice it'd be to load the ration in a feed wagon and drive along a fenceline auguring it out for the calves without so much as opening a gate.

Then I looked over at my boys, almost 4 years old and 1½ years old, who were in the granary with me trying to empty the pails I was filling. I looked at them and thought how awful a dad I would be to deny them the opportunity to fill pails with a scoop shovel and carry them to feed the calves while they were growing up.

As one rancher and father told me, one of the best things you can do for your children is teach them how to work. Too much automation on a place and you'd lose an awful lot of teachable moments.

So I'm going to hold back on the feed wagon and hold on to the plastic pails until my boys grow into them.

Breadth of education

To really give them a good schooling, I may want to do even more for them. Like get a couple of milk cows. You always can find a nice herd of dairy cows for sale somewhere when the dairy farmer's youngest kid heads off to college.

Sheep are a pretty labor-intensive piece of livestock. A small flock could teach young folks a lot about hard work, patience and disappointment. And it might encourage my boys to find a wife with those qualities if they want to stay in the sheep business.

Birthday shopping for the boys will be a cinch. A scoop shovel for their 12th birthday, a pitchfork for their 13th birthday, a posthole digger for their 14th birthday and so on. By the time they graduate from high school, they could have a whole set of wooden-handled educators.

If they grow up well, they'll probably be successful ranchers someday who can afford to finally automate the place that dear old Dad never did.

That is, unless they have kids of their own who need to learn about chores.

Sickness and health
A year for healthy calves and a sick family   March 31, 2008

This week, we've had more sickness in our family of four than we had in several hundred cattle the whole last year.

I wish I could keep my family as healthy as I somehow kept the cattle healthy. My two young sons had more nasal discharge than a truckload of freshly weaned heifers.

We do work hard at raising healthy cattle. We calve the cows when it's warm and dry, wean the calves in a familiar place when it's cold, and they get decent feed, several inoculations and relatively little stress.

The key to the calves' good health, probably, is they just don't travel much. No trips to town, conventions, conferences, coughing cousins or sniffling schoolmates. From birth to weaning, through the winter, and sometimes back out to grass, they're within three miles of where their mama dropped them on day one.

My family, on the other hand, likely would cease being a family if we didn't get off the ranch and see anyone but each other for 300 or 400 days straight. We are a family on the go. And the higher gas prices get, it seems, the more we go.

I'm not blaming any one individual for our miserable weeklong coughing, sneezing, aching, feverish sweats and chills, but my wife was the first one to get it after a recent 500-mile trip around the state.

Then we all got it, but we were lucky enough that my wife was getting better when I was getting sicker so our two little guys always had someone halfway healthy to take care of them through the long, whimpering nights.

Being self-employed, we don't have to call our boss and tell anyone we're sick. We just look in the mirror and admit it to ourselves.

On a ranch, you can limit your day's work when you're under the weather, but you can't eliminate everything that needs doing. So somewhere along the line in the day, you drag your sick, aching, shivering body outside and do the chores that absolutely need doing.

I used to think the ranch ritual of forcing yourself outside when you were sick was good therapy—a little fresh air pumping through the lungs and some sunshine to improve our outlook.

Now I wonder if the practice is a little sadistic. A barely coherent rancher slowly climbs out of the tractor to hack at the twine on the hay bales, feed buckets that used to swing from his arms drag along behind him and he struggles to clear the side of the feed bunk to empty them.

The fresh air brings on a coughing fit that might only end when his lung comes up completely and lands on the ground in front of him. The sunshine makes his head hurt even more.

If it was such good therapy, we'd have dressed our sick kids to go out and do chores with us. As it was, my wife and I each took part of the chores so one of us could stay inside to nurse the kids along.

But through a week's worth of the worst cold I ever had, we got the cattle fed and cared for. Maybe that's why the cattle's health has fared better than ours this winter—sick ranchers still feed and care for cattle, but sick cattle seldom feed and care for ranchers.

And, luckily, the cattle can't catch what we've got.

It's a girl! August 4, 2008

She's here! She's finally here, and she's a pink flannel-wearing, pink blanket-wrapped, heart-melting baby girl!

This is our third baby in five years of marriage, but this pregnancy and delivery was just as exciting, scary and amazing as the first one.

Our first two babies were boys – big boys – nearly 9 pounds each. Rough and tough, full speed ahead, no fear, no caution, nothing they can't bend, break or jump off of boys.

We've witnessed girl children in other families. Quiet, meek, gentle. Sit and play

14

with their dolls or color a picture for hours. We love our boys, but we've experienced baby girl envy when we've seen these little sweethearts in other families.

My wife's been looking at the pink clothes in the baby section for years. The outfits are cuter, she says, and there's way more to pick from. All a boy needs is a pair of jeans with holes in the knees and a favorite T-shirt. No need to do a lot of shopping for those items.

When we got pregnant this time, we thought this might be our girl. Of course, we were pretty comfortable with the idea of another boy. We already had all the gear.

My wife had an ultrasound a few months into the deal. We're one of those rare couples who don't ask the technician to tell us what the sex of the baby is. They say only 20 or 30 percent of us opt not to know. There're so few surprises in life these days, we see no need to spoil one of life's really good surprises.

We got through nine months of not knowing, willing to accept whatever we were blessed with, comfortable with the thought of another boy but kind of hoping for a girl.

Time's up

We were going to be surprised with the sex of the baby, but a little less surprised with the timing when the doctor and we agreed to induce labor once we'd gone full term. Seemed like the prudent thing with a 9-pound baby history and a 60-mile commute to the hospital.

The doctor suggested a little prostaglandin to start things out and, if that didn't work, some oxytocin.

I think I surprised him by knowing actually what he was talking about. I confessed to him that I was an amateur expert of reproduction in the bovine species. I told him I was using some prostaglandin myself on a group of heifers in a couple days for synchronization. I got a lot better deal on mine than what he was paying for my wife's.

The prostaglandin was administered. We waited and waited. Nothing. The next day, the oxytocin was administered. We waited and waited. It was right then that I knew this baby was going to be a girl. Only a female would make us wait like that.

When I was a kid, I remember getting ready to go somewhere with the family and we'd all be in the car sitting and waiting for Mom. I told Dad to honk the horn, but he advised, "No, son, she'd just make us wait longer if we did that."

I remember the first date with my wife when I went to meet her at her parents' house. I bet I sat and visited with her dad for 20 minutes before she came up the stairs. He told me I should get used to waiting for women.

A friend of mine told me that beautiful women always make you wait. Well my wife is beautiful, and never more so than when she was holding our brand-new, beautiful baby girl for the first time.

It was well worth the wait.

Upfront child rearing
For all to see   November 10, 2008

There're a lot of things I don't envy about the job ahead for president-elect Obama—the sliding economy and stock market, the wars and tension abroad, the need to replace campaign division with post-election civility.

But one thing that really makes me empathize with him and the new first lady is the challenge of raising your children in front of the media, the country and the whole wide world.

Everyone knows the new president is the first African American elected to the office, but he's also the first president since John F. Kennedy to bring more than one young child into the White House.

Speaking from experience, albeit with boys rather than girls, one kid is a lot easier to keep from jumping on the couch, racing around the table and sliding down the banister than two. Running and chasing just isn't as much fun when there's no one to race or pursue.

I suppose the temperament of their girls, age 7 and 10, versus my boys, age 2 and 4, likely will save the first family a lot of embarrassment. Kids are still kids, though. Maybe the new first puppy will distract the cameras from what the kids are doing.

Boys and baptism

We could have used some distraction last Sunday when our little rascals did a little entertaining for the entire congregation of our church.

It was our baby girl's baptism and we all headed up front, wife and I, god parents, baby girl, two boys and a pastor. I thought we had about the right ratio, five adults on three little tikes. We could have used a couple more hands.

The baby was exemplary, not even a peep when the baptismal water touched her head.

The 4-year-old wasn't too bad. He was mesmerized by the baptismal font and the water. He stood right next to the font with his fingers clinging, peeking over the edge to see what was going on. Our church's font is a narrow-bottomed, top-heavy piece of oak, so the pastor kept a steadying hand on it to keep it from toppling.

I held our 2-year-old for awhile until he wanted down. I figured there couldn't be much harm in that so I set him free.

He went over next to his brother, got a hold of the basin of baptismal water and proceeded to dump it out. I sprang into action at the speed of embarrassment and saved enough of the water for the pastor to do the intended job for our wee one.

Luckily, we Lutherans are sprinklers, not dunkers, or the spilled water would have spoiled the whole holy ceremony.

I got hold of our 2-year-old trying to look calm and cool to the entire congregation watching this family circus, yet stern and serious to the offending toddler who I had by the arm.

The pastor never missed a beat, reached in her pocket and pulled out a little toy car for him, all the while reciting calmly from the Lutheran Book of Worship. He spent

16

the rest of the baptism pushing the car around behind us by and on the altar. "Let the little children come to me, and do not hinder them," Jesus says in the gospel of Luke.

Well, I can say with certainty our children weren't hindered much, and we'll gladly bring them. I'm also glad we didn't have a press corps snapping photos throughout the whole ordeal.

Rough weeks
With tender, lovin' care   March 16, 2009

I guess it's our turn. Usually we're the parents with the healthy kids. The last couple of weeks, we've paid the price and served our turn as nursemaids and pediatric comforters.

My wife and I have had three straight weeks of sick little boys. Amazingly, we've stayed healthy, but we're tired. Our baby girl has rolled through things just fine thanks to mother's natural nourishment and the high immune status that results.

Our 4-year-old has a well-worn path going to the bathroom. He's learned to carry a bucket with him just in case he starts to heave when he's away from the commode. If nothing else, I figure it's good training for carrying feed buckets.

The 2-year-old's stomach is more affected on the diaper end. He just lets us change him over and over again throughout the day. He's at that age where staying little and lazy seems like a better option than being all grown up and responsible. Enjoy it while you can, I guess.

Tough symptoms

They're fighting fevers and chills, sallow-looking eyes and no appetite. We're thankful for electronic thermometers that display their temperature in seconds. Usually, the old hand on the forehead can tell us if they're hot or not but it's nice to have a number to gauge our required level of worrying.

The little fellas lay on the couch like limp noodles. They're so wiped out, they can hardly even fight. But they do summon just enough strength to thump on each other from time to time.

It went from a 10-day flu and strep throat to possible pneumonia for our oldest. His little brother went from the on-again, off-again, on-again flu to a wheezy, barking cough to tonsillitis.

We doctored the fever with the usual drugs that come in all the unusual forms for kids. You can get grape liquid, orange chewables or cherry meltables. They're bound to like one of them. It's a long way from the days of baby aspirin.

Their latest diagnoses has them both getting the liquid antibiotic that's supposed to taste like bubble gum but still tastes like medicine.

I much prefer doctoring calves to doctoring kids. Calves hardly ever whine or refuse to take their medicine. They barely flinch if you use a sharp needle to slip under the hide to make an injection. If the going gets tough or the cattle get bigger, you always can use a squeeze chute, or a rope or a balling gun to administer the big pills they refuse to swallow on request.

About all I can do with our boys is bribe them. I start by making a kind request for them to drink their medicine. Then I try to reason with them about "doctor's orders," the medicine's mode of action and the importance of them getting better. Reasoning with 4-year-olds and 2-year-olds is entertaining to spectators but wholly ineffective for the reasoner.

You can try to wrestle them to the ground and squirt a syringe full of whatever you're doctoring with onto the back of their tongue, but you'd be surprised how tough a determined 40-pounder can be. They're wiry and flexible. It's hard to keep them still enough to administer the happy, yummy stuff.

So I offer treats and privileges and things I'd never give them otherwise. Juice, fruit snacks, ice cream, even pop and candy. As they say, a spoon full of sugar helps the medicine go down.

I can't guarantee the health of their teeth, but I'm hoping I can get the rest of their body back on track soon.

Well dressed
Only the finest in pre-owned fashions   April 13, 2009

I have no hang ups about wearing hand-me-downs. I welcome them and I gratefully accept them for my children.

Getting married a little later in life and starting our family years after our siblings and friends started their families has given my wife and me a gold mine of slightly used clothes, shoes and baby gear.

We're pretty fortunate. Our kids have well-dressed cousins just a few years older than them. Our high-performance kids are starting to outgrow them now, but we've hardly had to buy a thing for them these first few years.

Some of the clothes were hardly worn. As fast as those little rascals grow, you're lucky to get two or three wearings on some of the dressier duds.

We even made a special exception to our prenatal ultrasound policy to grease the skids on a delivery of used apparel for our latest baby. A friend of my wife's had two extremely well-dressed little girls and she had the audacity to consider rummage selling them before we had our baby.

We've never asked to know the sex of our babies from the ultrasound technician, but if we wanted to save our friend's little girl clothes from the jaws of a neighborhood garage liquidation, we had to lift the veil of secrecy.

So we had the technician print out a revealing ultrasound shot, write down the verdict of the baby's sex on it, put it in a sealed envelope and we delivered it to our friend without peeking. She kept the secret from us and she kept the clothes to be delivered to us shortly after our little girl was born.

We've been awash in high-quality, brand-name little pink coordinates ever since.

Brothers that borrow

It's not just our children who know the pragmatic pleasure of a slightly worn wardrobe. My brother in California is much better dressed than I, and his income supports shopping habits in slightly more exclusive retailers than the local farm supply store.

We're about the same size, thankfully, and that means I'm first in line for the fashions he retires. I've gotten quite a few sweaters handed down to me by him. I'm not bragging or complaining, but quite a few of those sweaters are cashmere.

It's fitting that the word cashmere starts with cash because it takes more cash than I'm willing to spend to buy the soft, fine wool combed out from those little Asian goats. A goat can only crank out 3 ounces of the stuff each year, so it takes a small herd to make a sweater.

I can only use so many cashmere sweaters, so I've taken to wearing a few for work. He gave me one that works really well under my insulated bib overalls for winter wear. It's very warm.

When my brother was visiting, he couldn't believe I was wearing it for work. "That's an Arnys from Paris!" he exclaimed. "Oh, really," I said, ignorantly.

I looked up Arnys in Paris on the Internet. It's a pretty high-class men's store in Paris on the Left Bank, at 14 rue de Sevres in the 7th arrondissement, I guess. Of course, I've not been to Paris nor do I know what's on the Right Bank for clothing stores, but, by golly, the folks at Arnys sell a pretty warm sweater for feeding cows in North Dakota in the winter. I appreciate it almost daily.

Maybe the fashionable French haberdashers would like a photo of their sweater with a few foxtail beards and hay needles stuck to the cashmere.

Or, I'm guessing, probably not.

The wheels on the bus
Go round and round and round   August 31, 2009

It's been a long time since the big, yellow school bus has had our ranch on the route. About 21 years, if I'm reading the faded date on my high school diploma correctly.

We're finally on the bus route again with our 5-year-old trotting out the door each morning for another exciting day of kindergarten. He hardly could wait for the first day of school, but he was equally thrilled about getting to ride the bus. I hope both those feelings of awe and interest stay intact for the next 13 years.

I always liked school, and I don't remember ever complaining about the bus ride. It's a family tradition here on the edge of the school district to be the first kid on in the morning and the last kid off in the evening.

Our boy's got it a little better than I did, though. When he gets on the bus, another little boy with the tough luck of being the bus driver's son already is there so, technically, he's the second one on and the second to the last one off.

My bus ride used to be about an hour and 20 minutes. They've shaved a little time off in the last 20 years because my son's bus ride is a mere one hour. Still a plenty long ride for a 5-year-old, but I think he's kind of glad to get off the ranch and have someone else to talk to besides his little brother.

Sparser routes

Looking at the list of kids on the route, it's easy to see where they shaved off the time. They're making less than half as many stops and picking up a fourth as many kids as they did when I was a school boy.

There are eight children on my son's bus route. Heck, when I was riding, we picked up eight kids at one farm. Seriously. They had one in just about every grade. Of course, this was back before family planning got popular.

Things are a lot different now. We get married much later in life, if at all. And two or three children is about all most of us can afford. Those of us who farm or ranch spend the money we've saved by having small families on the bigger and better equipment that makes it possible to farm without bigger families. I'm starting to think it'd be cheaper to have a big family and small, old equipment.

Today, I was out in the hay field doing the same thing my dad did this time of year during his 20 years of having children in school. I was looking up the road to the north about midafternoon to see if the school bus was coming yet.

Waiting for help

At this age, I just want to confirm that my young son made it home, safe and sound, after another day of expanding his mind. In six or eight years, I'll be looking for the school bus to arrive so I can have a helper in the field to man the rake or a mower.

But I'll have to start talking up the good times and glory of helping his dad after school before all his friends start telling him how much fun it is to be in football, basketball, wrestling, track, soccer, baseball, gymnastics, swimming, band, chorus, piano lessons, guitar lessons, speech, debate, robotics, 4H, FFA, FBLA, FCCLA and everything else out there that keeps a kid from helping out his old man.

Maybe if we had eight kids, we'd have at least one introvert with an aversion to organized activities who'd ride the bus at night to come home and help. I pitched that idea to my wife.

I guess we'll just have to see what we can do with the three we've got.

Dress for the elements
Winterized kids   November 23, 2009

I suppose if we lived in Florida, we wouldn't even own a winter jacket, much less mittens, wool caps with ear lappers, snow boots or insulated coveralls.

But we have those four distinct seasons in North Dakota, and winter can be real distinct. As my warm-weather California brother told me, though, if the weather is always beautiful, it's never special. If it's 80 degrees and sunny every day, it probably doesn't seem real special.

In my neighborhood, 80 degrees felt real special after last winter. And if you've had a hot, dry summer, the coolness of autumn is special, the moist greenness of spring is special, and, although I hate to admit it, the clean, crisp whiteness of winter is even special.

The other truth confessed to me by semi-arctic expatriates who've moved to more temperate climates is that everything is easier when the weather is warm, at least in the winter.

Open roads that aren't slick with ice or snow, cars that start without any coaxing or strategically applied heat, the freedom of stepping out the door in your shirt sleeves without bundling up. It would make for an easier life, but probably less special.

Kids and cold

Life without kids probably is easier, too, but definitely less special. In winter, getting those little tikes ready to go outside is darn special. So special it just about drives you crazy.

Children come with milestones that mark their growth and maturity. Their first words, their first steps, the transition from diapers to big boy underwear. The list goes on.

The next stage I'm really looking forward to is when these little rascals can dress themselves to go outside in the winter.

I remember the day our firstborn got all five fingers in the right receptacles of the receiving glove as I dressed him. I felt like I'd just hit the jackpot on a slot machine. I just about jumped up and did a little victory dance. Now he puts his own gloves on. I'm so proud.

Our baby girl still is struggling with thumb placement in her mittens. As a parent, you have to work fast to manipulate their digits into position. Patience wears thin quickly on a kid as you try to get the gloves and mittens on.

Most every hand-me-down jacket we have for our kids has something wrong with the zipper, major or minor. Sometimes you have to switch to snaps or Velcro on the fly, or make an improvised zipper pull from a paper clip to get them out the door.

Right snow boot on the right foot, left boot on the left foot, pull the stocking cap down so that only their eyes are showing and push them out the door to enjoy the fresh air.

It's no wonder we're late for everything. But sometimes you get a hug in the middle of the process as you lace up their boots, or they smile at you as you zip their jacket up to their chin and, you realize: This, too, will be one of the things you miss when they have grown into insolent teenagers.

But I won't miss the mucous management when they return from their play time outside. I'll be a happy dad when all three kids quit sniffling and can blow their own nose. Another milestone to reach for a cold-weather family.

Full-time father
Flying parentally solo for six days December 7, 2009

I'm no skydiver, but I do some uncomfortable things on a regular basis. I stand in front of wild cows and tell them they can't go through the gate, I speak in front of large groups of people without so much as a podium to hide behind, I get on horses that aren't broke and I leap tall buildings with a single bound.

OK, I don't leap tall buildings, but I do the rest of that stuff. One really unsettling thing I've never done, though, is be a single parent to three little kids for six whole days. No, my wife didn't leave me permanently, just for a while to accompany her mother on a trip to New York to visit friends and see some sites.

When my mother-in-law asked if she could steal my wife for a week to visit some longtime family friends, I instantly thought of some advice given by my late father-in-law. There's a bond between a mother and a daughter, he said, and you don't ever want to get yourself caught in the middle of it.

So, when the trip was pitched to me, I was affirmative, but hesitant. "Yeah, OK, um, I guess so...." I'd have to figure out the details on how to run the ranch while feeding, dressing, changing, bathing, teaching, consoling, conversing and entertaining a 5-, a 3- and a 1-year-old for six days.

Feeding time

One thing about our ranch is it's a long drive to a restaurant, so you're pretty much stuck cooking for yourself when you're on your own.

I made a trip to the grocery store to lay in the needed provisions for my stint as chief cook and dish washer. It was like shopping for bachelor food with a preschool twist.

Frozen pizza, TV dinners, alphabet soup, macaroni and cheese and canned spaghetti in the shape of cartoon movie characters. My wife prepared some things I could stick in the oven (that's the square white thing in the kitchen that's smaller than the fridge). We had lots of milk and breakfast cereal.

As a fallback, I was consoled by a friend who said no one would be permanently damaged if we just ate ice cream for six days either. I checked the freezer. We had plenty of ice cream.

I didn't have to worry much about food for myself. I wouldn't have time to eat anyway.

Juggling act

Generally, the kids have been pretty good. Sometimes I've achieved 100 percent satisfaction—no screaming, crying or whining. Might have been the ice cream.

Other times, I've achieved 100 percent of them all wanting me to do something for them all that very instant. This would tip the scales of screaming, crying and whining to 25, 50, 75 or even 100 percent, if I joined in on the crying.

I have had help during the day with the oldest being in kindergarten and the two younger ones going in to day care long enough for me to get the cattle fed and the chores done. A 16-month-old girl just isn't very safe help around cattle or in the tractor.

We have a few days to go, but it looks like we'll survive. I haven't lost any kids yet to an avalanche of dirty dishes or dirty clothes, and everyone's gotten fed, watered and read to.

But I might do a little extra Christmas shopping to find something nice for my wife this year. Maybe concentrate on doing a few of those daily things that help a marriage last.

Because after this six-day experiment, I sure don't want her leaving us for good.

Little ranchhands
Next generation is eager to start   Summer, 2008

We added another member to the Taylor Ranch crew this summer. Our latest is a little girl who'll try to add a little class to the operation in the shadow of her two rough-and-tumble big brothers.

Mom stays plenty busy in the house with the newborn, so the big brothers tend to spend a little more time with Dad out and about on the ranch.

If I so much as lace up my boots or put a hat on my head and reach for the door knob, my 4-year-old shouts "Can I come?" cueing the 2-year-old, never one to be left out, to come at a run yelling, "Me, too! Me, too!"

I'm a big pushover, so I cave in and tell them to go jump in the pickup.

It doesn't matter what job I'm going out the door to do. I could tell them I was going out to neuter a horse trailer full of wild barn cats and they'd be on my heels, "Can I come? Me, too! Me, too!"

I could ask them if they want to help pitch manure, lance a lump on a cow or scrape gunk from the bottom of the water tanks, and the answer would be, "Yeah, yeah! Me, too!"

I can only hope they maintain that enthusiasm for chores when they get older.

Things take time

Having the dynamite duo, Can I Come and Me Too, with me all the time doesn't make me especially productive.

Just opening and shutting a gate that might take me 30 seconds by myself becomes a five-minute process as my crew jumps out of the pickup, collects sticks, hunts grasshoppers, runs a few circles and climbs back in their seats.

My 4-year-old is able to get some gates by himself though. I have a couple of those bungee cord gates on my electric cross fences. He knows to touch only the orange handle, lifts the hook out of the eye, and then goes shooting toward the other end of the gate like a slingshot. Kind of a short, earth-bound, horizontal bungee jump.

After I drive through the gate, he summons all 42 pounds of his strength to hook the bungee cord back up, and, if he remembered to put himself on the right side of the gate, comes trotting back to the pickup with a big smile on his face.

"I did it all by myself," he beams. I smile back at him and say "Yup, I saw that," sharing that parental approval we all yearn for.

They ask a million questions and I give them a million answers. I like to give them real answers to the questions I know. The 2-year-old can listen to my explanation of how a round hay bale is made with the pickup teeth, shafts, chains and belts and give a revelatory "Ohhh!," like he actually understands.

There's no quiet time when the crew is with me, but it is pretty entertaining.

Family ranch

The terms family farm, family farmers or family rancher are used a lot in the debate on the real value of rural America to the rest of the country.

I don't know if there's a single, good definition for what a family farm or ranch actually is. I reckon the operation would have to be owned by a family, rather than a corporation or some other disinterested non-agricultural entity.

I like the definition that a true family farm or ranch gets the majority of its labor from family members, not full-time salaried employees.

Our place has been run since 1903 by unpaid family members and poorly paid part-time help who must either like us, enjoy the scenery or appreciate the home-cooked meals.

And considering the 3-foot-tall crew that heads out the door with me most every day, I think we'll be a family ranch for a long time to come.

When I look at them, I'd add one more defining characteristic for a family ranch — along with raising cattle, it ought to raise some kids, too.

Horsepower or human power
Getting outside on our two feet   February 1, 2010

I've never been much of motor head. I accept the need for a little motorization to get things done on the ranch, but I generally prefer muscle energy — mine, my wife's, a horse's, anything that doesn't need diesel or gasoline or grease to do its work.

My mother could see that I wasn't immediately drawn to engines and noise when I was a kid. She also knew there's a lot of winter to try and enjoy when you live in North Dakota. I think that's why she came home with a pair of cross-country skis one day when they were clearance priced late in the season. I was only 10 or 12 years old at the time.

A few years later, I got a pair of the big, Alaska-style snowshoes for Christmas and a backpack trap basket to help me run my trapline for muskrats, mink and beaver. At an early age, I learned that my two legs were made for something besides folding up underneath me while playing video games or watching television.

I also learned early on that a guy could get somewhere in the winter without jumping in a pickup or getting on a snowmobile or a four-wheeler. I never once got stuck out on the prairie on my skis or snowshoes.

I'm probably blessed with skinny genetics and high metabolism, but even without those genes, I don't think childhood obesity would've been a threat when I'd ski or snowshoe a couple miles every day around my trapline.

Kids these days

Looking back, I feel awfully lucky to have been given simple gifts like a pair of long skinny boards to slide on and a couple of sharp sticks to push myself along. I never felt deprived for not having a snowmobile that I could fix on and fight with for two hours and ride for one.

My folks never had to push me out the door or peel me away from the glow of a screen or a video game. I learned to enjoy winter, and that's handy when you live where I do. I've always liked the Winter Olympics better than the Summer Olympics because of that early exposure to the sports of my Norwegian ancestors.

Now I wonder if I can do the same things, start the same good habits, for my children that my parents did for me. Kids are getting heavier and unhealthier, according to the statistics. In America, the states with the highest rates of childhood obesity are Mississippi, Arkansas and Georgia. Maybe it's the climate; those kids probably could use some snow and a pair of skis.

I'm sure us northern parents, and even Canadians, are raising plenty of overweight kids, too. But we do need to make the most of what we've got. If you've got lots of warm weather, teach the kids to swim. If you're covered in snow for a third of the calendar, put the kids on skis or skates or snowshoes.

I think I can get our tikes outfitted with some cross-country skis for less money that it takes to get them a video gaming console and the box full of games that plops them down on the floor next to the television for hours on end.

Humans were smart enough to invent motorized transportation and the technology of video gaming. Now we just need to be smart enough to get away from our inventions for an hour or two each day.

Daddy the draft horse
Paternity brings pack animal qualities   May 10, 2010

Of all the tasks I've taken on since I was kid, there's been one overriding constant — picking up stuff and carrying it from here to there.

I've carried feed buckets from the granary to the trough, grocery sacks from the car to the house, fence posts, lumber, salt blocks and sacks of mineral from where they're at to where they ought to be.

If I ever complained of the manual labor, my folks would assure me that hard work never killed anyone. Of course, I never asked them to cite any actual medical research to back up that claim.

Nowadays, we buy stuff in volume that comes on pallets so the folks at the farm stores can load you with ease using a forklift. But when I get home, sans forklift, I roll up my sleeves and start unloading my palletized parcel one box at a time. Pick it up here, carry it over there.

The years of training as a pack animal serve me well now as a father with three small children.

Carry me!

Packing kids around starts innocently enough when they come home from the hospital at a svelte 7 or 8 pounds. No problem, it's an easy and pleasant little package to tote.

Then they start growing and, before long, you're looking at a 40-pound toddler with outstretched arms pleading, "Carry me, carry me!" You start to think twice, and remember the advice about lifting with your legs as you bend over to get them.

Like all good beasts of burden, parents have devised various harnesses to handle the load. There are slings, wraps and something from the ingenious Swedes called a BabyBjorn to pack around the infants. They're expandable to the point where kids should start moving themselves around.

The harnesses adapt as the kids age. I got a homemade man harness from friends whose son used it to pull tires and weights around to strengthen his leg muscles for sports training.

I slipped it over my shoulders and used it to pull a sled full of youngsters across the snow while I was cross-country skiing. It makes me look a little like Roald Amundsen striding for the South Pole, except the supplies in my trailing sled are wiggling around and shouting, "Mush, Daddy, mush!"

Wheeled transport

Versatile horses and parents are broke to ride or drive.

Piggyback rides are great fun for the rider, but a little tough on the parental pony over long distances, especially in hilly country. Shoulder rides are best for the outdoors. Inside, the doorways are sure to catch you getting careless and result in some bumps and boo boos.

When not riding their father, the kids enjoy a nice buggy ride with Dad pulling the cart behind his bike. I pack 'em in, gear down my fat-tired prairie mountain bike and hit the trail.

Together, the boys are getting to be pretty heavy cargo. After our last trip, this draft horse daddy was all in. I put the boys on the scale, added the pounds, counted the axles and divided it all out. I told them we were breaking the spring road restriction rules and they'd have to start pedaling themselves on our trips. Don't want to damage the roads, you know.

They just as well start building some endurance to be a paternal pack horse themselves someday.

Dangerous jobs
Trying to balance the hazards with the learning   August 2, 2010

I wouldn't call myself a thrill seeker who hunts for dangerous stunts to try. But somehow, our family landed in the fifth most-dangerous job around.

There're plenty of lists that look at labor statistics, accident rates and fatalities, but they usually run something like this on rating occupational danger: fishermen, loggers, aircraft pilots, steel workers and then us, farmers and ranchers.

I thought I was playing it safe by not doing the bungee slingshot at the state fair or parachuting out of a perfectly good airplane. Turns out, just heading out the door each morning as a rancher puts me at above-average risk for death and injury.

I could find a less-dangerous occupation like office worker, but I don't think I could stand the paper cuts. Or we could reduce the risk on the farm or ranch some by how we do our job.

Old ways

I don't suppose it'd be recommended today, but I was 9 years old when I started working in the hayfield as a scatter raker. The tractor I started on was a "B" John Deere.

Safety features meant it had fenders and a steering wheel to hang on to. But it probably was safer than a lot of today's newer machines. It had a hand clutch to stop the tractor and change your gear. No shifting on the fly. If Dad put me in third or fourth gear, he knew I wouldn't be going too fast. The rake had few moving parts, no power takeoff shaft to watch out for. The job of "scatter raker" was not the most demanding job in the hay stacking operation, but I felt pretty important out there.

I used to dig a lot of fence post holes as a kid. Our old-fashioned ways made it pretty safe. No automated spinning post augers, just a clam shell, hand-operated posthole digger. The only moving parts were my arms.

I was fortunate to grow up with horses instead of four-wheelers and dirt bikes. Sure horses are big, strong animals, but they have a brain and most good ones don't want to hurt you or step on you. I've lost track of the guys I know who spent a lifetime with horses injury-free just to get hurt bad by a four-wheeler later in life. A horse will avoid a washout or a bull hole, but those machines will let you drive right in at whatever speed you want.

I'm sure I still did a lot of dangerous, stupid stuff as a kid, but I was able to work alongside Dad in relative safety. We were never in such a hurry that he couldn't take the time to point out the most dangerous things for me to look out for.

Different times

Today, we know there're lots of dangers on the farm and ranch. The machinery has more safety decals and warnings, but it's also bigger, more complex, more expensive and less forgiving.

It's hard to find a job for a kid to do that's safe. There ain't much summer fallow anymore, and in terms of safety and economy, it's hard to put a kid on an outfit that cost a quarter or a half a million dollars. Even on our ranch, I no longer have a relatively safe little bullrake for a kid to buck up hay to the stack, and I wouldn't dare put a youngster on a $30,000 hay baler—too dangerous and too expensive if they mess it up.

It's hard to raise responsible young people without giving them some responsibilities. I guess we need to choose those responsibilities carefully in our fifth most-dangerous environment. We just may need a little more time and a little less automation.

Follow the directions
But have a 6-year-old handy to help   October 25, 2010

Fatherhood is a humbling experience. Always has been, I reckon, since the early days when a dad had to ask his kid how to rub those two sticks together to start a fire.

These days, toys have a minimum suggested age on the box, like recommended for ages 5 and up. Not suitable for children under 3 years because of small parts, a choking hazard.

I've wrestled with the directions on some of these toys with my 6-year-old. They should have another age recommendation on there, like not recommended for anyone age 30 and older. Not suitable for adults over 40 years because of small details, a frustration hazard.

I'm going to drop some brand names here, not that I'm endorsing them, there just aren't many other ways to describe them. Play time starts innocently with Duplo blocks, then Legos, but before you know it, your floor is littered with tiny K'Nex pieces and your kid is poking a set of Transformer robot directions under your nose and asking for your help.

Parents tell themselves they're stimulating junior's brain activity and preparing him or her for a lucrative career in engineering or architecture. Then again, you might be raising a kid who'll be chronically unemployed but really likes snapping together Legos in all his free time because he's not working.

Either way, play time becomes a challenge for the parent committed to sitting down and helping with the latest Lego Star Wars Death Star and its 3,802 pieces scattered across the floor. Just completing the droid maintenance room might be a two-day job.

Artsy builders

It's a lot easier on us as parents if we can get our kids to freelance a little with their building toys. "C'mon, don't bother with those Death Star directions, let's grab all the long bricks and build a barn!" we plead.

I have completed the K'Nex carnival ferris wheel and had it turning freely but it wasn't real great father and son time. "Don't bother me now, son, I've just about got your toy figured out, go get Mom and the camera."

We're torn between wanting them to follow our directions as parents, and encouraging them to dump the 42-step directions for their toy and to go ahead and explore their creative, artistic side. Yo Dude, your Bionicle can look different than the one on the box, just build with your spirit, man, I mean boy.

Practical skills

The building skills we're working on in the toy room maybe should be encouraged and channeled to suitable places on the ranch. Yesterday, my 6-year-old wanted some help transforming his Descepticon Jetblade into Robot mode.

It reminded me of the time I had a box of 24 new roller bearings and races for the wobblehead on my hay mower. I really wanted to transform my box of parts into mower mode. If I'd honed my confidence as a kid with a few Transformer robots it might have gone smoother.

So I helped my boy get the jetblade into robot mode. He helped me figure out most of the steps. And I dreamed of the day when he could transform all of the broken down "descepticon" machines on the ranch into working mode.

When that day comes, it'll all be worth it.

Team ranchers
When your best ranchhand is also your wife   November 22, 2010

If you do a Google search on "teamwork marriage," you'll get 827,000 results in 0.2 seconds. When I want to work on the teamwork aspect of my marriage, I skip reading the books and articles. I just look across the breakfast table and say something sweet like, "Hey, Honey, wanna work some cattle today?"

The cattle-processing aspect of teamwork in a marriage didn't make the first 10 article hits on the Internet search, but it should have. A couple that works cattle together, stays together, I say. Of course, the success of that theory depends on the couple, the cattle, how they handle the cattle and how they treat each other while they're doing it.

If the details and personalities aren't right, the whole cattle-working activity could be disastrous for the marriage, bad for the cattle and ought to be avoided like the plague. If the ingredients are right, though, calmly and happily working cattle through the chute side by side with your life partner is right up there with a romantic dinner together.

Pick your partner

Knowing that your spouse may be called upon to help you work cattle adds a whole new aspect to the culture of courtship as you evaluate lifelong compatibility with possible mates. Somewhere along with physical attraction, emotional support, work ethic, desire to raise a family, molasses cookie recipes and such, you have to look deeper and ask your potential partner their theories on cattle handling.

I do have some gender bias when it comes to working cattle. I think most women are better at it, especially if you're trying to keep stress to a minimum.

Sure, there're plenty of men in my neighborhood who are good at working cattle, but I think us testosterone-clad guys need to work hard at it. We need to make conscious efforts to keep our cool or we go caveman and start screaming and thumping and slow the whole process.

Women who I've seen work cattle have a much longer fuse, and if they know a little about cattle and how they react to pressure points and where to locate themselves, they're 10 times the help of some guy yelling and screaming and grumbling about not having an electric prod to "make them go!"

Growth constraints

There are plenty of times where the work we do with the cattle requires more help than my wife and I, and we have a good neighborhood crew when we ask for it.

But our herd isn't so big that we can't vaccinate or wean the calves by ourselves in a couple different bunches if we get a baby sitter for the little ranch hands. When the two of us work the calves and nobody blows their top or throws a sorting stick at the other, I know I married the right person to support me in my ranching habit.

According to the so-called laws of economics, we ought to be growing our herd, renting more pasture, buying more machinery and hiring more help, but I don't like the thought of having so many cattle that I'd have to "cheat" on my wife by working cattle with other people, especially people who might not be as good at it as she is.

I think this was all in the vows somewhere, for richer, for poorer, in sickness and in health, to love and to cherish and to calmly work cattle together, until death or upon sale of the herd do us part.

But not until we've helped each other load the cattle truck.

Keeping up with the Jones (kids)
Tempted to keep kids sheltered   January 17, 2011

Every generation of parents probably has struggled with all the things their kids would like to have and what Mom and Dad actually can afford to give them. Or, if they can afford it all, struggle to rein them in a little so they gain a healthy respect for scarcity.

I never had to work at an appreciation for scarcity when I was growing up. It was just there, or not there as the case might be. Don't get me wrong, we had plenty of good gifts on birthdays and holidays, but we learned to get along without a fair bit, too.

Now, my 6-year-old sees a Web address on a box of cereal, goes to my computer, types it in and starts pining for whatever toy or game or brand of sneakers was being promoted. I guess we had the same temptation in the Montgomery Ward Christmas catalog when I was a tike. But it was a little less sophisticated, and didn't have the marketing push of cartoons shows paired with online games paired with character pajamas paired with the ad on your juice bottle.

I was lucky to go to a school with a lot of other regular kids in my class whose parents tried to keep them used to denial and disappointment, too. Now it seems like I'm the only one cultivating a good level of hardship in my kids by not indulging their video game desires – Wii, DS, PS3 and other combinations of letters or numbers that put kids into zombie gaming mode.

Clueless

For awhile, because of our remote location, we were able to keep our kids in the dark about what kids in the outside world had.

We were able to buy a used bike with training wheels for the boys for $10. Our oldest loved that bike, and being 3 miles from the nearest neighbor, no one was there to tell him that Dora the Explorer bikes were designed more for girls.

He was plumb happy riding that pink bike — it had tires that held air, pedals, a chain, everything you need in a bike. Then one of his school classmates came out and told him it wasn't cool for a boy to be riding a pink bike. OK, fair enough, we're keeping that one for little sister. We and found a used Spiderman bike, still $10, for him and his brother.

The kids figured everyone just played "I spy" when they were driving in the family van, entertaining themselves with what they saw in the passing countryside. Then they got in someone else's vehicle that had drop-down screens and DVD's they could watch while going down the road. Now "I spy" has taken a back seat to what they think is better back-seat entertainment.

Not having these things ourselves does make it more exciting for the kids to go to a baby sitter or visit other kids who have all the cool stuff.

It's probably too late to keep these kids under a rock so they're unaware of how other families live. As it is, they have discovered the outside world. My wife and I just have to remember a parent's No. 1 job — keep saying no, again and again.

Climbing the walls
Not just figuratively   January 31, 2011

I've heard of infants being referred to as "curtain climbers," but I don't know many kids who limit themselves to just climbing curtains. I know I never did. Besides, I grew up in a house with shades, and it's a lot trickier to climb a roll up, retractable shade.

As quick as I could, I started in climbing anything I could get an arm and a leg up on. I climbed corrals, then trees, then barns and windmills. I see my own kids on the same path to new heights.

Hay stacks were a lot of fun when my siblings and I were little. All lined up in a row, we'd jump from one to the next, but if we fell into the dark, scratchy void between four tightly spaced stacks, we were in a bit of a bind. If one of your playmates couldn't pull you out, you'd have to wait there and yell and hope someone missed you by suppertime. With a little luck, they'd bring a ladder for you.

Moving from stacks to round bales changed the game a little. More round edges to slip off of, but some twine you could grab to slow your descent. If you stack the bales three high, kids can get a little more altitude from which to ponder their surroundings.

These hay climbing games can take a bad turn, as taught to us by our toddler girl last summer when she tried to keep up with her two older brothers on a small stack of bales.

As explained to me by a 6-year-old eyewitness, "she just kept walking and then (shoulder shrug) … gone." Turned out the 5- or 6-foot drop off the edge, even though it was relatively soft ground and hay resulted in a fractured arm.

It gave our 2-year-old a little time in a splint and a fairly positive healing experience. She still describes the whole experience in two- or three-word sound bites. "Fell off bales." "Broke my arm." "Too bad." "Doctor fix it." It's one of those good 2-year-old tales, and we never know when she'll break into telling it.

Jungle gym

Modern playgrounds have all the cool things a kid might want. They go well beyond the standard swing set, teeter totter and slide. Now they have these multi-colored multifaceted multi-fun playsets.

Inevitably, they have a little climbing wall attached to them, complete with the cool, rock-shaped handles to grab or rest a toe on as they make their way up.

Our two boys really like the rock walls at the playgrounds. When I took them to a hotel for a banquet supper recently, I gave no thought to the way they see things from their small, scheming, climbing eyes.

We ate our meal, and while I was enjoying a cup of coffee, the boys asked if they could play quietly out in the hall. I didn't see much harm in that, so I turned them loose and started eating their leftovers.

Eventually, curiosity got the best of me and I went out in the hall to see what kind of game they'd devised. My reaction bounced between pride and embarrassment when I saw our two little rascals scaling the brick wall.

The 4-year-old was up about 6 feet when I got a hold of him and brought him back down to terra firma. I was pretty impressed with their strength as they curled their little fingers around a protruding brick and pulled themselves up.

Their mother wasn't nearly as proud. I suppose Spider Man didn't get much support from his mom either.

But it might be a good idea for us to stay close by to catch them if they fall. At least until their web shooters grow in.

Big screen entertainment
Family trip to the moving picture show   February 28, 2011

I think I could count on one hand the number of times we've taken our kids to the movie theater to see something up on the big screen. That's how we keep things special. Severe limitation.

However few their movie outings have been, it's probably more than my wife and I have gone on alone since we started raising a family. We're lucky if we have the time to sit down and watch one on the television or on a DVD these days. I guess that's why you're supposed to do those kinds of things in courtship, because you won't get to do them later.

Last week, we took the whole doggone family to the cinema. Even baby girl was invited along for her very first movie at the ripe old age of 2½.

The movie was animated, of course, and so was the level of excitement among the short people in our entourage. The movie was only 2D, so we didn't need to buy the special glasses, but our family was full on 3D and pretty excited as we entered the theater.

My brother came along so we'd have a one-on-one ratio with the kids in case they didn't mind their manners. It was matinee time, baby sister got in free, but I still plunked down $34 for the rest of us. My brother assured me that was a bargain compared to big-city California. Guess that makes me glad to be small-town North Dakota.

I bought a bushel of popcorn and a barrel of pop at the extortion snack counter for us all to share. Another $15, but they assured me I'd get free refills. We ate the corn like a pen of feeder steers and drank pop like we'd been trekking the Mojave Desert just so I could exercise the free-refill clause of our refreshments contract.

Like I said, we don't go to a lot of movies, and when we do, we wait longer than most folks before we break down and finally go.

It soon was obvious we had waited long enough to see this one, "Tangled," Disney's take on the old fairy tale of Rapunzel, her tower and her hair climbing hero. We walked into the theater just as it began, and, to our surprise and relief, we had the whole place to ourselves.

Now we could stretch out and give the tikes some free rein on our cinematic adventure! We had our pick of the seats, extra chairs to throw our coats on, and didn't have to worry about giving our kids the Shhh! for bothering any fellow movie-goers.

Of course, once the popcorn and pop made its way around and the movie started, you hardly heard a peep from them as they stared with wide-eyed amazement at the big screen of Disney-fied musical characters.

Even the adults enjoyed the movie. It was a cute show, but I got just as much entertainment looking over at the little popcorn munchers sitting on the edge of their seats, giggling and providing some 6-, 4- and 2-year-old commentary on the hairy plot as it unwound.

Of course, it had a happy ending. And after sharing the 55-gallon drum of pop amongst us, we were all happy when the credits started rolling and we made a dash for the restroom.

We may not wait quite so long to see our next movie — or to head to the restroom.

Life's a circus
Especially when you're at the circus   April 11, 2011

Every day is a family circus in our house. Three kids age 6 and under all trying to capture our attention at once, busy schedules where it seems like we meet ourselves coming and going. So, for a little Friday night relaxation we packed up the family and…went to a real three ring circus.

I think we just wanted to have a point of comparison for our daily circus. Thought we'd see how a professional traveling circus with clowns and tigers and high wire walkers would compare with our home life.

A friend gave me free tickets to the circus and that sealed the deal. How can you pass up a free family fun night? Well the tickets might have been free, but the family fun night was far from cheap.

Fortunately, most of the proceeds went to a good cause. I feel better about buying all the stuff kids want you to buy at the circus when the money makes its way to a children's hospital. Healthy kids having fun in one place and time making life a little better for sick children and their families in another place and time.

It was a pretty good little traveling circus. They had a ringmaster, a clown act, a trained dog act, tigers jumping through hoops, elephants that could balance on a ball, acrobats, high wire walkers and a woman who shot herself out of a cannon. You don't see that every day.

Even with the expectation of all those amazing and death-defying acts to catch a kid's attention as we walked in the arena, the first thing the kids noticed was hundreds of other kids carrying plastic swords and magic wands with batteries and lights and sound. So, of course, they really wanted an $8 plastic sword with batteries and lights and sound that was worth about a buck at the dollar store.

It was quite a sight when they turned out the lights in the arena and every kid in the joint had their sword lit up and swirling around as they engaged their siblings in hand-to-hand combat.

The sword fighting was strenuous and took a lot of energy from the short people in my family. The only way to properly recharge their nutritional needs was with three bags of cotton candy.

Between trips to the sword sellers, the cotton candy seller, the concession stand and the bathroom, we caught a little of the action in the three rings of the circus. Then when we really got settled in, it was time for intermission. Not just any intermission, but a long intermission where kids can go down to the three rings of the circus accompanied by a parent (and a wallet) to ride some ponies, take a picture with the trained dogs, jump in an inflatable castle or ride on the elephant. Now I was starting to feel a little abused monetarily with this subtle form of "Daddy, Daddy, please!" extortion.

I talked them into another sword fight until the intermission was over. Finally, after the cannon went off, the cannon lady shot through the air, landed in the awaiting net and the smoke cleared, I asked my two oldest kids what their favorite part of the circus was.

"The swords," they said. If I'd only known, I could've taken them to the dollar store and saved the $7 mark up on the imported Chinese made amusement peddled at the circus.

But then we'd have all missed seeing the cannon lady, and we'd have missed having a point of comparison for our family circus. Now I know. We are a different kind of circus. No one's been shot from a cannon at our house — at least not yet.

Color the eggs
Or risk losing them   April 25, 2011

North Dakota is one of those special places where you can hide your Easter eggs in a snowbank, even when Easter falls towards the end of April! Maybe the idea of coloring Easter eggs came from a country with spring snowstorms, since brightly dyed eggs were easier to spot than white eggs on snowy Easter mornings.

To look out the window as I write this, you'd think it was December, not April. I'm confident that spring will come eventually. That's the promise of Easter. Resurrection and rebirth. There's already plenty to pray for in church on Easter Sunday, but I'm going to throw in a small prayer for green grass and sunshine.

The weather is improving, so the snow may all be melted by Easter morning, but this year, there's always a chance for another snow squall and another few inches of snow to land on the ground.

More than likely, we'll be able to hide some eggs in snowbanks and tuck a few in the mud, but there won't be a lot of green grass to camouflage their hiding place.

Easter eggs aren't what they used to be in our house. I grew up with the hard-boiled eggs that we would dip in dye. I didn't even mind eating them after they had completed their festive tour of duty. I wasn't wild about the hard-boiled yolks when I was little, but I could eat a lot of hard-boiled whites with a little salt and pepper.

I always was better at eating hard-boiled eggs, Easter and otherwise, than Dad. He lost his taste for hard-boiled eggs after his cousin "preserved" a whole bucket of eggs by hard boiling them when they were chasing a group of horses 160 miles to auction in the 1930s. He claimed he ate enough hard-boiled eggs as they camped out on that trip to last a lifetime.

Dad would be happy with our transition from real dyed eggs to the plastic eggs that pop apart and reveal a few jelly beans, a couple malted milk balls or a quarter for the piggy bank. The switch to plastic is probably a hardship for the farmers with laying hens, but a boon for the jelly bean sellers and the always-growing plastics industry.

Holiday warmth

It builds character in our children when they have to wear their winter coats to hunt for eggs on Easter and stretch their Halloween costumes over coveralls and snowmobile suits to go trick-or-treating. It doesn't mean we don't have some pretty nice weather after Halloween or before Easter but our sometimes uncertain weather will give us different holiday memories than kids from warmer climates.

Sometimes the cooler weather is a benefit to the holidays that push candy onto our kids. When the temperatures dip down below freezing, you don't have to worry about the miniature chocolate bars melting in your Easter basket or trick-or-treat bag. That milk chocolate Easter bunny might look a little cold, but at least his whiskers won't droop and drip a chocolaty mess on your jelly beans.

I'm a four-seasons guy, and I truly like living in a land that has all four very distinct seasons represented on the calendar. But, as much as I like and respect winter, spring is a welcome sight.

And Easter is a welcome holiday. With or without the green grass. With or without snow or hard-boiled eggs and pastel dye or frozen chocolate bunnies. It's a spiritual thing found in church for many of us, not a commercial thing found on the aisle end cap of the local Wal-Mart.

It takes a lot more than a little snow to dampen that spirit.

Finding appreciation
The little things make the difference

May 9, 2011

I'm beginning to think I'm a "glass half full," not a "glass half empty" kind of guy when it comes to positive attitudes. Of course, I'm not altogether sure why the glass is at that mark, if it's to my credit for filling it up to that point or if it's my fault for sneaking a drink and draining it down to there.

Maybe it's because of my upbringing, but I'm pretty appreciative of the little things in life, and, in our life, most of the things we have to appreciate are pretty little. We don't often find ourselves having to react to a new yacht in the yard, an all-expense paid trip around the world, or a high-yielding oil well in the back yard.

There are, however, plenty of little things to brighten our day.

Time value

I've found that my level of appreciation grows exponentially the longer I've denied myself something, big or small.

The happiest part of my day yesterday was getting the trolley track hung back up on the front of our old, wood-framed barn that we still use for the horses and cattle. I think it lost most of its lag screws and anchoring a good year or so ago.

I finally got tired of lifting that heavy wooden door and dragging it open every time I wanted to go in the barn, so I took a timber to beef up the top framing and buried some 6- inch lag bolts to get things back on track.

We were working cattle nearby that day, and every time I looked over at the barn door, I smiled with pure satisfaction. Sometimes I'd walk over to it just to slide it open and then slide it shut again. I added some oil to the track, and the joy of it all was nearly overwhelming. Guess it doesn't take much to make me happy.

Playground please

I've passed that on to our children, too. Long-term denial of something simple to crank up their appreciation meter.

We have plenty of play space here on the ranch, but not a lot of playground style equipment. I did convert one of our old F10 Farmhands into something that would hold a couple of swings, but we've had no real swing set in the yard.

We've driven through the city neighborhoods where every yard has one of those $500 or $1,000 play sets from the local, big box home store. I always wonder if they considered sharing one of those elaborate play sets amongst a few families rather than have one after another in every yard. Would have been tough on the sales quota for the local big box, I suppose.

Our kids understood they wouldn't be getting the $1,000 model with the integrated rock-climbing wall for our yard, but we did buy an old swing set from some friends in town for $25 when they were dismantling it for an upgrade.

Being dismantled, it sat in our yard about as long as my barn door sagged on the ground. It laid there long enough for me to drive over part of it with the tractor while

I was pushing snow last winter.

My wife and I finally dug the bolts out of their water-filled bucket and put it together this spring, complete with a modification or two to account for the pieces I flattened.

You've never seen three kids happier to see a $25 swing set than ours were when we snugged up the last rusty bolt.

"Thank you, Dad, for putting our swing set together," my 6-year-old said as I tucked him in that night. "You're welcome, Son," I said, as I smiled about the simple pleasures of an old swing set that swung and an old barn door that slid.

Small concessions
Extra care for little critters   May 23, 2011

There's a lot of new life getting its start on the ranch these days. Every morning, I check to see how many new calves there are in the pasture, and, most every day, one of the more perturbed mothers lets me know I'm too close to her baby when I'm ear-tagging it.

It's a balance, and sometimes a sprint, to figure out my place in the whole deal as I put myself between mother and offspring. There is a certain amount of respect demanded by, and afforded to, a 1,200-pound mother coming at you with glazed eyes and flared nostrils.

Fear and personal safety is one way to motivate respect for maternity I guess, at least among ranchers. But, either by vocation or upbringing, that respect spills over onto other mothers and babies I come across that are smaller and less frightful, who can't put me in the hospital.

An even start

I was one of those kids whose mother would come unglued if she ever heard about or saw me messing with a bird nest or the eggs inside it. It didn't matter if it was a lowly barn swallow or something more revered like a sharptail grouse nest, you could look at it, learn from it, but don't you dare harm it.

Those eggs were the most important thing in that mother bird's world, and she taught me to remember that, even in my mischievous boy stage when I might have felt the temptation to crack an egg or knock down a nest. The lesson stuck.

My father taught me the virtues of orphan care when mothers of one kind or another couldn't feed or care for their youngsters. We learned from baby calves on the kitchen floor who needed shelter, a bottle of warm milk or a scratch on the back to bring them a little comfort in the absence of their mothers.

Once, he brought home a couple of orphaned baby badgers he'd found along the road. He probably wasn't heartbroken about the dead mother badger that had been digging holes in the middle of our driveway, but he felt for the two babies who still had their eyes shut and needed some nurturing.

We used a baby bottle to feed the aptly named "Howler" and "Growler," the baby badgers, and "Growler" actually lived to healthy adulthood with our surrogate mothering.

Both my parents had tender feelings for animals, and, I suppose that's why ranching and country life suited them so well. Sure we were in the beef business, and we knew how to hunt and trap, but springtime was about life's beginnings, not the ends.

Lessons extended

Those were the lessons going through my mind when I found a mallard duck hen nesting between two of our hay bales recently.

We're long on ducks and short on hay here, but I've steered clear of those two alfalfa bales to give that mama duck a chance at childrearing. I showed her nest to our wide-eyed kids who counted the eggs and inspected the way she drug a little hay over her nest to hide it while she was gone.

They're anxious to go back and soon see the nest left only with cracked egg shells, and find the mama duck in the nearby pond with her little brood paddling behind her.

Our kids may grow up to hunt ducks when they're older, and eat beef and curse badger holes, but I want them to know that everything gets a fair start in life on this ranch. At least that's what I was taught.

This day
For Father's Day and every day   June 20, 2011

My 4-year-old has his own way of saying some things. Instead of saying "today," he'll say "this day." Like, "What are we going to do this day, Dad?" Good question, son.

He reminds me, in his own cute way, that it's not just any day we're about to plan, it's this day. And when "this day" is over, we won't get another chance at it. This day will be gone forever.

There's plenty written in the motivational media about the value of a day. Set goals, make plans, check off your accomplishments as you capture each milestone on the way to your first million or your next promotion. Each day is a gift, for sure, and we ought to consider how we use each of those gifts.

My middle son isn't thinking about us reaching the next rung of some material ladder, though, when he asks about our plans for this day. He's just wondering if we'll get to do something together as a father and a son.

This all hit me as we approached Father's Day, and, like a lot of things, my 4-year-old helped me make perfect sense of it all.

Saddle up

Every kid is different, and every dad's relationship with his children is different. There is no standard instruction manual for the job, but there's a common denominator for the men most would call good fathers.

I think that denominator is like the tagline I read for an initiative promoting responsible fatherhood. It said "take time to be a Dad today." Simple enough. Take time.

The simple idea made perfect sense when my son looked at me recently with all his 4-year-old hope and earnestness and said, "Dad, can we ride horse this day?"

My generally consulted list of things to do that day had items on it like fixing fence, spraying weeds, entering cattle records and balancing the checkbook. I ignored the list and said, yeah, let's ride horse today.

He beamed as we went out to catch and saddle Dude, a 26-year-old gelding whose main job on the ranch is to eat grass and make little kids happy. He's the horse on the place that's not for sale, and I hope he has a few more years left in him to work his equine magic on our family.

Giddy up

Dude is a full-sized horse, making him about twice as tall as my son. My son didn't let that disparity discourage him as he grabbed a hold of the saddle strings and scrambled up and on to the saddle of his noble steed.

I saddled up another horse and off we went. I looked over at my boy and he beamed back at me with a grin that stretched from ear to ear. Dude is the horse that he gets to ride all by himself, full control of the reins to stop or steer or maybe even kick into a trot. He relishes the responsibility.

When we pulled back up to the hitching rail, I suppose the whole activity for catching, saddling, riding, giggling, talking and turning the horses loose again took an hour or an hour and a half of "this day."

My little boy slid off of that big horse and as soon as his cowboy boots hit the ground, he looked over at me with a big smile and a twinkle and said, "Can we ride Dude again tomorrow?"

What's a dad to say? I said, "Yes, I'd love to." And my heart swelled as I put the saddles away and I knew that "this day" was a good day, a father's day and a son's day.

Roughing it
In the great backyard   August 1, 2011

There isn't much of me that doesn't ache right now. That's because I just peeled myself out of a tent where I slept with my nephew and my two boys last night.

My wife asked if I was going to blow up an air mattress for our grand backyard adventure. I told her heck no, we were sleeping cowboy style, curled up in our blankets right on mother earth. Stiff and sore cowboy style, I've concluded.

My sons are at the age where building a campfire and pitching a tent a couple hundred feet from the house is something you can look forward to all afternoon. Having their 12-year-old cousin in on the deal makes it even better. They follow him around like junior woodsman interns, listening intently to his fishing stories and tales of Boy Scout camp.

It's good that the outdoors still can elicit excitement and awe in a kid. Dad talked about camping with his elder cousin when he was 14 years old and they chased 40 horses 160 miles to market. They camped out at night, ate hard-boiled eggs and created memories that stuck with Dad his whole life.

I remember my yard tent days and, later, riding horse off into a pasture with friends and neighbors to heat up a can of beans and boil some coffee.

There's a natural draw for a kid to want to roll out his sleeping bag and test his camping skills, but it takes some encouragement.

Outback mentors

I remember my uncle taking me fishing and camping, and, although the 6- and 7-pound walleyes I caught on Lake Sakakawea were memorable, the trip I most cherished was backpacking in Montana with him, setting up camp and casting for trout that would hit the frying pan just minutes after they were pulled from the Madison River.

Our parents never blinked an eye when friends and I wanted to saddle a horse and ride off into the hills with our saddle bags and mess kits. They would check on us once in awhile.

I remember the welcome sight of my mother walking into our camp one morning for coffee. She was a most welcome sight for my buddy and me because she was leading our two horses that mysteriously came untied in the middle of the night. I guess our knot-tying skills had not yet been perfected.

We did a lot of winter camping because Dad somehow decided to buy an old trailer house for $200 and pulled it into the trees for us to decorate as we saw fit and convert it to a boondocks boy's club.

A pretty good-sized group of boys got a return on that $200 investment many times over. We learned how to build a fire and cook on a wood stove, how to stoke the fire and go to sleep with the thermometer reading 100 degrees and wake up with it reading 20, how to hide in the blankets and hope one of your friends would take on the chore of building the morning fire. We learned to live in harmony with the many mice that made that trailer their home.

Mostly, we made a lot of memories. But the memories didn't just happen by themselves. They took an uncle, a parent, or an older cousin who took the time to get a kid out of the house and into the outdoors.

But next time I go out to sleep cowboy style, I think I'll go old cowboy style with an old cowboy air mattress to take the lumps out of mother earth as I curl up with the little campers.

Road trip
Family bonding on the great American highway   August 29, 2011

There's nothing like 3- or 4,000 miles together in a mini-van to bring a family closer together, but you do have to get out of the van once in awhile or you'll surely be driven farther apart.

Four-fifths of our family just finished a great American cross-country road trip from North Dakota to Oregon with several circular tours in between. We left one-fifth of our family, the 3-year-old girl, with Grandma to even up the odds for wife and I to keep track of the 5- and 7-year-old boy critters on our adventure.

Even at that, I'm not sure the odds were even, but we kept up as best we could. When the back-seat boy energy was about to boil over, we'd locate the closest city park or playground and siphon a little of that off so we could get back in the van and make another few hundred miles.

We had a mixed bag of lodging on the trip ranging from benevolent relatives to questionable tenting spots to motels driven by pure greed at the height of tourist season. We were treated best by the benevolent relative. No contest.

The city parks we found for playground time were pretty nice, but the RV park and city park we found to pitch our tent late at night seemed a little shady, and I don't mean shady like under a leafy tree.

One was bordered by chain link fence, piles of crushed asphalt, steel buildings and heavy equipment. I think the city figured their park district should group the industrial park and the tenting park together. We built a fire that night, hoping that there weren't enough flammable fumes wafting over from the industrial side to cause a problem. The donation box suggested $10 per tent, so the price was right.

Another tenting spot was located late at night on my phone's Internet connection and was one of those RV cities next to the interstate. We pitched the tent by the glow of our headlights, were lulled to sleep by the roar of the interstate traffic and woke up under a high-voltage power line. Our tent sites really weren't bringing us very close to nature, but they were affordable.

Luckily, there were plenty of other nature opportunities for the boys and us. We made a couple of swings through Yellowstone National Park, did some caving and hiking at Craters of the Moon National Monument and soaked up the serene beauty of eastern Oregon's high desert.

The boys got to see and do some favorite boy things — looking at, but not touching, live, poisonous frogs on display at the museum in Bozeman, Mont.; walking by burning hot, steaming water in the Yellowstone geyser basin; climbing around on some big, sharp rocks and going down into cold, dark, slippery caves.

They got to play with a whole bunch of other kids in an old barn at our beef co-op's 25th anniversary celebration. A homemade rope swing hanging from the barn rafters, along with a barrel of water and some water pistols made for a full day of fun that would rival any amusement park.

We got to spend time with good friends like my cousin and his family in Montana, my wife's cousin and her family in Idaho, our cattle ranching and retailing friends from the beef co-op in Oregon and our good friend who is 28 months into a diagnosis of inoperable pancreatic cancer at his high-desert ranch.

The trip was both meaningful and memorable. It's hard to ask for much more. Except maybe a shorter drive to get back home.

Child's play
That looks a little like work

Enjoy what you do and you'll never work a day in your life, or so they say. So I guess work is defined as anything we don't enjoy doing. But I know guys who don't enjoy leisure activities, so is that work? I don't know, it's more debate about words and semantics than I care to ponder.

The bottom line is this, I guess — work, or whatever you call it, goes better if it's fun. This is a place where our parenting skills are tested as we try to con our offspring into doing something helpful for the family unit, or the family ranch.

I must have been easy to entertain with ranch work because I spent a lot of time outside with Dad when I was a kid. Some of what I did out there must have been helpful. Maybe.

I pounded a lot of nails. To start with, I just pounded them for fun. I pounded 20 or 25 nails in the shape of my initials, RT, into a plank that was part of the walkway to the door of our house. It's pretty long-lasting nail art; it's still there 35 years later.

Eventually, the skill set I developed was put to use nailing up corral planks with long pole barn spikes, and nailing barbed wire to tough little oak fence posts with fencing staples that were a little less tough than the iron hard oak they were trying to penetrate.

When I take the kids to the shop with me, or out to the pasture, I make sure I have three hammers, a can of little nails and three blocks of wood. I also should remember to take some Band-Aids and a hanky to dry the tears because they are certain to hammer a thumb in the process.

But they are learning a little about hammering nails. And it keeps them occupied while I try to do my work, or play, or whatever it is depending on my level of enjoyment.

It takes some effort as a dad to find them a little job they can handle or an activity that'll keep them busy. Like keeping a pair of little grain scoops in the feed bin so they can help me fill the feed buckets. I could do it just as fast, or faster, by myself, but this way, they can help out and I have more fun when I here giggles in the grain bin.

Mini me fencers

I got the two boys helping to build a couple of electric cross fences in our pasture this fall. Nothing's quite as amusing as listening to a 5- and 7-year-old visit back and forth like a couple of little old men as they feed me fence posts and clip insulators onto them after I've pounded them in.

The best part is that the fencing tasks they took on were of real value. They saved me a lot of walking, and they were pretty darned entertaining co-workers.

It'd probably have been easier to give them my phone to play a video game, or to have left them home with their mother. But it was a beautiful fall day to get out and enjoy.

I don't think we broke any child labor laws because the boys had so much fun. And, like I started out saying, if you're enjoying yourself, it ain't work. Come to think of it,

I guess I didn't work much that afternoon either.

But somehow, at the end of the day, we did get a fence put up.

Nothing nice anymore
The things you can't have with kids and cattle   October 24, 2011

"I guess we can't have nice things" is a saying most of us have heard from a deflated mother at some point in the rearing of inadvertently destructive little people. Or an exasperated, "I have nothing nice left anymore!" when one her little angels has smashed the last of the nice dishes or knocked some other fragile heirloom off the wall.

A friend of mine told the story on Facebook of a Wii bowling game gone bad that ended up with a big, new, broken flat screen television. Can't have nothing nice. Others chimed in with stories of Wii remotes flying through the air, intersecting with a ceiling fan and being hurled just inches past a china hutch. Another mother's month-old flat screen was pulverized by a flying Lincoln Log. For some reason, only boys were mentioned as the perpetrators in the heinous destruction.

Maybe that's why we don't have a flat screen TV. Or a Wii. Just doesn't pay to have some of those high-tech and fragile things in a house with three kids under the age of 8, and two of them being boys, the aforementioned usually guilty party. It's the same reason my wife passes on the cute breakable glass knickknacks when she sees them in a store.

When we added on to our house, my wife had this thing about windows. I wasn't winning the argument using statistics on heat loss and R-value. I told her walls are a lot cheaper to fix when boys are wrestling and throwing each other into walls and/or windows. This ended like most of these discussions — we got the windows. So far, they're still intact, but fingers are crossed.

Cow destruction

I've used the same demoralized words of the Wii weary mother with our cattle the last couple of weeks. We've been hauling the hay in and stacking the bales nicely in straight, even rows. The bales were tied tight and looking good.

Then the cows who have plenty of grass and no reason to want anything more, broke out of one pasture and stood in the corner of the one next to the hay pen until some fence crawler got the gate knocked down and they all camped out in my hay pen for a day while I was gone from the ranch.

They ripped into my beautiful, green, second-cutting alfalfa and tore twine from my nicely tied bales all the way up and down those nice rows. "I guess we can't have anything nice," I muttered, and yelled a couple other observations at the cows as I chased them out of the hay pen.

A few days later, I was moving some bulls, and it goes like it often does if you're moving more than one bull anywhere. One bull is a walking bull, two bulls are fighting, bellering, fence wrecking bulls. Sure enough, when I was moving a half-dozen of them to another pasture, two got to fighting and CRASH! CRUNCH!

They demolished one of my better barbed-wire gates. "I have nothing nice left," I concluded as the horse and I broke up the bull fight and got them straightened out.

But even amid all the destruction, I like our cattle and love our children. It wouldn't be much of a ranch without cattle, and it'd be a much duller home without the children.

We may not have nice things, but it is a nice life.

Where'd that go?
Tracking things down   November 7, 2011

I think the key to having a few spare parts around the shop for the next breakdown is remembering where you put them so you can find them when you need them.

That's no surprise to the tidy operators who have the store quality parts bins in their shop all labeled, cross-referenced and organized with a Dewey Decimal System card catalog. I've made the attempt to have a few cupboards and little plastic drawers. I even taped some labels on some of them.

Of course, I have to remember when I've made a change to the contents but not to the label. Like the cupboard that says "1/2 inch drill," but when the drill burned out I converted the space to PVC pipe fittings. I just need to remember that the pipe fittings are filed under "1/2 inch drill."

Then there are all the little plastic drawers that aren't labeled but I usually can remember what I put where. This doesn't help anyone else find stuff for me. It sometimes doesn't even help me because I've nearly worn out the drawers by sliding every one of them open to find what I want.

I took a chance and bought a couple extra things at the implement dealer a week or two ago. I got a set of splice pins for the baler belts to start the season off next year and a half-inch drive ratchet that I needed. Haven't seen them since I bought them.

They may never have made it to the shop to be put in the wrong drawer or hid behind the wrong label, or no label whatsoever. It's possible they got kicked under the seat of the pickup, but that won't mean they'll be easy to find there either.

It's like the calendar cartoon I saw once where the cowboy's pickup got in a wreck and rolled a time or two with everything from wrenches to gloves to bull catalogs scattered hither and yon. The cowboy looks at the scene and figures his pickup still will run alright but he has no idea how he's going to get everything stuffed back under the seat! I got the same kind of seats in my pickup.

I'm afraid I've passed this poor memory for locating things on to my children. I had the kids out with me the other day while I was doing a little work out in the pasture. They were playing in some trees when my 5-year-old boy got all distraught about losing his cap.

I walked over and dedicated a fair bit of time to try and find the missing headgear. We retraced his steps. This is where we were playing in the trees, he says. This dead wood is where we broke off some branches to play with. This is where we walked to throw these dead branches into the water hole.

So we walked and looked and stared at the ground and looked some more. We weren't finding anything. Then I thought about this a little bit — this kid is five, he shares the same genes I do, he's got a lot of things on his little mind. I had a revelation. "Did you leave your cap on the seat in the pickup before you came out here?" I asked.

"Yeah, I did," he said and smiled. Lucky he smiled or I'd have been really mad. At least we finally found the cap. I'm still looking for the new ratchet and the baler belt pins.

Pay it forward
Surprise kindness

"Pay it forward," was a phrase I heard first in a movie by that name. From what I remember, it was about a kid who came up with the idea of doing something nice for someone and rather than take any payment or return favor, he just tells them to "pay it forward." Do something nice for the next person down the line and keep it going.

It's a good lesson to ponder as we turn the page on another year. Might even be a good movie to watch as you consider resolutions for 2012 and ways we might want to change our life, and the world, for the better.

Maybe you've had it happen to you. We do something similar to it when we help neighbors work their calves, or feed the mourners and family members after a funeral in a church basement. A simple act of food or labor that defines the meaning of community.

Those are a little different than a classic "pay it forward" act because we know the people well who we are helping. They're our friends and neighbors, not a random stranger. Good acts and efforts, but not quite as selfless as helping someone you've never met who won't have the opportunity to repay the favor.

Perkins people

A couple weeks before Christmas, we had our little family out to eat at a restaurant. My wife and I and the three little rascals flung open the door at Perkins restaurant and were seated at a booth. They seat families with little kids at booths in restaurants. It gives us more control. With kids tucked on the inside and Mom and Dad each guarding the bench-edged exit, you can kind of keep them from running wild.

You take every advantage you can when you're outnumbered, two of us big people versus three little people. We like to patronize restaurants that have a kids menu printed on an activity sheet/place mat and that give the tikes a three-pack of brand new crayons when they seat you. Whoever came up with the idea of giving kids crayons and a coloring page at restaurants deserves a Nobel Prize for keeping peace amongst hungry families eating out.

So we're sitting at this restaurant coloring some dinosaurs and visiting about whether they'd like pancakes for supper or the kids hamburger platter. The meals came and the kids did pretty well. Not too much food flying around, and no one had to get yelled at.

A single man, early grandpa age, sat at a table across from us and seemed to enjoy the break in the dining monotony that our family circus provided. I've eaten at a lot of restaurants by myself when I was a young, traveling salesman, so I know how it feels to eat alone and yearn for a welcome a little entertainment is.

Our 3-year-old girl made eye contact with him and commenced to engaging him in a little conversation. I like living in a place where I don't feel like I have to worry too much about creepy people who harm little kids. We know it can happen anywhere, and I worry a little about our kids being too outgoing, but we also want to raise children that can put a smile on someone's face and make their day a little brighter.

Well this friendly fella at the next table left, and when the waitress came to see how our supper was, she told us that the man had paid for our supper as he left. He said he appreciated how well behaved our children were and how he enjoyed dining next to a nice family.

I didn't know what to say. He wasn't even there to thank. The only thing I can think to do now, in this new year, is to pay it forward.

Chapter 2
Generations

Solid gifts
Christmas giving that lasts and lasts November 15, 2004

Picking out the perfect Christmas gift can be a tough job

As we head into the holiday shopping season, we all hope the gifts we buy will be keepers, the kind of gifts that are kept for years and years. Unfortunately, it's hard to find those heirloom-quality gifts in our disposable, plastic world.

Test of time

My father still has a couple of the gifts he got for Christmas as a young lad. When you're able to keep something for more than 70 years, it must mean a lot.

He's still got the tin model airplane that he and his brother got for Christmas from their uncle in Duluth, Minn. This is a toy with some heft to it. Uncles from Duluth like toys with a little steel in them.

The airplane says "The Spirit of St. Louis" on the side of it, so the gift must have arrived sometime after Charles Lindbergh's 1927 pioneering flight from New York to Paris. If a kid was looking for a hero in those days, Lindbergh probably was a pretty good one.

The other Christmas gift came from his mother in 1930 and it's sitting on my bookshelf to this day. It's called "Cowboy Dave," written by Frank V. Webster and published by the Cupples & Leon Co. of New York City.

They published other titles for boys and girls that were "clean, interesting, inspiring and educational," according to the inside cover. All their books were 50 cents plus 10 cents postage and included the Boy Rancher Series, the Baseball Joe Series and the Radio Girls Series.

It probably was a pretty extravagant gift for a young widow to buy her 9-year-old son at the beginning of the Depression. Dad took real good care of it, making a brown paper cover to protect the glossy book jacket that protected the hardcover book. He wrote his name in big letters on that brown paper so everyone knew who owned that copy of "Cowboy Dave."

It proves what we writers have always thought — books make good Christmas presents.

Wrap it up

Books can be meaningful, especially if they're autographed or personalized. Signed and dated from a mother to her son, they could become a family heirloom like my dad's copy of "Cowboy Dave," passed on from one generation of cowboy readers to another.

Books have a lot of practical gift value for the giver, too. One, they're nice and rectangular. This makes them a lot easier to gift wrap for remedial wrappers like me.

Two, they're easy to mail to loved ones far and wide. Books won't break or crack or crumble, and they even qualify for bargain-basement book rate postage.

Third, if you're going to the Christmas party with your nicely wrapped books and get caught in a blizzard, you can make a nice fire and stay warm while the blizzard passes over. I'd recommend reading the pages as you burn them though, it'll make the time go faster.

You must know this is all leading up to something and, yes, I do happen to have a brand-new book, "Cowboy Logic Continues" available for your gift buying needs. It's 300 pages worth of my latest stories and columns, along with a dozen catchy cartoons.

You can check this all out at my new website, www.mycowboylogic.com, or give me a call toll free at (866) 526-9269 for credit card orders.

The book happens to cost $15.95, but if you don't think it'll decrease the value too much, I will inscribe and autograph it for free!

Gifts of value
The difference between giving or just buying   December 27, 2004

It's not easy finding a Christmas gift for my father. Most people who have an 83-year-old rancher to buy for probably would agree that it's a challenge.

I used to buy him things for the shop or the barn or the horses, but now those gifts would just remind him that he can't get out to the shop or the barn, or ride or drive the horses anymore. Age and Parkinson's disease aren't kind to men who spent their whole life outdoors and active.

I used to buy him books about history and ranching and assorted old-timers. Now, his cataracts and eyesight don't allow for much reading.

He doesn't wear out clothes like he used to, and he doesn't get outside enough to warrant a new ear lapper cap or a pair of leather chopper mitts.

He's not someone who would want a new coffee mug if the old one isn't worn out. He's not one of those modern materialistic guys who want things just for the sake of having them or so other people can see that he has them.

Basically, there's not much you can buy for my dad. But there are things you can give him.

Giving time

Dad's not able to do much reading, but before his handwriting got bad from the Parkinson's several years ago, he did do some writing.

He handwrote a few of his memories from growing up in the 1930s to his start as a rancher in 1939. He wrote about horses and dogs and people from the old days. He wrote about cutting ice on the river and hauling coal with a team of horses.

He remembered what the winter of 1945 and 1946 felt like after he'd spent the last two winters in the jungles of the South Pacific in World War II, and he remembered the eight hours it took to get to town in the winter of 1948 and 1949 with a neighbor, a team of horses, 6 feet of snow and a mercury that read 22 below zero.

He wrote a pretty good story about chasing a herd of horses 150 miles to a sale where they sold for $40 or $50 a head. He was 14 years old and chased those horses with an elder cousin from Montana who became the father figure in his life after his own father died when he was just 2 years old. His cousin was a cowboy's cowboy, and Dad had more than a few good stories about him.

My Christmas gift to Dad this year was to gather all those stories, type them, organize them and make copies that he can share with others about the way things were.

Receiving

While typing up Dad's writings, I learned a lot about his life and his character. As usual, just when you think you're giving something of value, you receive something back of even greater value.

I learned something of untold value about our relationship that a lot of sons don't learn from their fathers until after they're gone.

He wrote on one of his pages 14 years ago, "I have one son at college who wants to ranch. Comes home and helps, is breaking a team this winter, likes to work with them and is a real good hand also. Will be nice when he gets done and can come home if he likes and take over, as he would make a real fine rancher. He is a good worker and is good to be with in all ways."

What started as a gift of time and typing for my father became my greatest gift this Christmas.

It made me wonder if I still had those traits he used to describe me 14 years ago. If not, my Christmas gift will lead to some important New Year's resolutions.

Hand me downs
Figuring out what's worth passing on   August 21, 2006

Every once in a while I get tired of the squalor that surrounds me and I start throwing stuff away. I threaten a rummage sale and donations to the thrift store.

I never get rid of everything, but it's a time-consuming process to try and figure out what I should keep around for posterity, or maybe throw away in the next sort. I like the sense of order I get afterward, but I often wonder if I kept the right stuff.

I have a few treasures from the past that make me glad my parents didn't throw everything away. I received a few of my late uncle's belongings from my aunt recently. I'm sure glad they hung on to those things through the years.

Funny how common little things from years ago become priceless.

Ordinary heirlooms

I never met my maternal grandfather, but my mother kept a pair of his blue-denim bib overalls. They're union made Pay-Day brand, and they were a staple piece in the wardrobe of this Norwegian immigrant farmer who brought seven children through the Great Depression.

Holding the soft, worn denim in my hand brings me a little closer to the grandpa who died of a heart attack in those same overalls long before I was born. I'm sure glad they weren't made into shop rags or sold in a rummage sale.

Dad still has his copy of "Cowboy Dave," a book that he got as a Christmas present when he was a youngster. I read it when I was a lad, and now I'm reading it to my boys.

When I'm turning its brittle yellow pages, I think about how extravagant a gift it was for a young widow to buy and give to her son when money was so scarce. It easily could have ended up in some used book store after Dad outgrew its adolescent audience. It means a lot to me that we still have it.

Just recently, my aunt gave me the Miles City saddle that my uncle had used for many years and that my dad had bought in 1939. It's an Al Furstnow Model 487, well worn but solid.

Dad was 18 years old when he and his friend, George, rode the rail to Miles City, Mont., to go buy the rig.

He kept his travel costs down by jumping the freight train and camping under a bridge in Miles City. They feasted on a big bag of day-old rolls they got from the bakery for a dime. He bought the saddle used for $30 instead of investing more than twice that sum for a new one. The saddle shop did throw it in a gunny sack and ship it for free so he wouldn't have to lug it back home.

I haven't ridden the saddle yet, but I'm anxious to pull up the cinch and give it a try. You can bet it won't end up on eBay as long as I have something to say about it.

Not for sale

It's good to have a few things that aren't for sale at any price. Most of the keepsakes I have are fairly common, but even if they were rare and valuable, I'd never sell them.

I wonder what things I might keep to give my children to remember this time in our family history. Maybe some broken imported gadget or a piece of undisposed disposable plastic?

No, I think we'll set aside the items that are homemade, handcrafted or locally built. That'll narrow the list down.

Most importantly, I'll make sure that anything we keep is handed down with its story attached. A book, a pair of overalls or a saddle are just paper, denim and leather. But attach them to people and places and stories, and they become treasures.

Paintings from the prairie
Breaking into the art biz   November 13, 2006

My family has a knack for doing work that's interesting, but historically low paying. Like ranching and writing. The kind of jobs that require a strong affection for poverty.

My mother spent most of her life ranching and writing as well. But, once upon a time, she had pursued another low-paying profession. For many years, she was a starving artist.

She was a pretty good artist. Her work wasn't abstract. When she painted a scene, you could recognize the subject matter right off the bat. She created familiar images from the ranch and the beauty of life in the outdoors.

But it can be a challenge to sell art for a profit. Some buyers figure the value of a picture for their living room should cover the cost of the canvas and the frame plus a little margin for the paint.

Art takes a lot of hours and a lot of God-given talent. That's a little harder to put a value on. In fairness, it needs to land somewhere between minimum wage and the hourly rate of a corporate attorney.

So, as much as my mother enjoyed the satisfaction of creating a pleasing image that could tell a visual story, she laid down her brushes and put more time into raising her family and, later, caring for her husband.

Friends and family members enjoyed the limited number of original paintings that came from her easel.

Time to share

This year, I decided to share Mom's talent with a wider audience. I pulled three of her paintings off my walls and commissioned a small run of limited edition prints for each of them.

It should be a little more economical for folks to buy a print than a piece of original art. They can decide if they want to frame it themselves on the cheap, or invest a little more to dress it up with a custom mat and frame job.

I like the subjects. One has a rancher feeding his cows in the winter with a team of horses and a hay rack. His kids are being pulled along behind on their toboggan. Feeding cows doesn't have to be all work and no play.

A second is a summer haying scene from her youth that shows her mother driving a team and raking hay. Mom, as a little girl, and her brother rode out to the meadow to visit and an overshot stacker is stacking hay in the background.

The third, I hope, will be a favorite with the fall deer hunting crowd and the "autumn widows" left at home. She painted it in 1958 and it shows a hunter sitting on a deadfall tree enjoying a cup of hot coffee and reading "100 Venison Recipes." His rifle is several feet away, and, behind him, two does and a nice buck are trotting out of the trees.

I think they're great, but I'm a little biased. I'm going to put them up on my website and see if there are a few takers. Like ranching, I hope we can cover our costs and put a little in our pocket to get us through the next year.

If not, we'll have 100 years' worth of gifts for family, friends and random acquaintances.

It's probably not too early to talk my sons into pursuing something profitable like medicine or law before they veer toward the joyful family businesses of ranching, writing or painting. No, there's lots of profit in the joyful things, it's just hard to put in the bank.

Our own Santa
Lessons in giving and generosity

December 25, 2006

Christmas is the giving season, and, with all that giving, lots of folks get hung up on the idea of receiving.

Growing up, I had my own personal Santa Claus to learn the lessons of giving. My family called him "Uncle Tony," a term of fondness since there was no blood relationship.

He was my first cousin's first father-in-law and he lived in a town called Downers Grove, Ill., a suburb of Chicago.

Uncle Tony liked our little North Dakota ranching community and he developed a great friendship with my parents when he came here to visit his daughter before I was born. I never had met him, but every Christmas since I was old enough to start remembering, there would be a box of presents on our doorstep from Uncle Tony.

My siblings and I would get toys and games, and Mom and Dad would get a check with instructions to "go out for dinner," his treat. A Christmas box from Tony came as surely as the holiday itself, year after year.

I learned how to write letters to thank him for the gifts. I'd mail those letters off to his Chicago suburb, a place that seemed as foreign and distant to me as Santa's North Pole. He became a loyal pen pal for our whole family.

Later, the boxes of toys gave way to checks written to Mom and Dad to buy us something we wanted for Christmas. I remember getting a pair of hockey skates that way, knowing I had Uncle Tony to thank even though they were purchased locally.

A real person

For me, Uncle Tony's existence was a bit surreal. My only contact was by written letter. He would send photos in his letters from time to time, usually from his flower garden that he grew with pride.

Finally, as a young man, I found myself in Chicago on business and decided I would extend my trip an extra half a day. I called Uncle Tony, told him I was in the area and got on the train in downtown Chicago headed towards Downers Grove.

The depot was just a block from his address. It was a nice, quiet neighborhood. I knocked on the door of Tony's modest little house. A modest little man in his 90s came to the door with the help of a cane. We visited like old friends for a good couple of hours until it was time for me to catch the train back into the city.

We walked together back to the depot and he waved goodbye as I stepped aboard. Tony was not a wealthy man. He spent his life working in a steel smelter for a working man's wage. He was a widower who lived rather humbly, but his generosity was legendary to at least one ranching family nearly a thousand miles away.

The letters continued to come after our visit until the last couple of years. I know he was getting more frail, but no one told us if he had passed away. My Internet search says he did.

Our relationship was built on letters and Christmas cards, but I'd have to say Tony was one of the finest men I've known.

For me, he was a Christmas miracle with a message of unselfish generosity. Because of him, I try harder to find ways to celebrate the season of giving.

We can all find ways to celebrate — we can pitch dollars into the kettle of the Salvation Army bell ringer each time we pass, we can lighten up the face of children with random acts of generosity, we can simply write a letter to an old friend or acquaintance.

Giving is learned. I hope I can teach it half as well as Tony did.

The week in words
Not an easy week, but a real week   March 19, 2007

A wise columnist always would have a column or two "in the can" and ready to go if, for some reason, he just couldn't get one written in a given week.

Get sick, have a family emergency or realize its deadline time in the middle of a romantic cruise with no desire to write a column? No problem, just pull that spare column written months ago out of the hopper and send it in. Easy as pie.

I, however, am not a wise columnist. Nothing written up and put on ice to use when needed.

Maybe I'm kind of like a fine chef who prides himself on making everything fresh, from scratch. My columns are written fresh every other week, usually scratched together minutes ahead of the absolutely final deadline.

This week, I'm not on a romantic cruise and wishing I had a spare column to fall back on. But I am coughing, sniffling, stuffed up, aching and battling through the fog of a cold and flu. And, this week, my wife's father passed away and I'm traveling and doing my foggy best to help her and my in-laws mourn his loss. On top of that, I'm trying to write this column.

Saying farewell

My father-in-law had been ill for a long time. He never really was healthy in the five years I knew him and even long before that. Bottled oxygen, oxygen concentrators, a lot of hose and an assortment of other medical advances kept him going from day to day.

We couldn't say it was unexpected, but that doesn't necessarily make it any easier. Still, the struggle is over.

I first met my future father-in-law when I had the ritual supper with the parents on an early date. I went to the door and my wife was still downstairs getting ready. We didn't see her for 15 or 20 minutes. He gave me a little advice about women, hair and makeup. "Better get used to waiting for them," I think he said.

But I sat down by the kitchen counter with this fella I'd never met and we talked the whole time without so much as an awkward pause. We discussed cattle, the markets and whatever else. He was a good visitor.

Our relationship always was cordial. He was Farm Bureau Republican and I was raised Farmers Union Democrat. We were both Lutheran and mostly Norwegian. We never let any of that get in the way of our kitchen counter friendship. He didn't even pause when I asked permission to marry his daughter.

He wasn't perfect. None of us are. But he picked a great partner to share his life with. And he raised a family that anyone could take a lot of pride in.

His funeral packed the white-steepled country church just up the hill from his farm. They came for him, and his wife, and his children and grandchildren. They brought food and fed the masses like only a little rural community can.

There were plenty of stories and memories, a few laughs and a few tears, as everyone said goodbye in their own way.

It must have been a good funeral because I heard a lot of people say, "he should've been here, he'd of really enjoyed it."

I think maybe he was, and I'm sure that he did.

Treasured obstacles
Mowing around the past
August 6, 2007

I just finished haying a piece that we call the "Koble Field." You probably can guess by the name that a family named Koble once lived there.

I wouldn't say it's my favorite piece of hayland. The hay grows pretty thin in places. It grows a lot of foxtail, and cows don't appreciate a lot of foxtail beards in their hay. But the field provides a little variety in our haying season.

You still can tell that people once tried to make a living there. Besides the farmstead itself, there're still a few fence posts on the property lines. And a little barbed wire an inch or two in the sand to catch on your rake if you hit it just right.

There're some nasty dead furrows that'll set your tractor to bouncing like a horse with a rough trot. We must not mind them too much or we'd have tried to disc them smooth sometime in the last 50 years we've owned it.

You still can see where they hauled the barn manure out and pitched it off. The grass grows dark green and thick as dog's hair there. Kind of makes up for some of the thin spots.

There's a pretty distinct ridge where a fenceline or something must have caught the topsoil before it blew out of the country in the hot, dry years of the 1930s.

The old farmstead is still there, or at least parts of it. All that's left of the house is the foundation and basement. The old two-story white house was moved to our ranch and my parents started their married life in it. The basement back on the farmstead is a handy place to throw a little rusty barbed wire as we rake it up.

The barn was moved off as well. But an old railroad boxcar, a chicken coop, a hog shed and a little shop stayed on the farmstead. They've fallen down over the years, but they're still guarding their spot with tire-piercing nails to detract hayers who might venture a little too close.

There're enough buildings and signs of inhabitation though, that you can begin to picture what the place was like when it had a yard full of kids running around.

The best part of the farmstead is a little grove of ash trees growing just north of the old declining buildings.

Those trees provide one of the best lunch locations across our hay land. I don't know how big they were when the family sold the place to us, but they're the perfect size now to provide some welcome shade on a hot day.

My wife lays out an old blanket in the shade of the trees and distributes the summer sausage sandwiches and Kool-Aid. Our boys toddle around and find a little grease to smear on their clothes, a little breeze rustles through the leaves, and I think to myself how nice it is my tractors aren't so modern that I'd be tempted to eat my lunch in an air-conditioned cab on the go in the field.

If I was a little more progressive, I'd have hired a bulldozer to push down the trees and pile up the buildings to be burned. The land beneath them might yield an extra bale of hay.

Me, I'd rather have something to mow around that reminds me of the homestead's past. And I'd sure rather have the shade of those trees for our family lunch than an extra bale of hay.

Executive skills
Management put to the test   September 1, 2008

Family farms and ranches don't get a lot of chances to demonstrate employee management skills. That's understandable since, by my definition, a true family operation gets the majority of its labor from family members rather than full-time, year-round, salaried employees.

Still, family farms and ranches employ a lot of folks. Generally, seasonal, part-time, benevolent friends, acquaintances, retirees and shirt-tail relatives who are kind enough to work for less than they could make in the oil fields, the trades or some fast food joints.

For more than 100 years, we've done most everything ourselves on our ranch. When we couldn't do it all, we've always found help from people who must either like us, the work, the scenery or the home-cooked meals. We know it's not the money.

Keeping hired help helping also requires some personality skills. You have to be kind of easy to work for.

The boss

I don't know if Dad would ever call himself the boss, but he oversaw the operation, so I guess he was. For us kids and the hired help, I'd say he was a pretty easy guy to work for.

We had some good wrecks. My sister tried to rake up a barbed-wire fence and challenged the territory of a deeply rooted telephone pole. I tried to buck up an old, sodden hay stack butt with the power bullrake and learned the bending point of seemingly strong steel.

Through it all, I don't once remember him yelling, screaming, bawling us out or belittling us.

I suppose he learned that yelling at the help is about as effective as yelling at the cattle. It might allow the person doing the yelling to release some frustration, but it doesn't do much to fix the situation, motivate the help or calm the cattle.

His demeanor may have mellowed with age. He was nearly 49 years old when I was born. Most of us wear out our hot tempers, impatience and anger when we're much younger. I know my fuse is longer than it was even 10 years ago.

Boss' son

I'm fortunate to have some of the same benevolent help Dad did. The fella helping me hay now first came out to the ranch when he was 16. He just turned 60. When he's not seven days on in the oil fields, he's several days on here at the ranch. And his wife comes out to help, too.

Last week, I went by the field to see how she was doing raking hay. I found her standing next to an amazing red-and-green steel pretzel.

The 36-foot dump rake, by design, is supposed to look kind of like a lower case "l". What I found looked more like a "Z" with the hitch high on the back tire of the tractor and two points of the "Z" planted firmly in the field.

My hired hand was OK physically but clearly distraught, pacing back and forth by the jumbled mess.

I got out of the pickup, didn't say a thing, walked a circle around the outfit and surveyed the damage.

Finally, I said, "It looks bad, but I don't think it's as bad as it looks."

With the energy I saved by not waving my arms and yelling, I went to work with a jack, a chain and some careful straightening of the tractor. The rake was smartly engineered with some critically placed hinges and u-joints. When it was all untangled, the only casualties were two half-inch bolts that sheered under pressure.

I told her not to let the incident rattle her and to watch the short left turns. "Thanks for not screaming at me," she said as we parted.

I smiled, waved it off, and, thinking about it, I realized it was just the way I was raised.

Generations
Trying to be a good father and a good son   October 27, 2008

There's a term for everything these days. The term they have for what I'm doing is "sandwich generation."

It doesn't mean I grew up eating summer sausage sandwiches in the hayfield, although I did, and it doesn't have anything to do with exotic vacations in the balmy Sandwich Islands, better known as Hawaii today.

The term is who I am, someone who's trying to care for his children and his parents at the same time. Little kids and aging parents are the bread, I'm that summer sausage in the middle.

My children probably are younger and my parents older than most in the sandwich. The fact that Dad was 48 when I was born and that I was 32 when I got married are to thank for my 87-year-old father and my 3-month-old daughter.

Dad has battled Parkinson's disease for nearly 20 years, the disease that steals your body with tremors and rigidity but leaves your mind intact.

Mom has been the classic caregiver, caring for Dad and ignoring her own health for years, until yesterday. Her aches and ailments were so unbearable she finally agreed to see a doctor. We're still awaiting more tests and more results, but the doctors are certain there is a cancer somewhere inside of her.

The family clan

So yesterday, we moved Dad into our house while Mom stayed overnight in the hospital. Neither of them were where they wanted to be, at home, but sometimes getting the care you need trumps the comfort of home.

Our boys think it's pretty neat to have Grandpa living in our house. I have to think that good night hugs and kisses from a 4-year-old and a 2-year-old are good medicine for any ailment. I'm sure Mom would like a dose of that, too, if we could drive to the hospital and get the little pajama-clad rascals up to her room.

I've read what others have written about the similarities between caring for your parents and caring for your children. Grown adults certainly aren't children, but I can't help but think of my children when I help Dad with the basics like cutting his meat, clipping his fingernails, getting him into his clothes, helping him into and out of bed, and the list goes on. Most all of the same things I do for our children.

I'm not yet sure what care will be required for Mom when she gets home from the hospital. Right now, she's getting the best care possible from the saints who don a nurse's uniform or a doctor's jacket.

I've seen people fight cancer, but none as close up as my mother. I don't reckon it'll be easy. But I don't know if I've ever met a woman with more grit or spunk than my mother.

The day my sister came and took Mom to the hospital, a lot of things changed on our ranch. The steady source of strength and support for our outfit was gone to get some support and care for herself.

Shortly after they left, I was driving away from the ranch and saw the most magnificent bald eagle I've ever seen in a cottonwood tree overlooking Mom and Dad's house. It's a rarity to see a bald eagle in our area, and I'd never seen one that close to the ranch.

He picked up his big wings, glided over their house and settled atop another tree behind the barn.

Some would say it was just another big raptor passing through the neighborhood, but, in my mind that day, it was a sign from the good Lord to let us know that he was with us.

I was glad to see it, I need Him in this sandwich with me.

Putting things in perspective   November 24, 2008

An early snowstorm dropped 22 inches of wet snow on my freshly weaned calves, socked in three-fourths of my hay bales on soft fields and diminished any hope for extended grazing to save a bit of the half a hay crop we got this year.

The surprise was that those little setbacks were terribly trivial on the Taylor Ranch. When it came to worries, we had bigger fish to fry.

A week before the storm hit, Mom had been diagnosed with late-stage ovarian cancer. The local doctors referred her to the Mayo Clinic in Rochester, Minn., for major surgery to try and help her rid herself of it.

The intense, six-hour surgery found most of the ovarian cancer but also found a colon cancer to try and fix as well. Days after the surgery, blood clots formed and tried to end her life. Days after that, complications with the colon took her back into emergency surgery. Throughout, fluid had been coming in around her lungs to complicate the basic act of breathing.

Twenty-two inches of snow? A couple sick calves? Challenging hay hauling? Just take a number you puny problems. You're not even a contender around here.

Bad news came in pairs for my parents. Dad's condition plummeted when Mom left for her initial diagnosis. Parkinson's is not something that gets better, but I didn't know how quickly it could get worse.

He already was bound to a wheelchair, needing assistance for every move away from it. For a man who spent his entire life on a horse or a tractor or his own two feet, it was heartbreaking to see.

Harder yet was the confusion and dementia that settled in like a rain cloud on my always sharp dad. And his diminishing ability to speak because of the Parkinson's stole our conversations together.

There were too many risks for us ever to consider leaving Dad alone, yet we still needed to work the ranch, raise our babies and help Mom fight for her life 600 miles away.

On one of those mornings when I "had Dad," my real Dad before the day's dementia overtook him, he asked, "What are we going to do, Ryan? I can't stay here, there's too much for you to do." As always, he was honest, and he was right.

So we began to talk about the thing that most farmers and ranchers always hoped to avoid, living in a nursing home. I learned that what we had been doing for Dad was called "skilled care," with his needs well beyond the "basic care" provided in most nursing homes. We had kept Dad on the ranch years longer than many would have, a fact that gives me a little solace.

When Dad and I went to the long-term care center, he granted me four clear fatherly words, saying, "I'll be OK here." Still, leaving him there and walking out the door was the hardest thing I've ever done as his son.

The next morning, I flew to Rochester to see my mother hooked up to a dozen tubes, lines and monitors in the intensive care unit, yet able speak a little through her oxygen mask. Sitting with her in the ICU wasn't nearly as enjoyable as the mornings we used to spend drinking strong coffee together across her table on the ranch, but it was precious time.

You see, it is hard to think about cattle and snow and hay, or even columns. Someday, those will seem like big concerns to me again. Not now, but someday.

Mama's boy
Getting used to life without her   February 2, 2009

Of all the blessings I've been given in life, I may be most thankful for the blessing of close relationships with my parents. "Mama's boy" and "Daddy's helper" probably were fitting terms for me growing up on the ranch.

On a family ranch, growing up doesn't necessarily mean leaving home or increasing the emotional or physical distance between yourself and the two people who raised you. For better or worse, the next generation to take over an outfit stays pretty close to the generation who's passing it down.

Aside from college years and some short-term jobs away from the ranch, I never got farther than a mile away from my folks when I built our little homestead down the road from them.

That makes it all the harder now to say goodbye to Mom. The lady who brought me into this world left this world on Jan. 17 after a 2½-month struggle with late-stage ovarian cancer.

Living large

Losing a parent, no matter what their age or ailment or circumstance, is a hard thing to go through. And most of us experience it if the common parental wish comes true — that their children outlive them.

One way we get through the grief is to remember the good years of their life. Mom wasn't always 76 years old and sick. She was an amazing person with a big personality, a broad smile and a quick wit.

She was a memorable lady with a memorable name — Liz Taylor. She was different from the Liz Taylor of Hollywood fame. She wasn't a movie star and she only had one husband, but she was famous, at least around these parts.

She was famous for her wit and good humor. She was famous for her fiddle playing. Self taught, Mom played her fiddle a little differently than most. Instead of holding the fiddle under her chin, she kind of held it between her hip and her rib cage. The uniqueness of it inevitably would invite someone to ask her why she held it there, and my gray-haired mother always would smile and say, without missing a beat, "well, it made for better tips when I used to play in a topless bar!"

She was famous for her divergent talents. She was a talented artist and writer who could set down her brushes or her pen, pick up a rifle or a shotgun and use them with equal skill. She taught me how to shoot a gun, she took me hunting and she helped me learn how to trap coyotes on the ranch when I was a lad. Not ordinary things for a mother to teach her son, but she was no ordinary mother.

She was famous for her Juneberry pie, her Norwegian doughnuts and her black boiled coffee. The Juneberries came from the sandhills where she loved to walk and pick them from the bushes, the doughnuts came from her mother's old handwritten recipe that hung on the wall, and the black boiled coffee came from hours of simmering and adding equal parts of water and coffee grounds as the day wore on.

The hardest part now is to think that I'll never share another cup of that coffee with her, or hear the laughter in her voice as she makes a wise-cracking comment or see the sparkle in her eyes that showed the true zest she had for her talented life.

But I have all the memories made before she got so sick, and I'll hold those memories dear as I share them with our children who will miss out on a wonderful grandma.

God bless you, Mom. And Godspeed your journey home.

Saving the trees
Wherever, however we can   July 20, 2009

I suppose it's the summer heat and the search for shade, but I've been thinking a lot about trees lately.

Even though I'm a child of the generally treeless plains, I'm a tree lover. I reckon you could call me a tree hugger, although being a Scandinavian Midwesterner with well-managed emotions makes me an unlikely hugger of anything. As with people, I'd be more likely to give a tree a firm handshake or a hearty pat on the back, but not a hug.

Some folks refer to all environmental activists as tree huggers, but there're a lot of us out here who've never chained ourselves to a grand old tree to stop bulldozers in the expansion of urban development but still have strong emotions for trees.

I chose to build our house next to about 10 acres of ponderosa pine that my father planted in 1979. We were as amazed as anyone that they'd actually grow in the glacial yellow beach sand where we put them, but they provide some nice shade and shelter from the wind. And they smell nice, too.

When I'm spraying for leafy spurge, I do my best to spare the trees in our pastures from the effects of the spray. My hate for non-native, invading weeds has to compromise with my desire to keep the aspen thickets and Juneberry bushes alive.

It still makes me sad to see the elm trees I used to play in when I was a kid dead from the spread of Dutch elm disease. It makes me smile when I see a new ponderosa taking root, thanks only to a dropped pine cone and some favorable weather.

These days, more and more people are talking about the effect on the world of destroying the rainforests in places like Brazil and Indonesia.

Ranchers know life is best when things are "how they're supposed to be." Native grass, growing forage, large grazing animals moving from place to place. We're basically doing what's been done throughout time, while providing some protein for the world's beef eaters.

Although I've never been there, I don't know if a cleared and burned rain forest fits that definition of "how things are supposed to be."

Of course, many of the people in those countries are poor, just glad to have some economic activity, a job and a way to provide for their families.

It reminds me of something my mother did 20 years ago in our neighborhood.

Driving our road to town one day, she noticed a fella she knew nicknamed Slugger cutting down some tall, massive cottonwood trees that had grown in the ditch. He had several of them down already.

She stopped to visit Slug about his new vocation of tree felling. Turned out the county commissioner had asked him to cut them down because he thought they'd catch snow in the winter and block the road.

Mom knew that a few single, solitary cottonwoods weren't causing winter road blocks. Shallow ditches full of scrub willows farther up where the road was lowest would be drifted over in winter, but not by these few stately cottonwoods.

"What's he paying you to cut these down?" she asked. Slug told her he got $20. Mom reached in her pocket, took out a $20 bill and said, "Here, why don't you quit cutting." With that, Slug packed up his chainsaw and headed home.

The big cottonwoods still are there today, shading cattle in the pasture next to them and reminding me of my mom, our local tree-hugging ranch wife, each time I drive by.

I suppose her motivational method could change the way things are going in the rainforests of Brazil and Indonesia, but I don't know if anyone has enough $20 bills.

Generation motivation
Trying to figure out the differences   October 26, 2009

I remember an old rancher friend of my father's who had the keenest interest in when people were born. "When were you born, sonny?" he'd ask, and I'd tell him I was born in '70. "Yes, nineteen a hundred and a seventy. Your dad, you know, was born in nineteen a hundred and twenty one," he'd say with a deliberate cadence and a voice I still can remember.

If you saw him a year later, he'd still remember you, when you were born, and he could probably tell you the birth year of everyone else sitting within 50 feet of him at the livestock sale barn diner while you visited.

Turns out, just knowing when people were born tells you a lot about them, their motivations and their personalities. Dad's old friend probably knew that.

I had the pleasure of hearing a speaker named Cam Marston at a recent meeting. He spoke about the four generations in our culture and work force and how we can work to understand each other a little better.

The generations are the Matures, born between 1909 and 1945; the Baby Boomers, born from 1946 to 1964; Generation X, born between 1965 and 1979; and the Millennials, those children born from 1980 to 2000.

Most of us have heard of the names of these generations. I hadn't given them much thought until I heard Cam's presentation. I started recognizing some of the traits that define each of the generations in myself and others.

I'm an Xer raised by two Matures, whereas most of my fellow Xers were raised by Boomers. That gives me a little different outlook on life, and I've always kind of known that.

My parents both lived through the Depression, my father is a combat veteran of World War II. They weren't afraid of sacrifice and hard work was a daily habit.

A good share of my neighbors, teachers and people I've worked with in various jobs are Baby Boomers. They're everywhere; it's a huge generation. They're loyal, hard-working team players.

Me, I'm an Xer. I don't like that anonymous generational moniker, but maybe it fits us. We're a little harder to define. We're more loyal to people than institutions, and our work ethic is geared more toward the job than the time put in at a job. We're skeptical, but self-sufficient.

My neighbors and co-workers who are a little older than me or married a little younger produced the Millennial kids in today's work force. A generation that has no idea a world once existed without cell phones, laptop computers or remote controls. They're the insulated, cared-for generation—from the five-point harnesses of their child car seats to the basement bedroom in their parents' house that they have a hard time leaving. They'll work, but they're motivated differently.

There is a difference in work ethic, though, as you cross from the Matures and the Boomers to the Xers and the Millennials. Cam told us he's found some exceptions to the standardized traits assigned to the younger generations. Farm kids, military families, immigrants and the children of first-generation immigrants have traits more like the older generations.

Maybe that's why I've often felt like an old man trapped in a younger man's body. Raised on a ranch by older-than-average parents with the lessons of limitless chores, limited recreation, scarce money and the realities of life and death gave me some Boomer traits.

I hope the countryside can keep raising farm and ranch kids, and not just kids whose parents happen to farm or ranch but don't pass on the lessons of the older lifestyle to the next generation.

There're worse things than being old for your age.

Historical perspective
Looking back a century   March 15, 2010

When things look bad, a lot of us have been raised to remember the old adage, "well, it could be worse."

There's some twisted sense of comfort that comes from that upside-down reminder of how good we have it.

I've been working on our ranch history for some time. Looking at the photo of my great-grandparents' tiny homestead shack with none of today's conveniences or technologies to battle the loneliness of a long winter, it makes me thankful for all we have.

The first homestead filed by my family on the ranch was in 1903, so the ranch is 107 years old this year. They weren't all easy years.

Another old saying you hear is that "the West was hell on horses and women." I tend to think that the horses maybe had it better than the women.

My great-grandmother left a pretty nice house in lush, green, settled Indiana to come with her family to a homestead shack on the semi-arid and desolate sandhills of north-central North Dakota. Family lore says she cried for a month straight. I don't doubt it a bit.

She had five children. She'd lost a set of twins at birth and a boy as an infant and brought her two living sons with her and her husband to become Dakota horse and cattle ranchers.

They survived all right, put together some land and livestock and began building up their ranch. Then in November 1921, her youngest son, just 20 years old, was hit by a grown steer when working cattle and died of the internal injuries 17 days later. He was the baby boy, the apple of their eye, a talented guy who could teach country school, play piano and cowboy.

Just a few months later, her husband died at 61 years of age from a rupture and blood poisoning. Her older son had married a local country school teacher, and he

63

worked hard to fill the void on the ranch with his father and brother gone.

That next winter, he went to visit a neighbor whose wife had just given birth. The home had smallpox in it, and he was unvaccinated. He got small pox and died in February at the age of 32. His two sons were 1 and 3 years old, and his wife was six months pregnant with a girl who would be born in May.

The West was sure proving hellacious for at least two women, my grandmother and great-grandmother. But they didn't give up, sell the place and move back east. They kept the land and kept some cattle to run with a neighbor. And, although they moved in to town with those three small children, the ranch still was intact when my father moved back out at the age of 18.

My family is pretty similar to my grandmother's. They had two boys then a girl in four years' time. We had two boys then a girl in four years' time. She raised hers alone with her mother-in-law with no breadwinner through the Great Depression. Our two-parent home with all of today's luxuries is no comparison. My wife and I know that no matter what, "it could be worse."

Our ranch is a contender this year for possible induction into the North Dakota Cowboy Hall of Fame ranch division. If we make it, I'd consider it an honor won not by the land or the livestock raised on it, but won by two widowed women who, despite broken hearts, everything else about them was pretty darn strong.

They already had seen the worst. They knew if they hung on, it would get better.

Words out loud
Early education, latter therapy   May 24, 2010

One of the best things you can do for your children, they say, is to read to them. I suppose it comes after giving them a safe place to sleep, healthy meals and a warm hug, but it's right up close to the top.

It's easy to take advice when it's something you want to do anyway. I want to read to my kids and I like reading to them, so if reading makes me a good parent, that's just icing on the cake.

Every night that I'm home, I put aside my latest nonfiction or historical novel to peel back the pages of "Go Dog Go" or something in rhyme by Dr. Seuss. The usual routine is for my wife to read to our little girl and for me to read to the boys.

We've got a shelf full of books, some from when I was kid, a bunch handed down to us from friends and family whose kids have grown up, a few we bought brand-spanking new. Despite that variety, our short, cuddly audience may request the same story every night for a week.

For our family, it's a seven days a week activity. I read in a recent report that 9 percent of children age 1 to 5 in my state of North Dakota are in families where they are read to less than three days a week. So 91 percent were getting ample story time. It put us in the top 10, on the good end.

The worst state to be a little kid wanting some family reading time was Texas. Twenty-six percent of those boys and girls were in families that read to them less than three days a week. I guess everything is bigger in Texas, but it's not all worth bragging about. I wish my state's 9 percent would be closer to Maine's 4 percent.

Our oldest son just finished kindergarten. I don't remember what all I was able to do at the end of my kindergarten year, but I was pretty impressed that my boy had learned enough to turn the tables at story time and he could read a story to me.

It was a proud moment for a parent, a child's first teacher.

Young and old

We spend a lot of years reading in silence, but it's OK to break out of that polite habit from time to time.

My Dad and I have had a hard time communicating lately. His Parkinson's disease has stolen his voice, and during some visits, I don't know what more to tell him in our one-sided conversations. So I pick up a newspaper or a book and I read to him.

It's a little different from my sessions with the boys. The reading material is more advanced and usually has to do with the cattle business, or old times, or old-time ranchers and cowboys like Dad.

But some things are the same. For the listener, young or old, it's the comfort of a familiar voice, hearing a story that can transport you to another time or place. For an 88-year-old cowboy in long-term care at a hospital, imagining another time or place is a more important part of the activity than if you're a 3-year-old boy snuggled in to Daddy's lap at home.

I'm not trained as a teacher, but if just reading to my children brings them learning, I'm happy to do it. And I'm not educated as a doctor, but if reading to my father brings him any kind of therapy or relief from his daily struggles, I'm glad to turn the page, clear my throat and read the words aloud.

Godspeed gentle father
The responsibility of carrying on his qualities   June 7, 2010

I once opened a Chinese fortune cookie and read on the little slip of paper, "A gentleman is a gentle man." I'm not usually struck with profundity when opening these mass-produced cardboard-like cookies, but that one stuck with me because it reminded me of my father.

A gentle man. A gentle man who treated people with an abundance of kindness. A gentle man who used compliments and suggestions to motivate us kids in our ranch work, kept any temper he had in check and never belittled us. A gentleness that suited him well in truly caring for the cattle and horses entrusted to him on the ranch.

I'll take that fortune cookie definition of the word over others I've read in the dictionary that refer to things like noble birth, superior social position or, the worst of them, "a man who considers manual labor to be beneath him."

No, my father, who only owned one suit, his "funeral suit," for carrying so many friends and neighbors as pallbearer, was not a tuxedo-clad kind of gentleman. He was the kind of gentleman of the remaining definitions — polite, considerate, gracious. One with little or no social position who dedicated his life to manual labor on the ranch.

My father's gentle soul left his body on the most beautiful and perfect of spring days on the prairie. We bid him goodbye and carried his casket to the cemetery by horse-drawn wagon to be laid next to the wife he missed so much on a day nearly as beautiful.

So here I am, nearly 40 years old, with both parents departed. I'm a far cry from an orphaned infant, but I still feel the weight of the void. Your parents get you raised, educated and on your way by the time you're 18 or 22 or 26. It shouldn't be so hard to let them go, but it is. With all the time with them we're given, we still wish for more.

Traits to aspire to

I spent much of my life trying to be like Dad, a pretty worthy goal. Anyone who knew him would say it was a goal worth shooting for. Granted, I've grown to be different than Dad in many ways, probably because of my mother's influence, but I hope I can carry on a few of my father's traits.

I often wondered how Dad became such a good father. His own father died when he was just 18 months old and his mother never remarried. He didn't grow up with a man in the house to learn from.

He did find a father figure in his father's cousin from Montana who took Dad in at his horse ranch for several summers starting when he was 11 years old in the early 1930s. Probably an important time for a boy to have the influence of a grown man in his life.

However it happened, Dad learned how to work and work hard, but also how to take time for family, friends and neighbors. He knew the value of a dollar and how to save a few by getting by with what he had, but he never let himself fall victim to the endless race for more dollars and more material goods to stack around him and brag about.

He put more stock in the value of people and relationships than material things, and that's why he'd always invite you to the house for a cup of coffee or take the time to visit. That's why he'll be missed. Because he took the time to know you and made time available for you to know him, his endearing smile, the timbre of his voice as he shared a story, his gentle nature.

And some of us will continue to try our best to be like him. God bless the memory of Bud Taylor.

Hall of Fame moments
A pretty big deal
July 5, 2010

There's a hall of fame somewhere for most everything from baseball to rock and roll music. In North Dakota, we have a hall of fame for cowboys and the horse culture of the plains. As of last week, our family ranch is in that hall.

It turned out to be a bigger deal than I ever imagined. It was an honor that would have made my homesteading great-grandfather proud. It was a point of satisfaction for my dad to know the ranch was to be inducted in the hall just before he died. It made me reflect on the value of this relatively small patch of earth to my children and, someday, their children.

The hall is in Medora, N.D., a little cowtown in the Badlands turned tourist destination. Tourists are those folks who take vacations from their jobs and walk around in shorts and flip-flops in the middle of summer.

But they spend a little of their hard-earned money to walk into that cowboy hall of fame and hear stories about men and women, horses and cattle, ranches and rodeo. Everyone who ranches ought to feel honored that our way of life still intrigues these people.

Induction weekend

My wife and I took in the whole two day affair for the hall of fame induction. Relatives were kind enough to watch the kids the first night so we could enjoy a steak and a couple cold drinks with other inductees and supporters of the hall. A cowboy and a guitar provided music for my bride and me to dance to.

We visited with old friends and made a few new ones. Rainfall, pastures, hay, cattle prices were topics of discussion. Old stories of the funny things that happen in ranching and life, perfected with age and retelling, brought laughter from deep within.

It was a perfect night.

The next day brought rain for the induction ceremony. Ranchers don't complain about rain; it's a lot easier to grow grass and raise cattle with it than without it.

My sister and her family came down. They brought our 6-year-old son along to represent the fifth generation being raised on our old homestead ranch.

The clouds cleared off and the sun came out.

A few words

I thought hard about what to say when we received the award for the ranch. The ranch is really just sand and dirt that grows grass and hay for the cattle and the horses that work the cattle. The award was really for the people grown on the ranch, their character and their stories.

How does a ranch stay in the same family for 110 years? I guess it just doesn't get sold. Not selling the ranch was surely a sacrifice for my great-grandmother, left widowed and childless by a series of tragedies, left with her widowed daughter-in-law and three grandkids under the age of 4 in the 1920s. My family enjoys life on the ranch today because she didn't sell it then.

Cowboy ranches stay cowboy ranches when someone teaches the cowboy ways to the next generation. My father, whose own dad died before he was 2 years old, learned those ways from his father's cousin, a real old time cowboy. Dad taught me. I need to teach my kids.

So ranches don't grow old by accident. It takes the sacrifice of a Mary Taylor, the mentoring of a Gordon Taylor. There's a sense of responsibility.

One of the last things I said to my father before he died was, "we'll take good care of the ranch, Dad." He gave my hand a squeeze.

We all have to take a turn at caring for this old ranch. And one other thing: It ain't for sale.

Ranch transition doesn't happen overnight. It seems to start the day the succeeding generation is born. It's especially evident to me now having lost both my parents in the last year and a half.

There're plenty of articles that focus put on estate planning and ranch succession, tax laws, relationships between farming and nonfarming siblings. This isn't one of those articles.

Don't get me wrong. If you haven't made those plans and talked about those topics in your family, you better do it—yesterday. The transition topic I've been thinking about are the stories that are passed on from one generation to the next, the traditions, lessons and one-liners that go with a place.

Our family is better off than most when it comes to having handed down stories. My mother wrote a column for the local paper for more than 20 years called "Meanwhile Back at the Ranch." Whenever I yearn for her voice, I can read one of those columns and hear it in my mind like it was yesterday.

Before Dad's handwriting got too bad with Parkinson's disease, he spent some time writing down some of his stories about growing up in the 1920s and 1930s. Writing wasn't as easy for Dad as it was for Mom, but those stories are worth more than gold to me now that he's gone.

I typed Dad's handwritten stories into my computer, some while I was sitting with Mom at the hospital in Rochester, Minn., reading them out loud to her as I tapped my fingers on the keyboard. I made a booklet of them to distribute at Dad's funeral last spring to share with his friends and neighbors.

Between Dad, Mom and myself, our ranch comes with more written records than most, but a lot of its stories are known only in the minds of those of us left behind to tell and retell them like they were told to us.

Our neighbors can help fill in the blanks on a lot of stories. I'm not sure how accurate some of the stories are, but I still like hearing them. It's like one of my neighbors said about his wife, "she remembers things that never even happened."

Along with the stories, I like remembering the expressions my folks used. Mom always would say, "times are tough everywhere, even the birds are walking." Dad always would advise "never hire a man who smokes or wears a straw hat. All they ever do is smoke or chase that hat around." I suppose the hat part comes from us living in windy country.

Dad used to look at me when my hands would be scratched up and bleeding from some fencing or building project and say, "boy, it looks like you chased a fart through a keg of nails." I'm too young to have ever seen nails come in a keg, but I knew what he meant.

As haying season slowed for one breakdown or another, Dad had a hired man who consoled him with, "Don't worry, Bud, you got all fall to hay." Might have been one of the same hired men who had some addiction issues and kind of liked going to town. Someone asked Dad if he was good help. "He's a pretty good hand," Dad would say, "but he draws his pay every night."

Another joke so old it puffs dust when I tell it was when we were harnessing up a mare for a cart ride and Dad would point to the strap that went from the breeching and then under the tail and he'd ask, "you know what that is, son?" When I said no, he'd smile and say, "that's a crupper, any horse's a** knows that."

Not stuff worthy of a stand-up routine in Vegas, but they bring a smile as we recount these quips and quotes with neighbors and friends. When a ranch goes to the next generation, it's good to hand down a nice set of cows, well-cared-for rangeland and maybe one tractor that'll start when you need it. But make sure it comes with some of its own character, stories and expressions. They'll last longer than the cows or the tractor.

Losing Liz Taylor
A tale of two Taylors   March 28, 2011

The big news this week was the passing of Elizabeth Taylor, Hollywood superstar and jet setter, at the age of 79.

When I think of Liz Taylor, I don't think of the one with eight husbands, who loved a horse in "National Velvet," who wore furs and diamonds and started a foundation for AIDS research.

No, when I think of Liz Taylor, I think of a woman who had one husband, my father. She loved horses too — real ranch horses — and she could catch every horse on the place that would evade the rest of us. She didn't wear fur coats, just a little fur strip on the hood of her winter parka, but she was an accomplished coyote trapper who added to our family income with her fur trapline. She was a charitable person, but without the notoriety to raise awareness like a popular actress. She did appreciate the other Liz Taylor using her fame to raise money for charities.

My Liz Taylor wasn't Liz Taylor until she married my father and took his last name. She knew that being a Liz who married a Taylor would give her a catchy name, and she relished the comparison to the Hollywood Liz.

She'd be in the checkout line at the grocery store, or Kmart, walking by the tabloids covered with pictures and supposed scandals of the other Liz Taylor, and when she wrote a check to pay for her stuff the clerk would invariably say, "Wow, Liz Taylor, right here in my store!" And, Mom, the 6-foot-tall, gray, curly-haired ranch woman invariably would smile and say, "I bet you didn't recognize me with my disguise, did you?"

Mom and the other Liz Taylor were both born in 1932, but, aside from an occasional trip to the local beauty shop for a permanent, Mom didn't do much to hide her age or cosmetically preserve her youth like the Hollywood Liz did.

Mom found satisfaction and a good life with just one husband. She stayed married to Dad for 49 years and 11 months before ovarian cancer took her from him.

When they were first married and Mom gave birth to my brother, the other Liz Taylor was married to Eddie Fisher. Mom was still under the influence of the drugs and exhaustion in the birthing room when the attending doctor thought he'd joke around a little with the Liz Taylor that was under his care.

"I suppose this baby has a body by Fisher," he said, referring to the other Liz, her husband, Eddie Fisher, and a reference to the GM cars of the time that boasted a "Body by Fisher" emblem on their door sills. "No, Doc," my groggy, but still-witty mother slurred, "this baby is Taylor made!" The doctor was tickled to see a woman with that much spunk right after giving birth.

Both Liz Taylors were beautiful women. My favorite Liz Taylor just didn't get the worldwide acclaim that the other one did. The two never had the chance to meet in this life. That's really no surprise as they couldn't have traveled in two circles that were more different.

But in the next life, the one we hope for after death, Hollywood's Liz Taylor could meet North Dakota's Liz Taylor. That would be a pretty entertaining meeting.

I kind of think Mom might make the bigger impression.

Intimate knowledge
Getting to know the lay of the land   September 12, 2011

There's something to be said for generational knowledge of a piece of ground — when you can steer around a boggy spot because your dad warned you about it when you were a kid driving through the field, or go right to a little known patch of Juneberries because your mom let you in on the secret of where to find them.

Ever since my great-granddad and his brother each homesteaded here in 1905 and 1903, we've been students of the intricacies of this small swath of the earth that makes up our ranch.

I was cutting hay on an 80-acre piece of Uncle Al's homestead land a few weeks back, appreciating that high sandy end where we were able to plant a little alfalfa, and not appreciating that boggy end that deceives you by looking dry but dropping from beneath your tractor if you dare cross it at the wrong time. This year, it's always been the wrong time on that part.

Using a little agronomic guesswork and generational knowledge, I carved out a curvaceous piece of hay land in that treacherous part. By following a line, and it wasn't a straight one, where the big bluestem grass was growing, I was able to get some good hay and keep from getting stuck.

I suppose my old range science teacher in college could tell me why that was, maybe big blue's affinity for better-drained soils or something to do with soil pH or alkalinity. Who knows, but it worked. I didn't get stuck.

Stacking hay on the meadow, Dad kept a year to year mental catalog of the good places to build a stack. He knew where the high spots were; maybe he looked for the big blue stem. He knew well the smooth spots because the hog wallows had swallowed plenty of his oak bullrake teeth as he tried to buck the hay from those rough areas.

We never had satellite photos in those days, but if we did, I bet you could lay one year's image on top of another and another, and find that Dad's big square stacks of loose hay almost always ended up in the same places year after year.

Now I just drive along with the baler and drop a bale whenever the little box beeps and tells me to. But I'll drive by those high, smooth spots and think to myself, "that'd be a good place to make a stack."

Over the hundred plus years that we've had parts of the ranch, I imagine there's been a boot print, a hoof print or a tire track of something worn, ridden or driven by a member of our family on most every square inch of the place.

In the dry years, we've even laid tracks on some of the slough bottoms. Dad would tell me about the dry year, I think it was '61, when they cut right through the sloughs for the hollowstem hay and pushed them out with his D4 Caterpillar. There still are some railroad ties in that one slough that were used to walk the Cat out when it got stuck in the mud.

Now it's wet, not dry, and we're making hay in our pastures to get some forage. With all the rain there's more grass than the cows can graze, and that pasture land is drier than the hay meadows. I'm adding to my knowledge of the terrain as I mow, rake and bale around each bull hole and sand dune in the pasture.

It's paying off with hay and treasure. I've found a few hundred bales of hay and two ear-tagging tools that bounced off my horse years ago. They're a little weathered but workable.

Maybe if I keep studying, I'll find that fencing pliers I lost back in '95....

What makes you, you
Recognizable features   March 26, 2012

It's funny, the things that people notice about you. Whether you're tall or short, smiling or scowling, overweight or underweight, crisply dressed or sloppily dressed, the color of your skin or your eyes, what you have on top of your head.

There's more to the list I suppose — glasses or not, moustache or beard or scruffy or clean shaven, long hair or short hair or no hair, ears that stick out or ears that tuck in, big nose or sharp nose, strong chin or no chin, the list just keeps going.

If I were to pick three things about me that most often are noticed, it'd be my height, my smile and my cowboy hat. They're all mostly genetic for me. My frame came from my 6-foot mother and my 6-foot-2 father.

Those who knew my mother say I got my smile from her. She used to tell the story that when she was born, she had no mouth, so her mother told the doctor to just cut one for her from "here to here." But the doctor thought she said from "ear to ear," and so became my mother's broad smile.

And the hat, well, you can pick one up in a variety of stores, but, for me, I got that tradition from my dad. Cowboys wear cowboy hats just like baseball players wear baseball caps and green berets wear, well, green berets. Dad was a cowboy, a real one and a good one, and at least a couple generations before him were, too.

There's a saying, "all hat and no cattle." But Dad and I were "hat and cattle," or "hat justified because of cattle." And horses, too. Riding, roping, raising a few colts and then training them as they grew older kind of went with the broad-brimmed lid atop our head.

Father and son relationships can be tumultuous, nonexistent or perfectly matched like a good team of work horses, but with one older horse and one younger horse hitched alongside to learn how to pull. Dad and I were the well-matched team in our relationship.

So it would be no surprise to those who watched me grow up to know that I would emulate my father in every way I could, including the hat. Treat people with kindness, especially the very old and the very young; have a healthy attitude toward hard work and those who work hard; keep your word and honor a handshake deal because, rich or poor, honesty is a trait you'd be known for regardless of how many coins you had in your pocket. Those are a few things that came from under Dad's hat, and I've tried to tuck them under my hat, too.

Sure, the hat would come off from time to time. We never slept in our hats. Dad wasn't a stern man, but if you kept your hat on while eating or at the supper table, he'd knock it off your head. It came off in church, at times of prayer, for the flag, the national anthem and the pledge of allegiance. The hat would come off when you met a lady. Maybe it was just a matter of "truth in advertising" to let the ladies know that the handsome cowboy they thought they were meeting was just another average balding male with a receding hairline.

I don't presuppose much about folks when I meet them from how they look or what they wear. It's always best to start a conversation and learn firsthand. And, I suppose, that's how we'd all prefer to go through life.

So when someone notices me, tall, smiling, wearing that cowboy hat, and says, "so what's up with the hat?" I have to say, "Have you got a minute?" Because it's not just something I picked up in a store.

Chapter 3
Ranch realities

Keep or cull
Tough winter decisions

It ain't easy being the boss. Especially when you have to fire someone — like one of your cows.

It's that time of year when we decide which cows we keep another year and which cows get the pink slip.

I'm not just speaking figuratively; the cull cows do really get a pink slip. When I drop the culls off at the auction barn, I get a pink slip from the yard hands documenting my recently unemployed culls and their back tag numbers.

After we pregnancy check the cows, it's easy to know who gets fired from the herd. The culls all have a big "O" painted on their hip for "out of here."

Once all the open cows have been sorted out and shipped, the decisions get a little tougher.

Stay or go

I start walking through the herd trying to identify the cows that are ready for retirement. I usually can find a few old girls with wide muzzles and toothless grins who might not make the winter.

I look for the limpers and gimpers, a lump or a bad eye.

I walk through the calf pen where I kept a few peewees and fuzz balls who didn't quite make sale weight. It doesn't take much of an investigation to correlate the runts with the mother who raised them and break the news to her that she didn't quite reach goal for the year.

Some things you can't see, so I consult my calving book to check for other cullable traits jotted down throughout the year.

Attitude factor

While I'm out in the herd with a keen eye, my wife is out there with a wary eye. She likes nice cows. I like a cow that raises nice calves, never mind the attitude.

My bride graciously runs the gate when I'm sorting cattle and cuts the plastic twine off the round bales while I'm on the tractor rolling them out. She notices things that I miss.

Like when a cow takes a swipe at her as she goes through the gate, or when a cow comes snortin' and stompin' at her out in the feeding pen. She especially notices when it's the same cow in both instances and she does it more than once.

My wife doesn't always remember tag numbers, but she can remember a black cow with beady, little eyes, a blood-curdling beller and one left horn sticking straight out of her skull.

She pointed her out to me the other day and told me I should sell her. "That's 064," I said. "She's a pretty good cow. She's just 4 years old, calved early, had a nice calf this year, bred back and she's in good shape."

"I don't like her. She's mean. Sell her," she said, rather sternly. I told her I'd think about it.

That's when I went back to my calving book to do a little more research on that good cow. Next to her number and the calf stats in the comments column, I wrote a word that I won't repeat here.

I wrote "major" followed by a word that began with a "b" and it wasn't beauty. I began to remember tagging her calf.

After she tried mashing me in the ground while I was on foot, I roped her from the horse. She started knocking my horse around, then I got her in a poplar thicket, wrapped the rope around a half-dozen trees like "cats in the cradle" and got her calf just out of reach to tag and vaccinate while she bellered and slobbered and shook the branches off those trees.

I didn't get my rope back for three days.

In consideration of the evidence, I think I might sell 064, maybe even before Christmas.

I've been having a tough time coming up with a Christmas gift for my bride. I think 064's pink slip might make the perfect stocking stuffer.

Tagmanship
Numbering with a personal flair   May 2, 2005

It's time for me to practice my penmanship again. It's ear-tagging time on the ranch, and that means a lot of handwriting that'll be up for neighborhood scrutiny. And it's done with real permanent ink, so no "do overs."

Most every ranch has an official ear-tag artist. My mother is an artist by trade, so it was natural for her to be our designated ear-tag numberer for many years.

Dad would bring in his tally book and she'd get to work on the kitchen table with an assortment of colored tags and bottles of white, yellow and black tag ink that would take forever to dry.

Sometimes, she'd hurry the process along with a hair dryer to speed up the drying time, but they'd generally spend a couple of hours on the kitchen table, propped up level to reduce drips and runs while they dried.

The finished products coming off of Mom's kitchen table were a genuine bovine work of art.

It wasn't easy to achieve work-of-art status with that old-time ink. It would blotch in a heartbeat if you weren't on top of your game. If you didn't squeeze the bottle with just the right amount of pressure, you'd end up with a big solid ink-filled "O" on the tag, which isn't real handy if you were trying to draw a zero-free number like 174.

Things have progressed some since those days. From the old, slow bottle ink, I spent a year or two writing on the tags with a little hand grinder that would expose an opposing color hidden in the middle layer of the ear tag. You didn't have to wait for the tags to dry, but I'd cough up plastic shavings and dust for a couple hours. And hand cramps were an issue after 10 or 12 tags.

From there, we began to trust an ink pen that dried quickly and claimed to last. I began writing out the ear tags right on location with the cow staring back at me with instructions of what number to put on her calf.

I inherited some of my mother's artistic talents, and I have to say most of my tags are nearly picture perfect.

They're so good that I'm tempted to carefully extricate them before shipping the calves and reuse them. But it's tough to sort through a bag of used tags and find the one you need when you need it.

Sometimes I can pull out a 124 and convert it to a 424, or, with a little fancy pen work, turn a 173 into a 788. But, after laboriously pulling a few tags from heifers that I kept for replacements, I decided to let my 80-cent masterpieces go on to the feedlot without removal and recycling.

Tags aren't a legal mark of ownership, but around our neighborhood, most everyone can tell where a calf belongs by the artistic tagmanship of the owner.

There's different numbering and lettering schemes, tag colors, right ear or left ear and handwritten versus factory-stamped numbers to differentiate one herd from another. Most times, we just use a little local handwriting analysis. Sometimes when I'm gone during calving, my hired hand does the ear tagging. I guess that's why I still brand my calves, in case there's any confusion with the handwriting.

One rather intellectual neighbor was going to go with Roman numerals to set his herd apart, but when he realized that calf 369 would become CCCLXIX, he knew he'd never get it all on one tag.

Gated community
The finest in exclusive grazing enclaves   May 16, 2005

Whenever someone talks about a "gated community," my mind conjures up images of the rich and famous sealing themselves and their property off from the troublesome regular folks in the neighborhood.

But just last week, I was cinching up the gate rope and laying a double half-hitch on the barbed-wire gate that crosses our gravel driveway when it struck me that I, too, live in something of a gated community.

And, like rich kids whose chauffeur drove them through the wrought-iron gates of their mansion grounds on the way to school, I grew up thinking that everyone had a barbed-wire gate going across their road.

Our school bus driver wasn't a big fan of our gate when we closed it to facilitate a little spring grazing. He didn't care to open it and often dropped us off at the gate, a little less than a half-mile from the house.

I suppose those spring walks down our road, dodging cows and cow pies, helped me steer clear of childhood obesity. Genetics, high metabolism and other physical chores probably helped, too.

Good grazing

In most places, gated communities are designed to protect property. On the ranch, our gate was put up to make more efficient use of our property.

The cows and I hate to see good green grass go to waste in the spring, and ditch grass looks especially delectable after a long winter of chewing on dry hay. In a dry spring like this, the ditches are about the only places that collected enough snow and moisture through the winter to sprout any early green shoots.

Our gate isn't manned by a live security guard or any electronic surveillance. It doesn't even have a Rottweiller or a Doberman pinscher pacing back and forth behind it.

But it usually is calving season when the cows graze along our driveway, and I know a few ol' girls in there who'll put you up a tree as fast as any guard dog if you get too close to their calves.

We're a pretty welcoming bunch around the ranch, and although we shut our gate once in awhile, we've never hung up any signs next to it saying "Keep Out!", "No Trespassing!" or "Beware of the Ornery Cow!"

Our little four-wire gate is enough, though, to turn back a few salesmen glued to their car seat, traveling Jehovah's Witnesses unsure of the cow on the other side of the fence and my old bus driver with his aversion to our double half-hitch on the gate post.

Gateless options

I suppose if we'd put in a "Texas Gate," or a cattleguard, we could graze along the driveway and not have to open and close a gate every time we left the place.

But then we'd lose that gated community status, and some real agents say houses in gated communities have a higher resale value. Never mind that the old shack only has one bathroom, no air conditioning and 1950s wiring, it's an exclusive reclusive ranchhouse complete with its own gated access.

Of course, resale hasn't been a big issue for us the last 100 years. As a matter of fact, I can't recall a single prospective buyer ever driving into our yard to offer us any big bucks for the homestead.

They might have tried, but I suppose the gate was shut.

Tying up
And lookin' for a tree   May 30, 2005

My part of the world isn't known for a lot of forested acres. When people ponder North Dakota, they generally think of wide open prairies with nary a tree on the horizon.

Granted, we have a few areas where there are plenty of trees. And we can grow trees if we plant them and care for them, but they don't often sprout up and grow on their own.

We have a few pastures that are pretty well wooded with cottonwoods and poplars. And we have a few pastures with nothing more substantial than an especially stout blade of grass.

This can pose a problem from time to time.

Hitchin' help

Most of my horses aren't big on "ground tying." I can't dismount, drop the reins and trust them to stick around to give me a ride home later. So I kind of need the occasional random hitchin' post if I want to dismount in the pasture and do something on foot for a few minutes.

Sometimes I'm close enough to a fence to throw the lines around a steel fence post. If my trusty steed is hungry for green grass, I can tie him to a well-anchored piece of brush and let him graze while I wander.

If I try letting him graze without anchoring him, I usually end up walking home.

Cattle management on the Taylor Ranch works best with a few trees. As one of my veterinarian friends told me, good animal medicine is all about proper restraint.

So when I'm by myself and I rope a cow that needs some doctoring, I'm usually on the lookout for some of that proper restraint to tie my 1,200-pound patient to.

This calving season, I had a cow trying to calve that needed a little assistance. I wasn't having much luck chasing her in to the home corrals, so I stuck a loop on her and looked for somewhere to anchor.

I looked high and low in that tree-free pasture. Finally, I got her close enough to a rural electric highline pole to tie her off, and then I rode home to get the calf puller. I'm sure this is not approved of or recommended by the utility companies and electric co-ops, but we saved the calf.

I had another cow under a lot of strain that I discovered with an upside-down hoof protruding from under her tail. The calf was breech and time was of the essence, so I roped her and looked for the nearest woody plant.

I found one, sort of. I'm not enough of an arborist to know what it was called, but it was a thorny thing with stickers on it about 2 inches long. My hands looked like they'd run through a keg of nails when I got done dallying her to this thorny monster. Backward calf and distressed cow looked fine when it was all done, however.

Snubbing options

I should find some other options for my calving-season cow restraint.

I could put the cows in a muddy corral and monitor them next to my squeeze chute and headgate, but I kind of like calving cows out on green pasture.

Committed to pasture calving, I think the best option in my treeless pastures is to go out and dig in a big treated wood post every couple hundred yards. Then I'd have something solid to tie those laboring cows to and I wouldn't risk the thorns or the off chance of causing a neighborhood black out.

And, if my neighbors ask why I've got those nice posts stuck out in the middle of my pastures? I'll just tell them that those treated corner posts had gotten so expensive I decided to plant a few to see if I could grow a crop of my own!

Memory missed
Knocking some sense into this cowboy's skull

I work hard at remembering things. I've committed to memory important dates like my wife's birthday and our wedding anniversary, I write down commitments I've made and places I need to be, I sort tasks out in my mind as I go, and I even sort a few bills out on my desk so I don't forget to pay them.

One thing I can't sort out is a period of time about 24 hours long surrounding a little horse wreck I had this week.

Witnesses tell me I caught a mare that wasn't real well broke and made the not-so-wise decision to ride her the mile from the ranch to my house with just a halter and a lead rope — no saddle and no bridle.

I guess the mare beat me home. Next anyone saw of me, I came walking into my yard missing a little hide off of my forehead and acting even more peculiar than usual.

My mother was baby-sitting our 13-month-old boy at our house while my wife was in town. I walked in, sat down and asked her what day it was. She answered. Then I asked her that same question 11 more times and she decided to call our local nurse practitioner.

The next day, I woke up in the local hospital stiff and sore and more than a little confused. I guess they'd brought me in and given me a CT scan and said that aside from a few bumps and bruises and a receding hairline, my head was as normal as could be expected for an aging cowboy of Norwegian heritage who had suffered a concussion.

My only real deficit is that I'm missing the memory of a day or two from this week. It's a spooky feeling; losing your memory and having people tell you what you did or said and having no recollection of it.

I have learned a few things from the event. I learned a new word, perseverating. It means repeating the same thing over and over, despite being told the answer each time. After asking what day it was 12 times in two minutes, my phrases of choice were, "Was I riding Babe?" and, "Is Bud OK?" Babe is the rather sweet name for that wicked mare that knocked my lights out, and Bud is the nickname of our son.

I learned that a CAT scan actually is a CT scan, and it doesn't involve a feline walking around the exam room and looking you over. In the next month or so, I'll learn how much the bill was to have one done.

I learned that concussions are cumulative. Each time you have a concussion, it's easier to get another concussion in the future. This is actually the second one I've had. I wonder how easy they'll be coming in the future. Just in case, I'm going to be careful not to stand up quickly in places with short ceilings and I'm going to quit banging my head on the wall when confronted with the frustrations of the markets, machinery and weather.

And, now, I have something to blame my absentmindedness on. When I can't find a wrench I need in the shop, can't remember where I left my jackknife or seem to have misplaced my wallet, I'll just blame it all on those few hours of cognitive dysfunction surrounding my concussion. I'll be sticking with that excuse when things are lost for years to come.

Haying help
Small crews and big jobs

It's a pretty small haying crew on the Taylor Ranch this summer. I'm pretty much it.

But, when we can line up a babysitter, my wife comes out and doubles the manpower of our haying outfit by adding her womanpower. It sure is nice to see someone else in the field. Hay fields are a pretty lonely place if you're the only hayer.

It wasn't always that way. The ranch used to run a good-sized crew of kids, hired help, retired friends, vacationing relatives and any other passer-by who could be talked into joining our little chain gang of mowers, rakers, buckers, stackers and scatter rakers.

Family planning was really a function of filling out the hay crew for some ranching parents. If they had five tractor seats to fill, they'd make sure to have five kids before they called it quits with the procreation.

Lunch was a real social event when you had a half-dozen helpers gathered around the sandwiches and doughnuts. Nowadays, farmers and ranchers eat lunch on the go in the tractor cab or hurry through it sitting by themselves in fields far from anywhere.

Good help, or even bad help, is hard to find. Families are smaller, relatives are lazier and retired friends say they're truly serious about retirement and recreation.

So we did what every modern agriculturalist has done for the last 50 years, we bought bigger equipment.

Wider, longer, lonelier

Last winter, I bought a new sickle bar hay mower. There's nothing like a strong calf market to stimulate the machinery sales.

It's a shame that rich folks who never buy anything have all the cash. To really stimulate the economy, what we need is more money in the hands of ranchers.

Whatever money most ranchers have during good times is quickly spent and pumped into the economy. Give us a dollar, and we'll go to town and spend two.

That's what I did after we sold the calves last fall. Now I have a double 9-foot mower out in the field whacking down 18 feet of forage with every round. It's a far cry from the 4-foot horse mower or the revered John Deere No. 5 that clacked and banged and cut the meadows around here 7 feet at a time.

It's nice to be able to do a little more work with one tractor instead of two, especially since you have to take out a second mortgage to fill the farm tank with diesel these days.

Somehow, Dad was able to keep a whole fleet of little green tractors going when we had the big crew. Of course, they only had two cylinders a piece and you generally could fix them with a pliers and a screwdriver.

The fleet got so big they even painted white numbers on the front of those old tricycle tractors. That way they could tell the newest member of the crew to "go get on No. 4," or "hook up to No. 1," and there'd be no mistaking the machine they meant.

There's no denying that times have changed. One person with the right equipment probably can get as much done in the hay field as three used to. That's progress, I guess.

But when I sit down on the stubble in the shade of the pickup to eat my lunch, those two other hayers would provide a lot better conversation than that big new mower.

Fleet prognosis fails
The other high cost of gas on the ranch   January 23, 2006

One of my favorite ranching adages is, "If you don't have any, you don't lose any." This is meant to soothe the pain of livestock death loss with the logic that we should … actually I don't what the logic is, but I like it just the same.

And I use it from time to time when my meager veterinary skills fail to keep all creatures great or small alive and kicking on our ranch.

For a layman, I know a little more about animal health than some, a little less than others. I usually can diagnose the sick ones, often times with the blanket diagnosis of "ADR" taught to me by one of my veterinarian friends.

For the uneducated, ADR is "ain't doin' right." I can spot an ADR in our pastures and pens just as if I'd gone to school to learn how.

My treatments of ADR aren't nearly as accurate as my diagnoses. If I can't find what I'm looking for in my little bag of miracle drugs and pharmaceutical panaceas, I break down and call a professional.

Bloating blimp

My last foray into animal medicine allowed me an even more accurate diagnosis than ADR. I had a calf that was a chronic bloater, and he was becoming more chronically bloated than not bloated as the days progressed.

Even I can call a bloat when I see one. But I do have a copy of the Merck Veterinary Manual that I like to refer to it from time to time for sheer entertainment and intellectual vocabulary building to help with my Scrabble game skills.

The bloat my calf had was called "secondary ruminal tympany." I was encouraged to learn that "chronic ruminal tympany is relatively frequent in calves up to 6 months old without apparent cause; this form usually resolves spontaneously."

That's what I was looking for, some spontaneous resolution, my kind of low-cost, no-hassle treatment regiment. Over the last couple weeks, I'd run this little guy in to put a hose down his throat and let off a little excess gas, but he'd be bloated again in a day or two anyway.

This calf had a couple of underlying factors that weren't necessarily in his favor. His mother had died last summer and I brought him back to the ranch orphanage and put him on a costly, labor-intensive diet of powdered calf milk replacer and creep feed pellets.

You put that kind of care and money into a critter, and they're bound to die on you. Increasing dollars are a sure predictor of decreasing health.

The other big negative he had going against him was that my wife decided to give him a name to reference him as she bottle fed him and carried pellets to him.

I bet you could conduct a scientific study and learn that named calves, especially bum calves, have a much higher likelihood of croaking.

Chip was down but not out the other morning. I got him up and thought he might move around a little and work up a good belch. I checked on him a few hours later with the thought of poking him with a trocar to allow some rumen release.

He outran me, so I gave him a positive prognosis. Nine times out of 10, if a calf can outrun me, he doesn't need doctoring.

Chip must have been number 10.

I should have known. The Merck manual said "ruminants may die of bloat if they become accidentally cast in dorsal recumbency."

Chip, our costly little orphan, got recumbent on his dorsal and died. I should have run a little faster last night.

Calving surprises
Our very own side show   May 15, 2006

Whoever said "two heads are better than one," sure wasn't talking about a two-headed, breech birth, Charolais Angus cross heifer calf.

The Taylor Ranch had its first two-headed calf — that's a dicephalic bovine for you scientists — in its 103-year history this spring.

I was out checking the cows when I spotted an old black cow with two hind legs and a tail protruding from her backside. I went into assisted delivery mode, roped her, dallied on to the ball hitch of the pickup and put the chains and puller on the backwards birthing baby.

I began ratcheting the puller and the calf was coming out nicely. She hung up at the shoulders a bit, but I worked the puller up and down a little and out she came. Or should I say out they came?

The calf/calves was/were quite a surprise when the two legs I was pulling on came out attached to two backbones leading up to two fully developed heads.

Unfortunately, the calf was dead and I'm not sure if it had been alive when the birthing process started. I do wish our two-headed calf had come out alive though.

Malformations abound

I did some research on two headed calves. From the papers I found, it probably was a set of twins that didn't quite twin.

Dad said there was a stuffed two-headed calf in a bar in our hometown many years ago. I've seen plenty of stuffed deer, buffalo, moose, longhorn steers, you name it, in small town taverns, but I guess nothing will bring thirsty cowboys into your saloon like a taxidermied two-headed calf.

Seems like everyone's got a mutant calving story. One neighbor told me about his five-legged calf, another had one born inside out, you know, guts on the outside, hide on the inside. You hear a lot of weird stuff from your neighbors when you open a conversation with, "Hey, we had a two-headed calf last week!"

The great thing about living today and having the Internet in our homes is you can Google "two-headed calf" and spend hours reading about other bovine oddities. I got 1,210,000 hits on my Google search for two-headed calves. After reading the first page, I began to think that I should dig up that malformed heifer, find a taxidermist and put a sign out on the highway to fleece curious passers-by.

There was one called "Billy Boy" in Indiana, born in 1938 and believed to be "the only one of its kind in the world." Obviously, they didn't have Google back then.

Another, born in Ohio in 1941, was stuffed and its owner charged a dime for tourists to come and see it. Luckily, his farm was located on a major highway. Locals claim the calf's owner would go to town and buy new cars with buckets of dimes.

I found a stuffed one in New Zealand that had been sold in an Internet auction to appease the owner's wife who didn't want it in her house. Another one, nicely taxidermied, on Ebay was supposed to have sold for $3,000 plus $50 shipping.

There's one on display in a Ripley's Believe It Or Not museum in San Francisco, and one was born in Pennsylvania near Three Mile Island ... hmmm. Some try to link the birth to radiation or some local toxicity; others consider the calves a statistical anomaly.

Dairy farmers in Russia had one and feared it would bring misfortune, but the corpse of another one was being carted around Cambodia and its owners were raising money for a shrine because they believed it would bring prosperity to those who saw it.

I don't know if ours will bring us misfortune or prosperity, but I do wish it had lived. It'd have been nice to have a calf on the place that would have doubled my chances of catching it in a roping contest.

Dead and dying wood
As boards retire, steel steps in   June 12, 2006

I made another trip to the bone pile in our east pasture this week to deposit the remains of two old friends on the ranch.

No, this bone pile doesn't hold the carcasses of dead critters. It's the last stop for the remains of old corrals, busted gates and rotted off posts. I call it Deadwood, except our Deadwood doesn't have South Dakota's blackjack tables, slot machines or colorful history of Wild Bill Hickok and Calamity Jane.

The two old friends I took out there were the last two wooden gates we had left in our sorting pens. They were 8 feet long and built with two-by-sixes. They were some real swingers in their day, but, in the last year, they'd become a serious drag on the cattle sorting system.

Like all the retired sticks and timbers in the pile, they had character. They were gray, weathered and twisted from a hard life in the elements. They'd taken some hard knocks and their broken limbs were patched up with an occasional new crosspiece and a few more nails.

Transitioning

In the last 10 or 20 years, every time a section of wooden corral fell down or a board built gate collapsed, I replaced it with a chunk of processed steel or a welded up salvage sucker rod panel.

For a while, I almost encouraged the cattle to snap a few planks or bust up an old wooden gate. The shiny steel replacements had a powerful allure, aside from the price tag.

The steel is nice — lower maintenance, more staying power, fewer slivers. But I kind of miss my old, gray, brittle friends. I remember building them with Dad. There was a lot of satisfaction in turning a pickup load of fresh, new, yellow wooden planks into a gate or a section of corral that you could stand back and admire at the end of a back breaking day.

When I was little, I didn't have a "Bob the Builder" DVD or video or plastic play tools. I had Dad, a bucket of real tools and corrals that needed fixing. I hit my thumb, bent some nails and made a few crooked saw cuts, but I learned. Come to think of it, I'm still learning.

Wiring up a steel panel or drilling the holes for a ready-made gate just doesn't have the same satisfaction of swinging a hammer and driving home a can of nails. But the days and weeks are full enough without my going back to more labor-intensive methods or higher-maintenance setups.

Leisurely future

With all the steel gates, steel corral panels and steel posts in our fenceline, you'd think my days of patching corrals and fixing fence would come to an eventual end. It hasn't happened yet, and, if it does, I suppose the steel will have rusted through and the cycle will start over again.

For now, though, I think an old-time ranch needs at least one old-time wooden gate. There's one left, a little walk through going into the corrals built of salvaged oak bullrake stacker teeth, bolted together and hung on homemade hinges.

If I was a betting man, I'd say a cow could pop the weld on a piece of sucker rod or bend a tube of 16-gauge steel before she'd put as much as a scratch on that oak gate.

It's comforting to know I won't be the only thing hanging around the ranch getting gray and weathered without being forced to retire.

Turn 'em out
Another branding in the books   June 26, 2006

Every year I say the same thing when we're done working the cattle at branding time. "Boy, it's good to have that job done." I say it with the same predictability as Paul Harvey says, "now you know the rest of the story."

There are lots of jobs that I'm glad to have done throughout the year. I like wrapping the twine on the last bale of hay, having the last bale hauled in for the winter, getting the cattle gathered up in the fall, getting the calves weighed and sold for the year.

But getting the calves branded, vaccinated and castrated in the early summer seems to top the list and require verbal confirmation that I'm glad to have the task behind me.

I guess it's because it's one of those jobs that I'm never sure we'll get done until it's done. Everything needs to fall into place. The weather needs to cooperate, the cattle need to allow themselves to be captured, the neighbors and friends who provide all the labor need to show up.

I guess a lot of the jobs we do are dependent on good weather and cooperative cattle, but independent, Lone Rangeresque ranchers don't always find themselves depending on other people to help them out.

Sure, I help out the neighbors whenever I'm asked to lend a hand with their branding, but I still feel like I might be imposing on them when I get on the phone and start putting our branding together.

I know everyone's as busy as can be with other projects and paying jobs. There are weeds to spray, fences to fix, hay fields to cut, families to tend. Everyone's glad to help, but I still apologize as I ask for assistance.

I sometimes use the negative assumption proposal. "Say, I don't suppose you could come help us work calves next week. ..." Other times I say, "I reckon you've got a hundred things to do next week Tuesday. ..." Then they can give themselves an easy out.

Every year, though, the crew comes together in miraculous form. And this guy who spends most days by himself, doing things alone, revels in the presence of a dozen or more good friends and neighbors who've come to help.

I can credit a couple of reasons for the good turnout. First, we rope and drag the calves with horses to the ground crew for their jobs. So, it's not really work, it's more of a loosely structured play day for cowboys.

If I asked the crew to throw them by hand or push them through a calf chute one at a time, I think they'd quit answering their phone this time of year for fear I might be calling to ask for help. None of us are getting any younger, and roping the calves by both hind feet keeps us from getting ironed out and trampled by our little sharp-hooved friends.

Second, my wife is a good cook. Somehow, she finds a way to both help in the corrals and put on a tremendous supper at the end of the day. For some in the crew, working calves is a small price to pay to partake in the food and drink afterward.

It's a good feeling when everything comes together. I call six or eight people to come help and it warms my heart to see a dozen show up. Extra hands make the day a little more festive.

And when the calves get mothered up and go to nursing with a new brand on their left hip, you can't help but feel good. We couldn't have done it by ourselves, and we wouldn't want to. But it is nice to have the job done.

Now, if I can just get motivated for the other dozen jobs around here that we need to do by ourselves.

Let the wind blow
And the water run

September 4, 2006

I'm not sure if I'm a visionary who's way ahead of the times, or a curmudgeon stuck in the past. But, either way, I like the windmills on our ranch.

The ranch has been using wind power since it was homesteaded, but only recently has wind power become all the talk in the alternative energy circles.

For the most part, wind is a hateful weather phenomenon on the prairie. It blows dirt in your eyes, makes it hard to cut hay, speeds up wildfires and saps the strength right out of you when you're buffeted by it.

But wind does have a saving grace. It can really can make the windmill wheel turn, and when the wheel's turning, it can pump more water than a thirsty herd can drink on a hot day.

This year, the windmills and tanks were significantly more appreciated by the cows than the slimy, muddy excuses for waterholes that we had in the same dry pastures. Given the option of drinking the dirty water from their bovine bathtub and bathroom, the herd would head right for the windmill to sip some cool, clean water from the tank.

High-wire mechanic

The windmills do take a little more high-level maintenance than a waterhole. Not advanced, just high up in the air. Luckily, I've never been afraid of heights, so I've enjoyed the scenic view from the top of a windmill since I was a young tower climber.

I've learned a couple things in my career as a high-altitude windmill mechanic. First, there's no shame in a cowboy wearing a plier holster on his belt. When you're working without a net, easy access to your tools is essential.

Second, if you drop something, don't make a grab for it to try and rescue it. It's a lot healthier to just hang on tight, watch it drop, listen for the thud and make a mental note of where to start looking for the slippery pin when you get back to earth.

It's also a good idea to put on the wheel brake before climbing a windmill. Only you can prevent fan blade decapitation when the winds blowing 20 or 30 miles an hour. The brakes on our windmills don't work so well, so if I can schedule the windmill work, I shoot for a calm day.

Likewise, I try not to climb windmills or golf when there's a lightning storm.

Pins and gears

In general, I'm not very mechanical. When I pop open the hood on a car and peer underneath, I'm pretty clueless. I do know what propels most machines forward and keeps them going — a big checkbook or a high-limit credit card.

But, windmill motors, I can see how they work. Wheel turns a shaft, shaft turns some gears, gears lift and lower a rod that pumps some water.

You can pop the top and fix what needs fixing with that plier hanging from your belt. If you can pull a cotter key from a pin, you're a qualified level one windmill

86

mechanic. No electronic sensors or sensitive computer modules to rewire.

The worst part of the job is the 50 years of old oil and grease built up on and around the motor. You can get rid of it if you scrub off the layer of skin it's attached to.

It's hard to complain, though, when the entire fossil fuel requirement of your water pumping system is a couple quarts of old oil. I reckon that's why our old windmills have found new favor.

Stomachs of steel
Ranch-dog diets

April 16, 2007

Pet food's been a hot topic as of late. There've been product recalls, contaminated wheat gluten, salmonella-laced pet treats, and lots of recipes for "homemade" pet food.

When we heard the news on our ranch, we didn't have to rush out and check the label on our dog food. I guess you could say our two ranch mutts have been on a bit of a homemade diet their whole life.

I wouldn't say their diet is free of contaminants, but it's never killed them.

I don't know that I could recommend the ranch-dog diet to anyone who's concerned about the safety of off-the-shelf dog food. But I'll share with readers the ingredients that keep our dogs well fed and happy.

Carnivore canines

Our dogs have a varied, seasonal diet. In spring, they roam the calving pasture in search of the expelled placenta of parturition. I know it's pretty gross, but I'm sure I'm not the only rancher with dogs who prefer afterbirth to dry dog food.

In summer, they travel the calf-branding circuit to gorge themselves on what we daintily refer to as Rocky Mountain oysters. They'll eat all day long on the byproduct that results when bulls are turned into steers. They'll have a bit of a hangover the next day, but they're always recovered by the next branding.

Throughout the year, they trot up and down the byways in search of fresh roadkill. Sometimes they settle for less-than-fresh roadkill, or carrion as they call it. Rabbits, deer, raccoons — I know what they're grazing on because they usually drag a drumstick or two back to the yard.

Ranch dogs don't mind eating wild turkey once in a while. I've never seen this myself, of course, but I've heard of ranches where a turkey will mysteriously die on occasion when there're a hundred of them lined up on the feed bunks every morning.

Like all good ranchers with impeccable management, I, of course, never lose a cow or a calf to sickness, weather or chance. But I've heard of guys who lose calves and have a ranch dog or two helping with the carcass disposal.

Their dogs will disappear behind the hill for a couple hours every day, drag back a leg bone or two, and they see a noticeable decline in the draw down on the 50-pound sack of co-op elevator dog food they keep in the shop.

Not for all

Nobody needs to write and tell me how dangerous the ranch-dog diet is for a loving pet and companion. I'm certain that these free-roaming eating activities are completely out of balance with the required nutrients, vitamins and minerals.

But I'm not about to chain them up. Part of the joy of country living is letting your dogs be dogs and enjoy some freedom. Of course, running free does have them eating like a coyote most days.

I think the diet does toughen them up a bit. They fend off salmonella, scoff at bacteria and might even survive a dose of melamine in a contaminated batch of wheat gluten.

And, in light of everything that's been in the news, I'll let them take their chances out on our meaty domestic range before I head to town to buy any imported Chinese wheat gluten.

Green grass sensors
Cows are ready even if pastures aren't   May 14, 2007

Ranchers can hardly wait to see green grass in the spring. The only ones more excited than the rancher would have to be the cows.

All winter long while they're grazing old dormant grass and feeding on dry, crunchy hay, they dream of tasty, tender, juicy blades of grass. Cows seek out that new grass like kids clamor for ice cream. And they pitch just as big a fit when you deny them that treat.

You might have the straightest, tightest barbed-wire fence in the world, and, come green grass and springtime, the cows will have the posts bent and the wires stretched as they lean forward to wrap their tongue around a little succulent ditch grass.

The crafty cows will walk right through the barbed-wire boundary and head for the spring smorgasbord. If you're lucky, the whole herd won't follow her through her hole in the fence. You hope for the sake of parental nurture that the grass-crazed cows will remember to come back and get their newborn calves.

Shock factor

When green grass comes around, I do my best to keep the cows in. I've tried reasoning with them, explaining the damage they'll do to the warm-season native grasses if it's not at least in the 3½-leaf stage with a minimum leaf height of 8 inches as recommended in the range science guidebook.

I've had about as much luck with that as scientists who explain global warming to a herd of suburban car drivers, or doctors who explain the ills of obesity to folks standing in line at the doughnut shop.

The cows aren't buying into the 3½-leaf vegetative stage argument. They want their grass and they want it now! It makes no difference how long the barbs are on the wire, or how close the posts are spaced, just get out of their self-indulgent way.

Then I discovered the power of electricity, or, more specifically, electric fence.

String a little smooth wire around the cows, send a little pulsating electrical current through it and — Bingo! — the herd is contained, even when the grass is truly greener on the other side.

The key to electric fence, though, is keeping it electrified. Some say that once cattle are trained to it they won't even try to touch a nose to the wire. When green grass comes in the spring, I think my cows test it every day.

I could have saved the expense of a digital voltage tester for my fence by just observing the cows. Last week, I went out with my offering of dry, crunchy hay and found grass-drunk cows walking though an electric fence that should've knocked them back on their heels.

My electronic gadget confirmed the failure. The lead wire had gotten unhooked from the fence. Or, perhaps, some super-dextrous, cloven-hoofed cow unclamped the wire to free her corral mates.

If our pastures are ever going to make it to the 3½-leaf stage, I better check my electric fence several times a day.

But, looking at the diminishing size of my hay pile and the drool coming from the mouths of the cows who've tasted the green goodness of spring, I may just have to hope for 2½-leaf leaves before flinging the gate open for 2007.

Independence Day sale
Equine commerce on the Fourth of July   July 9, 2007

I've always had horses, but I've never been a very good horse trader.

It takes skill to be a good horse trader. Skilled like a card shark, or a carnival game operator, or a pickpocket.

There's a difference between being a horse seller and a horse trader. I don't do much of either. Most of our horses are keepers, or at least they're kept. Having just celebrated the Fourth of July, America's Independence Day, I always think about my single best horse trade.

I had a red roan colt named, of all the original names in the horse-naming world, Red. I bought Red as a weanling at a local production sale when I was 12 years old.

I cracked the piggy bank, emptied my savings account and told the owner I was looking for a $250 red roan stud colt. Usually, it's a cardinal horse trading sin to lay your top bid out on the table like that.

The sale was averaging $300 or $400 that day. But when this particular roan colt came in the ring, the owner yelled "Sold!" after I mustered the courage to raise my hand and bid my whole $250. Other people still were trying to bid when my colt left the ring and I was declared its new owner.

First horse

Red the roan was the first horse I bought and paid for with my own money.

It seemed only right that I train Red myself. I hadn't learned about "horse whispering" yet when I was 14, but I tried to put a lot of miles on the horse to make up for my limited horse training experience.

The miles never quite did it for him. He could be plumb fine, then blow up and start bucking. He had some spectacular explosions. I never got hurt, but I never trusted the bugger.

I was too honest to take him to the sale barn and sell him as a "kid horse" just because I was a kid and he was a horse. So I did the most honest thing I could imagine, I decided we should buck him out at the Fourth of July rodeo in my hometown.

I came up with this grand Fourth of July idea on the night of the 3rd. I needed to find the rodeo stock contractor after the evening performance. This was before cell phones.

I tracked him down the old-fashioned way, I called the bar and asked for him. Sure enough, he was there. This stock contractor — we'll just call him Dean — said to bring him in and they'd put him in the draw for the Fourth.

I figured we'd start him out with an exhibition ride to see how he'd do. They must have been short of bareback-bucking horses that day, so Red's debut would be in the performance.

The lucky rider was the current bareback riding champion in the state rodeo association. He didn't recognize the horse's name when he drew it, and when he heard it was a local saddle horse, he had to be pretty disgusted with his luck.

I wasn't sure how he'd buck, but in a few seconds, Red had the state champion bareback rider thrown to the ground.

The stock contractor gave me $500 for my strawberry roan. In the horse business, you call that doubling your money because you never count the cost of hay, grass, oats, training or transportation in an equine transaction. It's a rule.

And although I've never ridden broncs in a rodeo, every Fourth of July, I can tell folks I rode one horse that a champion bareback rider couldn't.

Llamas on the loose
Exotic imports make a local appearance   July 23, 2007

These days, you never know what kind of livestock might wander into your yard. Most days, it's just a stray horse or a few fence-crawling cows.

This week, we were visited by a couple of llamas out roaming the neighborhood. Llamas, you may or may not know, are South American camelids who originated in North America 40 million years ago.

About a year ago, they migrated back to our part of North America via a local sale barn, an exotic animal sale and a neighbor's hired man with an itchy bidding finger. He must have figured they were going too cheap. He came home with eight or 10 of them.

I've been tempted with livestock auction bargains myself, but I've never brought anything home more exotic than a pair of Belgian draft horse colts.

He took them to his boss' ranch, threw open the trailer gate and proclaimed them to be the new guard animals for calving season. Personally, all my cows are mean enough to chase off their own coyotes, but llamas have a reputation for canine hate that might be helpful to more timid bovines.

New neighbors

My first contact with the local llama herd was along our adjoining fenceline when I was riding pastures on my horse one day.

Me and my gelding topped a little rise along the fence and found ourselves face to face with one of these South American imports.

My horse was more than a little surprised by the encounter. If I hadn't been sitting deep in the saddle when he jumped sideways, I'd have looked like the cartoon Wile E. Coyote in midair holding a sign that said "Oh oh" and waiting for gravity to take hold, a crash and a puff of dust.

The llama followed me along the fence for a half-mile or so. Being a savvy stockman, I deduced that this one was an intact male when I saw him from behind. That may have explained why he was a little aggressive, stopping every now and then to hiss at me.

A little-known fact about llamas is that they breed lying down. So I did my best to make sure my horse didn't lie down in sight of this male.

He finally went back to his llama friends and my neighbor's cows.

Exotic visitors

I hadn't thought much about them again until two of the critters came trotting down the road to our ranch yard.

When I called my neighbor, he said we could keep 'em or shoot em'. Apparently, he'd had his fill of llama ranching in the past year.

I contemplated roping them; after all, they're mostly neck. If you can't catch a long-necked llama, you're not trying very hard. Of course, I didn't know what I'd do with them once I caught them.

I've heard stories about their spitting ability. The last thing I wanted was to have a llama on the end of my rope and have him turn around and launch a wad of llama spit at me.

Luckily, I didn't have to rope them, chase them or get in a spitting contest with them.

My mother thought they were making a move toward her garden, so she grabbed a hoe, took a few steps toward them, questioned their parentage and told them to "shoo."

We haven't seen 'em since. Smart llamas.

I walk the line
Because I have to   September 3, 2007

I used to fancy myself a marathon runner. Nowadays, I'm mostly a hayfield walker.

By luck and perseverance, our ranch has been in the same exact spot for 104 years. We've never gotten real big, but we've stuck with it long enough to put together a couple contiguous sections of native hay land.

It's pretty handy to have all our hay in one spot. I hate to say that too loud because

I know lots of ranchers aren't that fortunate.

I once told a ranching friend of mine that the wheels on my rake were stuck in field position because I couldn't remember ever having to put them in transport position. I thought he was going to deck me.

We don't spend a lot of time on the open road dragging our equipment along in high gear. But I do spend plenty of time walking our two sections of meadow moving our copious collection of equipment every 80 acres or so.

Power walking?

I wouldn't classify my walking style as power walking. Power walking is what you see the soccer moms doing on the city streets, clipping right along, arms swinging like they're about to fly out of their sockets. They kind of resemble harness racing horses that go as fast as they can without breaking into a lope.

My style is more "have-to walking." I walk because I have to start moving my equipment from one end of the field to the other. I have to leave a tractor here but the pickup is back there. I have to walk because I'm usually out there by myself and no one's around to give me a ride.

"Have-to walking" is purposeful. It's not super fast, but it ain't slow. I try to use every inch of my 6-foot-3 frame and stride to my advantage. I don't dawdle because I want to get to the pickup and get home for supper and a shower.

Some city walkers carry dumbbells or wear wrist weights to add to their workout. I've been known to pack a grease gun or lug a couple of balls of baler twine, and they'll add some strength training to your cardio session.

Walking hay stubble and hogwallows in work boots isn't quite as free of resistance as walking a paved path in athletic shoes. You try for the efficiency of a straight line route, but sometimes you have to walk around a slough or dodge a few hay bales.

Again and again

I get to make the trip several times per field because I have separate tractors hooked up for mowing, dump raking, wheel raking and baling. Making the walk three or four times in the heat of midday to ferry equipment back and forth can get tiresome.

I should wear a pedometer on my belt to check my mileage. I'm sure it adds up. I guess you could call it part of the wellness plan here on the ranch. I expect it'll pay off with a long, healthy life.

My favorite hike is the end-of-day walk. With the coolness of dusk descending on the meadow, a setting sun, a rising moon and the smell of fresh-mown hay, you hardly have time to feel sorry for yourself and the fact that you have to walk back to your pickup in our age of physical ease.

We do get to know a piece of land pretty well. We get to think about the generations who walked those fields before us and we get to wonder about who'll walk those fields when we're gone.

I kind of hope no one gives them a ride. I think they'll enjoy the walk.

Hauling for home
Going like hay on wheels

Every fall, I question the progress made in haying methods, especially the day we quit stacking our hay and began rolling it into big, round bales.

Used to be you put in your hours in the summer making a nice bunch of hay stacks that weighed six tons or more. Sure, it took a long time and a big hay crew to run all the needed equipment, but the autumn chore of moving it in was a cinch.

What we used to accomplish with 150 sparse stately stacks of hay we do today with 1,500 round bales littering every available acre on the meadow.

The wise, old ranchers in our neighborhood told us "when you bale your hay, the work's only half done" and warned us about the extra hay moving time with our fancy new round balers.

Getting 150 stacks home was pretty easy — back under one, drive it home, chain it off. Put in a good week and call it done.

The mere thought of moving 1,500 round bales is so intimidating, I'm almost afraid to start the job. Then I see the neighbors out moving bales, and the peer pressure sets in.

For awhile, I justify my procrastination with the old theory, "I hate to move the hay in too early and have it all piled in one place in case of a fire. We really should wait until there's a little snow on the ground."

Of course, the last big fire I remember was 30 years ago and it was in a field. I guess the hay would've been safer hauled into the yard.

One benefit of waiting until after the go-getters have moved their hay is having our narrow gravel road to myself. No pulling over to meet another hay mover or a semi if you let them finish up first.

Getting it done

On our place, we whittle away at our 1,500 bales 11 bales at a time. I know there're bigger hay trailers, but the hay's close and, like Dad used to tell me, poor people have poor ways.

It could be worse. At least I don't have a bigger herd and 5,000 bales to ferry in.

As it is, I load up 11 bales and head down the road. Job proficiency is mostly about driving and watching the minutes tick by.

The biggest decision is picking the 11 bales to put on the load as I walk from the mover to the loader tractor.

I can hardly drive by a field of hay without analyzing the spatial location of bales, sloughs, soft spots and prairie trails and partitioning it into 11 bale increments. I quickly calculate the short load of five left over at the end.

A lot of haulers get to handle their bales one at time twice, loading them onto a trailer and picking them off of a trailer. My little chain mover only makes me handle them once, but then I have the challenge of lining up my bale stacks when I back up and chain them off at home.

Sometimes, I can line them up nice and straight stack after stack. I know the cows will eat the hay just the same whether it comes from a straight row or a crooked row but there's some pride involved.

My wife lets me know when she drives by one of my crooked rows. I assure her that by next spring, we'll never know where the crooked rows were.

Today was a tough day. I couldn't get within 6 feet of even on a 12-foot stack.

Maybe by the time I'm done with the next 1,400, I'll have it straightened out. Either that or the snow drifts will have evened out the lines.

Simple tools
Character building chores   December 10, 2007

Sometimes it's the simple things that bring a little satisfaction to my day.

Granted, I like new fangled gadgets and gizmos. They're nice to have, but they usually come with as much frustration as satisfaction. Just think about cell phones and computers.

But you know what I really like? A pitchfork with a new handle. Or a freshly sharpened double bitted axe. Winter time on our ranch lets me use both tools a fair bit.

On our ranch, the water gets pretty hard in the winter. We call it ice. And getting the cattle watered in the winter usually means handling some ice.

Human Deicer

We don't handle as much ice as we used to. I remember Dad used to start every day chopping the ice out of a water tank in front of the house and pitching it over the fence into a pile. It was as regular a ritual as boiling the morning coffee.

The calves would drink, a squeaky pump jack with a little electric motor would fill the tank back up, and, the next morning, Dad would chop and pitch a brand new ice crop.

You could tell how tough the winter was by the height and size of Dad's ice pile pitched out of that tank come March or April.

These days, most of our tanks have frost-free water inlets and electric heating deicers. All you have to do is make sure they don't get unplugged. For winter entertainment, we stand by the power pole and see how fast the electric meter gets to spinning.

But I still have a tank or two that needs to have some ice chopped and pitched. And, for a few weeks in the fall, I cut a few holes in the ice of a lake for cattle to drink from.

There's something I like about simple, regular chores. I like to start the day with a mundane, mind-numbing task. Don't think too much, just grab the axe and the fork, swing and chop, fish and pitch.

Almost makes me want to revert back from the frost-free systems. Almost.

Antique tools

I don't suppose everyone keeps a supply of pitchforks and axes on their farm or ranch. They're a little outdated, but I'd hate to try and run a place without them.

Our barn still has a hay mow, so you need a pitchfork to get some hay poked down into the mangers for whatever animals might be in there. Our chain saws never seem to run quite right, so a sharp axe is still a must-have.

I don't feel the need to feed the whole cow herd with a hay rack and pitchfork instead of a tractor and loader, but every real rancher ought to know how to handle a pitchfork. There's some learned skill to move a pile of hay with three healthy fork fulls instead of 30 little bites.

It's high praise to say a fella "pitches his own hay and saddles his own horse." If you're the boss, it says something about your character to do those things yourself.

I strive to be that kind of rancher. And in the winter, I like to chop my own tanks and pitch my own ice.

PG Time
Winter predictions for spring   January 7, 2008

Not everyone knows what it means when a rancher says he's going to have his cows PG'd. Hint, the P and G doesn't stand for a Proctor and Gamble personal care product.

I've been accused of sharing more information than necessary at times in this column, so I'll just say, on our ranch, PGing means bovine rectal palpation to determine pregnancy. I'll leave it at that.

So when we want to find out which cows are in the "family way" for spring, we run them through the chute in the fall or winter to palpate the presence of junior developing in the womb.

There have been advances in pregnancy detection. Cows can get an ultrasound exam, kind of like human females do at the hospital. It's more expensive on a cow scale, but still a lot less than the human exam. It can pinpoint the pending birthdate and tell you if the calf requires a baby blue or pink ear tag.

A friend of mine ultrasounds cattle and has performed at least one human ultrasound with his machine. He claims to have bested the hospital technician in accurately predicting the baby's sex, and I'm fairly certain he had a lower copay for the procedure.

Another friend claims he's seen a fellow witch for bovine pregnancy, just like finding a well site with a water witching rod of some kind. I'm skeptical, but I'm sure if a herd usually runs 90 percent bred, the pregnancy witcher can call nine out of 10 of them right.

Reputation preg check

I may be able to forget the palpation and call the cows bred or open based solely on their demeanor and reputation.

I'm not too proud to admit that there're a few cows in my herd with some attitude problems, especially after they've calved and I'm attempting to do a little animal identification on the baby.

Every time I'd see a cow come into the chute who charged my horse or chased me up a tree, over a fence or into the box of the pickup during calving season, I'd kind of hope for her to be open. No way; every mean, rotten cow on the place was bred right on schedule.

On the contrary, when a nice, little mama cow who'd let you scratch her ears while you tagged her calf came through the chute, she'd test open just to make room in the herd for an ill-tempered replacement heifer raised by the mean cow.

I'm not sure why this happens. Maybe nice girls do finish last in the breeding pasture. Or the bulls prefer a cow with a bad attitude. I think that was a subject once on "Dr. Phil."

At any rate, pondering the random role of attitude, age, body condition or the year's weather on the cows that are bred or open gives the crew something to visit about while they're working the cows.

Funny how conducive the PG process is to visiting with one fella in a plastic glove covered with manure, one moving cows up the alley covered with a little less manure and a third guy with the relatively clean job of running the headgate. But to hear them visit, you'd think they were in a downtown coffee shop.

Sometimes the visiting is so good you kind of hate to run out of cows.

Some slow technology might improve the social aspect of the task. If they could make those home pregnancy tests a little more economical and the cows would pee on cue, the crew could pull up a table by the chute, deal a game of cards and have 10 minutes per cow to chat while everyone waits for those two pink lines to appear.

A full freezer
Ready for a recession   February 18, 2008

One thing about being a cattle rancher, you always have a little beef in the freezer. Sometimes you have a lot.

Of course, it's not always the very best beef produced on the ranch. A good, young, well-fed steer is worth a lot of money, and the one thing a ranch needs even worse than a full freezer is some cash for the banker.

Generally, we eat our mistakes, like an open heifer, a bum calf or a critter whose hair or hide color wasn't quite what the buyers were looking for. We make lots of mistakes on our place, so we always have plenty of meat.

Sometimes, we find an old cull cow or a bull with a limp to harvest at the local locker plant. But they're good hamburger, and it's fresh as can be.

The way things worked out this year, we doubled down on the ranch's beef inventory. We had a gimpy bull produce a boat load of burger, and we had a steer that was as close to normal as anything we've ever kept to feed the family.

A bacterial infection as a calf left this steer's ears hanging as limp as a beagle's. The steer got over the infection and was plumb healthy, but his ears never did perk up nice and straight again. I knew he'd be a prime candidate for some cattle buyer to give a drastic discount so he could cheapen up a load of higher-priced, erect-eared cattle. So we kept him, grazed him, fed him and now we give thanks and dine on him. He turned out pretty good. If it weren't for his limp ears, we'd probably be chewing on some stringy, old cull cow, so I'm thankful for his beagle-like look.

Cold storage

We're a two-freezer and four-refrigerator ranch between us and my parents. City folks would have a hard time understanding our abundance of cold storage. But out here, the grocery store is more than a few blocks away.

Depending on what you're looking for, the drive is from 16 miles to 60 miles for most of our provisions.

We have plenty of cows, but not a single milk cow. Some of our cows barely can support a calf, much less a family of four with two growing boys. So we usually walk out of the grocery store with six or eight cartons of milk to get us by until the next trip to town.

We're Norwegian, so we buy butter by the case when it's on sale and toss it in the freezer. We freeze a few gallons of ranch-picked Juneberries to remind us of summer, along with a few vegetables from the garden, but no zucchini.

The two big chest freezers usually can get us through the year with a little room for popsicles in the summer.

However, harvesting the two beefs within a month's time pushed our freezer space to the limit. So we did what most farmers and ranchers do with their overproduction — we started giving it away.

We can close the lids on the freezers again, but if we produce many more mistakes, we may need a third freezer.

From what I hear, we're all supposed to go buy something we don't need to keep the economy out of recession. Maybe the purchase of a third freezer will be our contribution to the economy, or at least to the local appliance store.

If the economy really does hit the skids, it may not be a bad idea to have a surplus of life's necessities. We could hunker down and make it through a short recession nicely eating fine steaks and roasts, or, if it's an extended downturn, a whole lot of hamburger.

Land man
Reading abstracts a lesson in history   April 14, 2008

Owning land is a fairly new concept in my neighborhood. Homesteaders started the practice here about a hundred years ago. Before that, land was mostly shared by the people indigenous to this part of the country.

With the advent of land ownership came some paperwork, and courthouses were built to hold all the documents. It's an amazing system where a little piece of paper tells everyone who owns what.

And even more amazing is that people honor what that paper says. No more gunfights to settle land disputes, just a couple sheets of paper, an attorney or two and the rule of law. Saved a lot of cemetery space when the system took hold.

I've been looking over the paperwork on our ranch. We call the stack of papers "abstracts." It's a fitting term.

One definition of abstract is a summary, and abstracts summarize all the actions recorded on a piece of property at the county Register of Deeds office. Another definition of abstract is, "not easily understood." After reading our abstracts, that definition fits, too.

There are lots of grants, conveys, acknowledges and assigns language about places described as romantically as the southwest quarter of the northwest quarter of section three of township number 154 north of range number 75 west of the fifth principal meridian.

Common recordings

After looking at pages and pages of abstracts from our ranch, there's a fairly common chain of events. The government got the ball rolling with a patent deed for some homesteader. As quick as they could, the new owner would mortgage the land to some financier to secure some dollars.

Mortgages turned pretty quickly. Pay one off in a year or two, mortgage it again, pay it off and then back in the hole again and again. If things went bad, there'd be some recordings by the sheriff about a foreclosure and a public auction at the front door of the courthouse, another new owner and, of course, new mortgages shortly after.

Sometimes the county ended up with the land for nonpayment of taxes. If you hung in there and still owned the land in the 1930s, the popular mortgage holder was the Land Bank Commissioner in St. Paul, Minn.

Looking at the course of hard times, death, estates and mortgage history, it's nothing short of miraculous for a family that homesteaded a piece of land to still own it 100 years later.

Looking at those abstracts makes me appreciate my ancestors even more.

Heavy reading

In North Dakota, there're a lot of people studying abstracts. There's a good-sized oil boom going on, and courthouses in the boom areas are full of newly minted "land men" from the oil companies poring over documents to figure out who owns the mineral acres on the prime land for oil exploration.

We're a good 100 miles away from the heart of the new oil activity, but you never know, a little oil might have accidentally seeped this way without knowing any better.

I haven't quite figured it all out yet — the entries are pretty abstract you know — but it looks like some of our mineral acres made it through the Depression, the Land Bank, past oil booms and slick mortgage holders.

I'm not banking on it, but an oil lease would make a nicer recording than another bank mortgage on our debt-worn abstracts.

With luck, a lease out here on the fringe of the boom might bring in enough cash to fill both gas tanks on my pickup.

High speed I.D.
Tagging calves and dodging cows   May 26, 2008

Individual animal identification might be a great thing for the cattle industry, but it's definitely a younger man's sport. At least it is in our cowherd.

As a matter of fact, if the government ever mandates animal identification at birth, they ought to exempt every rancher older than 50. Or maybe even over 40, if they're a little slow or overweight.

Seems like every other calf I ear-tagged this year had a mother who was less than pleased with my presence. I usually could tell when I walked toward the calf to tag and vaccinate it if I should be running the other way.

I can understand a little maternal concern when I've got a cow's calf between my knees to poke a tag in his ear and a needle in his neck. I don't even mind if the cow sticks her nose in my back pocket or nudges me a little to keep me from dawdling too long with her baby.

But when they let out a blood-curdling beller and run over the top of their calf to try and knock you down and grind you into the dirt, I get a little cautious.

I'm a long-distance runner by my build and experience, but I've developed a pretty fast 50-foot dash out in the calving pasture. Most cows won't go much more than 50 feet from their calf to try and snuff you out. If you don't see another column after this one, you'll know I met a cow with a 51-foot range.

I asked my 86-year-old dad what I should do about getting the calves tagged out of these mean mamas. He said I might want to try wearing tennis shoes. Sound advice, but I prefer the challenge of running in high-heeled cowboy boots.

I've noticed that other ranchers must have a few cows like mine, too. They're packing around little corrals on their tractors and four-wheelers. When they spot a new baby, they lower the pen down on the calf and work in peace while the mother's pawing the dirt and butting against the steel bars. I think they got the idea from watching those shows where divers are lowered into the ocean in cages to take pictures of the sharks.

Me? I tough it out without a cage. But I have roped and pulled calves under the loader bucket of the tractor, into the back of the pickup and onto the seat of the four-wheeler to try to discourage the mother's killer instincts while I work with her calf.

Occasionally, one of the ranch dogs will serve as a decoy to distract the cow. That works well until the cow tears after them and the dog runs and hides behind me.

I do know usually what I'm getting into as I check the cows. Each year, I score the cows with a bad attitude and put together a "look out list" from the previous year's high-scoring hell cows. I check the list as I make out the ear tags to get my adrenaline pumping and my fast twitch sprinting muscles cocked and ready.

I suppose I should just sell the cows once they've made the list, but they always breed well, raise big calves, stay fat and are as pretty as a picture from their udder to their eyes.

If the drought persists and the pastures fail, this may be the year to cull some of the troublemakers.

I'm afraid to think what the freight will cost me if I load up the mean cows and take them to a sale barn.

It'll be darn high because these aren't the kind of cows you dare sell too close to home.

Haying etiquette
Field location boosts quality   July 21, 2008

It's a good thing we don't live on too good a road. Our haying is getting a later-than-usual start this year, and if the whole county was driving a highway by my unmown fields, I'd be overwhelmed with guilt.

As it is, the road by our place isn't too well graveled or traveled, so the only witnesses to my unharvested hay land are the neighbors, and most of them haven't been in the hay field very long themselves.

There are some benefits to a boondock ranch location. The scrutiny of running a ranch on a major highway would stress me out.

Fences would have to not only be tight, but straight and pretty, too. You'd have to keep your barn painted, your cows fat and your mailbox decorated for each appropriate season.

Crops would have to be seeded, sprayed and harvested on time, or better yet, early, like being the first one done.

Hay never should get rained on, and the bales should look as good as the ones in the glossy brochures where they sold the baler.

Thanks to living far from the beaten path in our area, we can pretty much let things slide as much as we dare.

But even though our main thoroughfare is just a remote township road, I still make hay a little differently near it than I do when I'm a mile or two further inland.

Tied up tidy

I do my best to make the bales along the road tall and firm, with a good square shoulder. If the twine tie malfunctions and I kick out a fluffy bale with little or no twine on it, I unroll it, bale it up and try again to get the twine to take.

I use a little extra twine on my road bales, too. Nothing makes a poor bale look better than a lot of twine. If you use enough. it's kind of like net wrap without the expensive attachment, just a lot of expensive string.

I guess Dad's the one who taught me my road-haying skills. He'd make his stacks a little taller and straighter where people might see them. We'd rake up every stick of hay that was scattered, and we'd park our machinery perpendicular to the road at night fall like a well-managed parking lot.

Haying along the road requires good machinery operation. Straight windrows, no skips when you're cutting and clean up your corners. It means steering a little straighter and looking back a little more often, all the time being ready to take one hand off the wheel to wave if someone drives by.

Waving is a requirement if you hay next to the road. No one likes an arrogant hayer, so if you see a cloud of dust coming down the road, you get ready to wave.

As I work further in on the field, I'll still wave just in case the traveler in the car is looking my way. Sometimes I can't hardly see the vehicle or even tell if it's a person or a dog doing the driving, but still I wave.

This year, there's plenty of time to wave. The drought really has knocked the hay back, so I only need to trip my rake every 100 feet of so. The hay's so sparse and thin, most observers wouldn't know if I left a skip or a streak while I was mowing, or if I even cleaned up the corners when I finished.

It's been a forgiving year for haying, but a terrible year for hay. The bales I've made look good, but there aren't near enough of them.

If I end up buying some hay this year, I'll be sure to look for bales close to a road. They are tied a little better, you know.

Sink or swim
Teaching the horse to dog paddle   September 15, 2008

There's a reason — several reasons actually — I don't have much love for bulls. There's probably a reason or two why my horse doesn't much care for them either.

Bulls that'll turn away, put one foot in front of the other and head away from you are pretty lovable. Bulls that'll turn toward you, paw the dirt, put their head down and charge are plumb hateful.

It's the hateful bulls that my horse doesn't want much to do with. He's been hit, pushed and bruised enough to now run backward, sideways, any which way he can, to get away from them when they turn and charge.

I had one of those hateful bulls to bring home for a trip to the sale barn this week. Surly and ornery, he didn't even make an attempt to cooperate. After charging me and the horse several times, I thought I saw a glimmer of hope as he took a few steps away from us next to a water hole.

Wet and wild

It was a fairly new water hole in one of our pastures. Our water doesn't run down hills, it comes up from shallow water veins, so we have "dugouts" or "water holes," not "stock dams" like my friends in creek country.

When we dig out these water holes with a back hoe, they get pretty deep pretty suddenly as you go in from the shoreline. When I started moving that bull away from the water hole, he turned and charged my pony. My trusty steed figured the best place to go was in the drink. He forgot that he'd never learned how to swim.

Down, down he went. The water was up to my armpits and I was sitting straight up in the saddle. When the horse hit bottom, he decided to start paddling. His head came up out of the water like the Loch Ness monster as he lunged toward shore.

I lost one stirrup but stayed in the saddle because the thought of being in the water dodging his hooves didn't appeal to my sense of safety. Years ago, a neighbor boy had gotten killed that way when he swam his horse into a water hole. Every parent has warned every kid in the neighborhood about the dangers of horses and water holes since then.

We came out the other side of the dugout looking like a couple of drowned rats. I looked back toward the water hole kind of impressed that it was deep enough to submerge a horse and rider as dry as it's been this year.

I was thankful that it wasn't cold and windy for my wet horse and my wet clothes.

There wasn't a squeak or creak left in my saddle, but it did kind of go "squish, squish" as we rode back toward our friendly sire.

It's a wrap

We finished the job we started by roping the hateful bull and tying him to a tree until we could return with a pickup and horse trailer.

I suppose the bull could have choked and killed himself before we returned, but neither the horse nor I much cared at that point. I've tied a few bulls to trees in the past, and if you leave them there long enough, they're practically halter broke by the time you load them in the trailer.

I came away from the experience with a renewed preference for fresh pumped water and stock tanks. They're not only better for the health and growth of the cattle, they're harder to drown in if your horse decides to jump in while he's retreating from a bull.

And maybe replacing the herd of hateful bulls with a comprehensive program of artificial insemination isn't such a bad idea either.

In Crisis
The economy gets an overdraft   October 13, 2008

The economy seems to be on everyone's mind. Especially if you're knocking on 60 years old and planning on cashing in your retirement savings. There's probably about 30 to 40 percent less in that account than there was one short year ago.

I've got a little money in that same kind of account, but I'm a long ways from retirement. Hopefully things will straighten out by 2030. I can hardly imagine the sick feeling you'd get if you were making withdrawals for retirement and learned that what was there yesterday is gone today.

It'd make you wish you'd put your money into something dependable like a cream can or something a little less risky like a racehorse. Today's market seems to make "poor" the new "standard" in the Standard & Poor's 500 Index.

For the most part, though, my worries are related more to the livestock market and less to the stock market. Unfortunately, the market on hooves is following the market on corporate paper down into the basement.

But it'll have to stop somewhere soon because people still need to eat; even down-and-out stockbrokers can't live on bourbon alone. I just hope they can pay enough for their steaks, roasts and hamburgers to make it worth my while to round up the cows and haul the calves to town.

On the up side, the feed grains and fuel prices seem to be going down with the price of cattle, so it'll cost a little less to add some pounds to the cattle and send them down the road for their eventual loss.

Silver linings

It ain't easy finding a silver lining in today's clouds, but it does remind me of a story my dad told when our local bank closed down in 1976 for a sudden and extensive

102

audit. It put the community in quite a bind when they woke up one morning and found the doors locked on their deposits.

One of Dad's friends was really in a blue mood worrying about his savings account and certificates of deposit he had at the locked-up bank.

Dad lent a sympathetic ear but wasn't really able to join in the lament. You see, the very week the bank closed, Dad got an overdraft/ That's what I call good timing.

No need to worry about federal deposit insurance when all you have is a big loan and an overdrawn checking account. Of course, they could have called in the loan and put the ranch in a major bind, but they didn't, and eventually, a new bank was chartered to honor the deposits of the savers like our friend and provide credit to the borrowers like Dad.

Today's mess is more widespread than one local, small-town bank, and the national financial community obviously encouraged too many overdrafts and not enough savings accounts, too big a home mortgages backed by too little an ability to pay.

Where it all goes from here nobody seems to know. Absolutely nobody.

With winter on its way, we'll just have to treat the economy a little like a North Dakota blizzard — hunker down and wait it out. And, sure enough, the sun will shine again, but it might take awhile.

Improbable situation
Stretching the laws of physics   December 8, 2008

I never was tempted to go to school to be an engineer, but I remember kind of liking the sampling of physics I was exposed to in high school. There were laws that could not be denied. A way things were supposed to work. Somehow, our ranch seems to exist in a third dimension where the usual laws always work against you, but never for you.

Last week, we got the kids borrowed out to others so my wife and I could do a little cattle work. We brought in the calves to boost their vaccinations and apply a little pour-on dewormer. We were just about done when it was time for my wife to go pick up the kids from preschool and day care.

I told her I could finish the last few by myself. She barely was to the end of the driveway when I was in full crisis mode with one of the very next calves to hit the chute.

My chute has a little door on each side to give you access to the neck of the cattle for vaccinations and injections. Open the door, give the shot, shut the door. Sometimes you don't get the little door shut.

I had two calves come in the chute. One stuck his head in the headgate, the other stuck his head through that little neck door that I didn't shut. I quickly vaccinated the one in the headgate so I could get him out and do something with the knucklehead that stuck his head through that little door.

Hairy Houdini, almost

The one calf went out the chute, the other calf, a 550-pound bovine contortionist escape artist, somehow pushed his 15-inch-wide shoulders and rib cage through that 8- or 10-inch door until he hung up on his 15-inch wide hips. In the world of physical laws, old Sir Isaac Newton would apply his three laws of motion and explain this unsatisfactory situation with terms like acceleration, force and mass.

The calf started bellering and jumping up and down. I started bellering and jumping up and down. Eventually, all the bellering and jumping wore us both out and we took a little breather.

The calf was stuck, stuck, stuck. His hips weren't coming out forward and he wasn't going to pop his rib cage and shoulders backward. I couldn't get him to repeat the acceleration and force he'd applied to his mass a little earlier.

Chute depreciation

I needed a trump card to overcome the physics. I don't know what Sir Isaac would've done, but I went and got the acetylene cutting torch. I gave it some critical thought. The price of calves was going down. The price of steel squeeze chutes was going up. I think I paid $2,500 for the chute years ago, the calf might fetch a little better than $500.

Eventually, compassion overruled economics and I decided the torch was the only chance to save the calf before he gave up. I made three strategic cuts without barbecuing the critter I was saving. I took the steel I had dismantled and put it in the spare parts pile to be reattached another day.

When the torch made its last cut, the calf sprung out of there like a rocket. If only he'd have had that kind of reverse acceleration to remedy our predicament before I had to turn part of my chute into scrap iron.

Maybe next time, the laws of motion and physics will work in my favor. Or, maybe I'll just remember to shut that little door.

The hay maze
Looking for the cow's reward   February 16, 2009

Tedious jobs don't get any easier if you wait to do them after 7 feet of snow has fallen. Actually, I can't think of any jobs that are easier after 7 feet of snowfall. Maybe snow sledding gets easier, but that's more of a recreation than a job.

Misery loves company, so it warms my heart every time I tell someone about the couple hundred bales I have left out in the field and they confess to me they have as much or more left out as I do. Maybe they're just saying that to make me feel better. If that's the case, it's working.

The snow doesn't seem to be melting much, although it has settled some and blown around enough to leave just a couple feet of hard, crusted snow on the level where my hay bales are inconveniently stored out on the field.

Last weekend, I worked four hours with a front-wheel-assist tractor to dig out eight bales. Drive and push until you start spinning, make a pile of snow, take another angle, spin down and pile. Find a bale with 4 or 5 feet of snow drifted around it and pry it from its snowy vault.

It's not exactly an efficient operation to push snow for a half-hour or an hour to dig out a single bale and get it home. The pounds-of-hay-per-gallon-of-diesel ratio isn't looking very good at all this year.

Of course, the cows don't care how much diesel it took to get dinner delivered, just that it gets delivered.

Snow circles

I've heard of the crop circle phenomena where a farm field ends up with some unexplained geometric design in it where the grain is knocked down or bent over. Usually, aliens and UFO's get the blame.

If someone flew over our hay meadow after I'd been digging out snowbound bales, they'd surely figure a winter hardy band of martians had made some crop circles in our snow. The designs may not be completely geometric, but some aliens are better drawers than others.

Or, I think it might kind of look like a giant play area for a game we used to play when we were kids called the fox and the goose. You'd trudge a maze of trails through the snow and the "fox" would chase the "goose." You just had to make sure you never strayed from the trails.

Instead of fox and goose, now I play tractor and bale, and when there's 2 feet of hard snow on the level you definitely have to stay on the trail. Once I catch a bale, I'm bound to taking the same circuitous route back out to the road that I made coming in, zigging and zagging from bale to bale.

If the snow digging and pushing didn't burn enough diesel, a trip to the road a hundred yards away might take a mile of meandering back through the maze. It's worse yet if you take a wrong turn in the maze and hit a dead end.

Now I know how the lab mice feel in the experiments on their memory. But I wander through the snowy maze looking for hay not cheese. And the reward isn't for me but for my cows.

Maybe I'll just set up a little sensory perceptive experiment and turn the cows loose out on my maze in the snow. I'm willing to bet a hungry black cow can find a hay bale quicker than a little white rat can find his cheese.

Ravages of ranch time
No more replacement postponement   June 22, 2009

Nothing lasts forever, but we have a few things on the ranch that are doing their best to buck the rule.

We have tractors still sputtering beyond their expected useful life, pickups still rolling but so far gone there's no chance of qualifying as a trade-in vehicle, a couple cows that might remember the first Bush administration and a barn with centenarian timbers still holding it somewhat erect.

All good things must come to an end. And this last winter seemed to be the tipping point for a good portion of the fence on the ranch that's supposed to keep the cows on our place, off the road, out of the neighbor's herd and away from our bulls until breeding season.

I don't know why the wires finally broke. Some of them were only 50 or 60 years old. They had a good layer of protective rust and lots of years of experience at holding cows.

Ready, release, fix

This summer seemed like a good time to replace a little barbed wire on the ranch. Now that the $40 barbed wire is selling for $70 a roll, it must be time to start buying it.

I make the decision to replace by a quick tally of the number of breaks in the wire per 100 feet of fence. The snowdrifts we had last winter did a good job of identifying the weak spots.

I knew some of the fence was on its last legs. Seemed like there was a splice between every post from the repairs of years past.

Since our ranch went to managed grazing and pasture rotation, I've gotten on a fix-as-I-go fencing routine. Instead of fixing lots of fence for big pastures across the whole place, I fix a little fence on small pastures as I need them. I'd like to fix the fence on a paddock and then turn in the cows, but this year, we seem to turn in the cows first and fix the fence later.

So far, there's been enough grass to entertain the cows for a day or two while I try to catch up on mending the fence that surrounds them.

History on a roll

The wire I've been replacing is old, and I have a pretty good idea about how old it is. Dad called this wire "Army surplus wire."

He said they put the fence in after he got back from World War II, or, as sitcom character Archie Bunker would call it, "The Big One."

Whether the wire was surplus from World War II or World War I, I don't know. I don't know if it was ever any good, but it's sure not much good now, 60=plus years later. Depending on the integrity of the military contractor, it may not have been top quality when it was made.

It had four pretzel-knotted points on it, and I wonder if it ever was galvanized. You couldn't bend it more than 17 degrees or it'd break in two, which made splicing a real trick.

But now it's rolled up and filed in the ranch's historical pile of old wire. Maybe I'll give a roll to each of the kids for high school graduation to remind them of their roots. The pile is bigger than just our three kids though. We may need to mass produce some rusty-wire western art to peddle it all.

For now, I just need to mass produce the rolls of old wire, unroll the new and tighten, splice and prop up the rest.

By the time I get done mending this year's broken fences, I'll be just like the old-timers lamenting for a return to the days of the open range.

106

Rodeo ranch style
Friendly little competition

We have a nice little grocery store in my hometown. The kind of place where you can find the basics, order 500 pounds of lutefisk for the church supper and get recruited to be on a ranch rodeo team all in one stop.

That's what happened to me when I dropped by my friendly, neighborhood Towner Foods store. My experience with ranch rodeo has been as a partially distracted spectator at two of them. I've spent a lifetime working on the ranch part of the equation, but the rodeo part … not so much.

Despite that, I still was game to give the team a go. It's hard to say no to your local grocer, especially after he's cut you a good deal on 500 pounds of Norwegian fish.

Ranch rodeo is one of the ways we entertain ourselves in small communities without professional sports teams, Broadway musicals or big name concerts. It's got kind of a Roman gladiator twist to it as neighbors turn out to see if any of their friends get run over by a Longhorn cow or fall off their horse.

No one on our team was a ranch rodeo regular. We weren't afraid to learn on the fly though.

The trailer relay was easy enough to figure out. Jump out of a pickup, unload four horses, run a little relay race as fast as the ponies will go, load up the mounts and jump back in the pickup. Fairly simple, unless you have a horse that's not used to people, or excitement, or being loaded in a trailer under the duress of a stopwatch.

Then there's a few roping events where you don't have the advantage of an even start like you do in normal team roping with the steer in a chute and the roper hovering next to him in the roping box.

In the trailer loading, I got our steer roped pretty quick like, dallied and pulled him over to a trailer sitting in the arena. That's when my two big, burly teammates dismounted and ran at him to load him in the trailer. That 300-pound Longhorn looked at the 500 pounds of combined cowboy headed toward him and knew he was beat. He jumped in like a trained circus animal.

In the steer mugging, we roped our steer, got him on his side and tied up three legs only to watch him wiggle loose in less than the six seconds he needed to stay tied.

The wild cow milking was the event where the spectators leaned ahead in their seats in anticipation to see if any of their neighbors would get trampled, gored or kicked in pursuit of a few drops of unpasteurized, non-homogenized, longhorned whole leche.

Our cow was pretty easy to handle once we got a rope on her and a couple guys on her tail. The challenge was in her October lactation. She was no Holstein. No relative of the Brown Swiss. She was a straight-up Longhorn who probably only milked decent for the first month or so after her calf was born. After that, she stuck with her calf more for companionship than nutrition.

Somehow our designated milker found a few squirts from one-quarter of her udder and I sprinted to the judge as best I could in chaps and cowboy boots.

When we packed up at the end of the day, we weren't weighed down with any prize money or trophies, but it was sure fun. It wasn't exactly how we do things on the ranch. It was just different enough to seem like play, not work, and that's why I'd go do it again sometime.

Tough fencing
Stringing wire and planting posts   February 15, 2010

Fencing is one of those jobs best done when the temperatures are tolerable and the ground isn't frozen. But sometimes we don't have a choice.

I had a small fencing project to keep two groups of cows separate that I feed in the winter. I roll some hay out for the cows out on the range. I figure it's easier for them to scatter their own manure out there in the winter, than for me scoop it out of a feedlot, haul it out and scatter it for them next summer.

My older cows get fed pretty good, but my heifers and youngest cows get fed a little better including some distiller's grain from an area ethanol plant. The generational segregation of the haves and the have-nots was accomplished with three strands of loose barbed wire that was beginning to drift under the snow.

Pretty soon, I was feeding the young cows their distiller's, and then I'd stop and look around and realize there were more and more mature cows in my pampered herd. I guess an old cow doesn't get old without being smart enough to figure out where the good groceries are.

Actually, it isn't much of a trick to walk across a drifted-under, barbed-wire fence, but I was holding on to the hope that they wouldn't figure that out.

So, with tractor, snowmobile and snowboots that sunk the full length of my 38-inch inseam at times, I commenced to stringing an electric wire and attaching insulators to make my point on the separation of cows who needed a little extra protein and those who didn't.

Harder jobs out there

After watching the news of events a couple hundred miles south of our ranch this winter, my little one-day winter fencing job was pretty darn easy.

Freezing rain and sleet, followed by high winds, brought down high-line electric poles like they were toothpicks in parts of North and South Dakota. Several thousand homes, farms and ranches were without power for a few days to more than two weeks.

One estimate I heard said that 3,200 poles had snapped. That's a lot of "fencing" for lineworkers to do in the middle of winter ... when the ground's frozen ... and you have to bulldoze away several feet of snow to get your equipment in to do your work ... and the temperature's below zero.

I'm plenty leery of electricity. It's one of those special things in life that, in modest doses, can toast your bread, or, in abundance, it can kill you.

I don't even like ticklish jolt from an electric fencer or the static from dragging my leather-soled boots across the carpet. I can't imagine putting on the big leather mitts and pulling electric transmission lines (did we really get them shut off?) out of the snow like a lineman does.

So, here's to the best winter fencers in the business, the lineworkers who dig in and tamp tight the 40-foot fence posts and stretch up the heavy wire with a potential bite worse than a red point barb.

We all might cuss a little when we see our electric meter turning and start adding up the dollars in our head of what those revolutions cost. But we have a lot more to cuss about when that meter quits turning altogether, the house goes dark and cold and the cattle start to go thirsty.

Thanks to all the people who get those meters spinning again.

Cow pie patrol
The less glamorous side of modern ranching   August 16, 2010

What goes up, must come down. That's gravity. What goes in, must come out. That's the rule of mazes, freeway tunnels, and, in bovine and all other species I know of, digestion.

I've been combining my knowledge on the two rules of digestion and gravity as I venture into a new area of modern ranch management and cattle nutrition.

Here's the deal. I walk nonchalantly into a herd of my grazing cows and look for five or 10 fresh cow pies, really fresh cow pies. I reach down for a little piece of each pie, so to speak, about a spoonful, and put it in a resealable plastic bag for a little laboratory analysis.

According to the folks at the lab, the sample would be even better and fresher if I could catch a spoonful in midair, or next best, from the pie that just hit the ground that very second. I want to send the best sample I can, so this becomes a waiting game for me and my cows.

I stand there amidst the herd with sharpened senses, my eyes furtively searching for a rising tail or a look of alternating bovine concentration and relief, my ears tuned keenly to listen for the sound of a "plop, plop, plop." It's like a stakeout in law enforcement; it's tedious.

The reward is a nice bag full of … used grass to send to the college lab down in Texas.

Analyze this

I always thought Texans were a little full of … used grass, and now I know why. It's because ranchers from all over the country and continent bag it up and send it to them. It has to be part of the reason for their reputation.

Actually, they are smart enough to have created some high-tech economic development by analyzing the seemingly low-tech cow pie.

Brace yourself for some technical language. The Texans in the lab use near-infrared reflectance spectroscopy to judge the fecal samples for the protein and energy in the grazing cow's diet and plug the data into the nutritional balance analyzer to help ranchers make nutritional decisions for the cowherd. But it all starts with 10 spoonfuls of fresh cow pie.

You see, the cows are out there grazing plants ad libitum, which, I think, is how the old Latins used to say their cows got to eat whatever they wanted and as much as they wanted. Clipping and analyzing a square of grass in a pasture and figuring that's what the cow would eat really would miss the mark. It'd be like heading to the family dining buffet and figuring a kid would eat a little bit of everything when it's really just noodles and ice cream.

So the cows pick what they want to eat, and today's astute cowboy just follows them around with a Ziploc bag.

Forget what you've heard or seen in the movies about the cowboy up on the hill sitting tall on his horse, a fresh breeze blowing over him as he watches his herd graze off in the distance. Today's cowboy who wants to fine tune things for a little finely tuned profit needs to ride down that hill, listen for the tell-tale plop, get off his horse and get down on the ground.

The things we do in the name of science.

At least we can get back up on our horse once the bag is full and resume our post back up on the hill.

King of hay
My first second cutting   August 27, 2010

When I was in college, an animal nutrition professor always called alfalfa "the king of hay." Whatever you measured — crude protein, relative feed value, taste, smell, bovine yumminess — alfalfa had it going on. Of course it had to be put up right to get all that.

Our ranch never had much for alfalfa acres. Most all our hay ground was native meadows. Low, sub-irrigated marshes and bogs and hogwallows dotted with sloughs full of ducks and muskrats to watch us get stuck while we hayed.

If alfalfa is the king of hay, then our bales of meadow and slough grass are kind of the "peasant serfs of hay." No royal nutritional qualities, but common, plentiful and able to get you through the winter without a lot of fanfare.

Alfalfa valley

When our area was homesteaded, one of the posters from the railroad's boosters who wanted more settlers, train business and land sales called this country "alfalfa valley." Lush, prosperous and aromatic — made you want to move right out here.

Growing alfalfa wasn't quite as easy as they made it out to be. The best time to plant alfalfa in our sand is right before a nice rain. That's hard to predict. If you get some rain and get it growing, the best time to cut the alfalfa is right before a warm, dry spell. Almost as tough to find as the rain was when you were planting it.

Dad planted a dab or two of alfalfa on some sandy ridges of our hay meadow years ago. One stand was at least 50 years old when I reseeded it last year. As ranchers, we're a little afraid of our farming ability, so we're not in that crowd of hay raisers who replant their alfalfa stands every five to seven years.

Even reseeding that 50-year-old stand was questionable because I still could see a few alfalfa plants out there. Hate to give up on a growing legume in our country even if it is 50 feet to the next one.

I got lucky on my alfalfa seeding venture last year. It rained last year, and it rained a bunch this year.

New experience

I turned 40 years old this year, been haying since I was 9, and this year was the first time I ever took a second cutting of alfalfa. Maybe this wasn't "alfalfa valley" after all.

It's kind of like the old story about the eastern farmer who was bragging about getting three cuttings of alfalfa every year and asked his western friend if he got three cuttings. "Sure, I get three cuttings," the arid westerner said, "but it takes five years to get those three."

But this year it all came together. Just barely blooming, I laid down that second cutting with visions of protein and energy.

Day after day went by. Too green, too green. I raked it in the morning to try and keep the leaves intact. Stems still were too green. Then suddenly — if six days can be suddenly — it was too dry. The alfalfa guys told me this was when you tuned up the headlights on your tractor and started baling at night when the dew comes out.

I thought maybe I could use the old grazing strategy of "take half, leave half." The half I'd take would be the sticks and stems, and the half I'd leave would be those tender leaves to help enrich the soil. That way I could sleep at night like regular folks.

If I did that, they told me, I could say goodbye to the king of hay. I never was much for high-maintenance royalty.

I'll be glad to get back in the bogs with my peasant hay again.

Getting late
Hay and harvest drags on
September 27, 2010

I had to use ether to start my rake tractor the other day. It made me wonder what happened to the old-fashioned idea of making hay when it's 100 degrees and sunny.

The misery of trying to hay and harvest in a balmy 45 degrees with 75 percent humidity has a lot of company this fall, and, although misery loves company, I'd rather be done with it all.

We froze hard last week — the ice-in-the-water-tank at daybreak kind of hard. Made me think I might need to start blending in some No. 1 diesel or fuel conditioner in my mowing tractors as I go forward. A fella should be able to finish haying on No. 2 fuel, you'd think.

The night we froze, I was driving to a pasture at midnight to wrap insulation around the brass pump cylinder on a windmill we use to water some cattle. I knew we were heading for a frost when I almost could do that job by the light of the stars.

I suppose that's a northern thing when you look up at a night sky so clear you can see every star and, rather than gaze at its beauty, you run around looking for pumps that aren't drained, hoses that might burst and pressure washers that need to come inside where it's warm.

Clouds mean insulation for the earth at night, and without them, the mercury doesn't have much to stop its freefall.

Our meadow hay that's been too wet to put up all summer is now too wet and frozen. The quality is far from premium now, but we're going to keep the mowers attached, wait for a dry spell and get what we can until the grass boards on the end of the cutter bar start ridging up snow.

Frozen meadow hay doesn't have the protein or energy that it did before it froze, but Dad had a theory on the quality of frozen hay. If someone asked him if frozen hay was any good, he'd say, "well, it depends."

If everything went good and you got all your hay up before the first hard frost then, most certainly, frozen hay wasn't worth a hoot. Hardly worth putting it in front of the cows.

But, he'd say, if things got late and you had to put up some of your hay after it froze and that's all you had to feed, well then that frozen hay wasn't so bad after all. It's all a matter of perspective.

Or, as another rancher told me, the frozen hay should be just as good as the grass we've all got our cows grazing on out in the pasture after the frost. You don't see anyone hustling the cowherds home after the frost to start feeding them alfalfa because that darn frozen grass isn't any good.

I don't know if I have any feel good theories for the farmers who still have small grains standing out in the field though.

If it's any consolation, they won't be the only ones fighting Father Time and Mother Nature to get everything done before the snow flies.

And if you hear the hum of a generator out in the hayfields, it's just guys like me plugging in the block heaters on our haying tractors to save on the starting fluid.

Liquid form
With the aid of alternating current   February 14, 2011

It always gets warmer after a cold spell. Of course, that cold spell could last five or six months in some parts of the world. This winter, in North Dakota, the cold shifts from tolerable to intolerable about once a week.

Even when it's intolerable, like 25 degrees below Fahrenheit, we still tolerate it. We don't have much choice in the matter. But thanks to all our modern conveniences, we can tolerate it pretty darn well.

Water is one of those things that is a lot easier to manage when it's above, say, 32 degrees. Cattle like to have a little something to wash down their hay in the winter, and, in my country, water is the cheapest input we've got for their daily diet.

It's not so easy to keep it in liquid form in the winter, but we don't have to dig deep to get it and it'll flow as fast as you can pump it. But if it sits still in a water tank for awhile when it's 25 below, there're some issues.

That's when we start to appreciate our rural electric cooperatives. And the co-op board members who have to balance the books appreciate us when we plug in every possible 1,500-watt warming device we can find in the farm supply store to keep our water watery.

We hardly have to swing an axe anymore to break ice. Just stand by the electric pole, lean on our retired axe handle and watch the meter spin around and around.

I've got sinking heaters that sit on the bottom of the tank and floating heaters that swirl around like a toy tugboat on top of the water. I've got a 20-gallon tub for the barn with its own internal heater and a plug-in cord. I refuse, however, to buy a heated dog dish. If the lion can lay down with the lamb, the dogs can drink water with the cows.

I also have an open-loop geothermal heating system on a pasture tank where my cows water in the winter. Open-loop geothermal means I just let the water run all winter, overflow and sink back into the ground. But it does the trick, and the cost of running the pump to constantly circulate the 50-degree water is about the same as plugging in a couple thousand watts of electric heat.

I like the idea of using free heat from the ground, but sometimes, it's hard to get enough of that heat to keep the pipes from freezing on my tanks where the water line comes up through a section of culvert that serves as a heat riser.

That's when I get another cord and send a good old 100-watt light bulb down the culvert. Throws off a fair bit of heat and works wonders. There's always a little risk of fire, but the way I see it, if a good fire gets going, it melts the water line and the hole in the water line acts like a cheap emergency fire sprinkler. I thought about going with a compact fluorescent bulb that doesn't get as hot, but then you're back to frozen water pipes.

So far, so good this winter. Whenever we've froze up, we were able to fix it in short order with 5 gallons of warm water and a little propane torch.

Combined with a lot of electricity, we should be able to make it to May.

Planting posts
Tough digging, easy pounding   July 4, 2011

The only job where a common fell gets to start at the top is digging post holes, I've heard. I've had the fortune, good or bad, of starting at the top of a lot of those jobs.

I always took three things with me — my Ph.D. (post hole digger), a spade and a tamping stick. Two tools for digging and one for packing the dirt back in a space half the size it came out of because I displaced it with a post.

Digging post holes, especially the big, deep holes for fence corners, corral gates and railroad ties, is a contemplative business. You have to pause once in a while to catch your breath, gauge your depth and straightness and ponder why you chose such an occupation for your life.

When the job is done, though, it's one of those things where you can stand back, take a look and see that you've made a difference. Measurable results. Quantifiable progress. The little things that bring satisfaction to physical jobs.

Sand sans rocks

It's hard to complain much about digging postholes when you live in sand country. No rocks and the digging is easy. Except when the sand gets so dry your digger can't hang onto it long enough to get it out of the hole. It takes awhile to finish a hole when you only get a few tablespoons of dry sand to the top each time you send your digger down.

Dry isn't an issue for us now. Having a 4-foot post hole fill halfway up with water is though.

When we're not on the high sands of the ranch, we're digging in the low ground and meadows. There, you can't get the blue clay and gumbo to come off your digger without scraping it off with your foot. And as hard as you might tamp it, if you don't bring in some outside sand or gravel, those posts in the bog are going to float and wiggle.

Still we've always had it better than the country where Dad spent some of his youth in the Missouri River breaks near Culbertson, Mont. He always said you could get a job fencing in that hard pan and you could choose your pay — 10 cents a hole or a dollar a day, and anyone who knew the country would take the buck a day.

Hydraulic help

Now, technology has come to the post digger's rescue. I had a good number of posts to plant for a couple of projects this summer, so I borrowed my neighbor's hydraulic pounder. These machines have been around awhile, but we're just catching on here in the easy digging country.

With this outfit you can take a 6- to 7-inch post and drive it in the ground 4 feet just by working a hydraulic lever back and forth about a dozen times. A 20-minute job done in a couple of minutes and you move on to the next one.

Our ground is so soft this year with the rains and moisture, you can even drive blunt railroad ties into the ground. No need to sharpen posts here.

I only see one drawback with this hydraulic post pounder, and that's the way it inflates the cost of a project. No, my neighbor didn't charge me to borrow it and it only took a couple gallons of gas to run the motor.

But it greatly inflated the post cost for the project because it was entirely too easy to make the corral longer and put the posts closer together.

You can bet if I had to dig all the posts by hand, there'd have been a lot fewer posts planted. But if a stronger fence is the price of progress, I guess it could be worse.

At a loss
Valuable, vulnerable data   December 5, 2011

Anything smaller than a sledgehammer or lighter than a house jack probably has been lost at least once on this place. I even might have lost the sledgehammer once, but the grass was tall that year.

So it makes you wonder why I'd trust myself with something as small as a calving book that has as much important and irreplaceable information written down in it. Or makes you question why anyone would let me walk out of a store with a tiny, expensive, handheld communications device.

I guess the reason the cell phone store lets me leave with one of their phones is because whether the phone is lost or found, the bill still comes once a month for the life of the contract. And the value of the phone is all on my shoulders unless I take out their insurance for $10 a month.

I don't know anyone offering insurance on calving books. I suppose because it's hard to nail down a tangible value on the little red book that rides in my pocket from pasture to hayfield and from horseback to pickup seat. I get the book for free from either a vet clinic or a feed dealer, but by the end of the year, the numbers and words I scratched down inside of it are infinitely more valuable.

It'd be interesting to know the loss ratio, the difference between premiums paid in and claims paid out, on cell phone insurance. At its core, insurance is simple business — everybody pays, some collect and some don't, but everyone gets a little peace of mind.

I had insurance once on my phone. It escaped from my coveralls when I was out feeding cattle never to be seen again. The insurance worked and I got a new phone. Actually, it wasn't a new phone, but rather a replacement phone that was exactly like the antique one I lost that was out receiving calls underneath the hoof of some cow.

So, statistically, I figured I'd carried enough insurance and didn't renew the plan. What were the odds I'd need it again?

Honestly, I haven't lost another phone, at least not for more than a few terror-stricken days, but things do happen that make me wonder if I should renew the protection plan.

Last week, after weaning calves, I was cleaning out the water tanks and fixing the floats and valves, doing a lot of bending over and darn near standing on my head from time to time. And, bending over like that, you'd wonder why you would put important stuff in open-topped pockets without so much as a flap or a snap or even a safety pin to keep things secure.

I skirted tragedy when my cell phone plopped out of my pocket a couple times, but it was retrieved and maintained working order. But a few hours into the day, I couldn't find my calving book. After trying to blame my wife for misplacing it in the house, I realized it was in the open-topped pocket of the vest I was wearing that morning.

Like we tell our kids to do, I retraced my steps. Nothing. I stewed about it all day and just before dark, I looked again. There in the muck and manure next to one of the water tanks I saw a little glimmer of red. I turned a few cartwheels of glee on the way to the tank to retrieve my soggy-edged but safe calving book.

I suppose I should start logging all my important facts and figures electronically and upload them to some "cloud" I hear tell of to keep them safe. Either that, or I should poke a safety pin through the top of that vest pocket.

That one paycheck
When the trucks roll out
January 30, 2012

The past year had its ups and downs, but luckily for the family, one of the ups has been the cattle market. Having just sold last year's calves and having close to 20 years of cattle markets to compare since I came back to the ranch after college, I can say I much prefer selling into an up market than a down market.

Watching the markets is a nerve-wracking pastime. When the market's going up, you wonder when it'll start going down. When the market's down, you wonder if it'll ever start moving back up. If you sell your calves or your corn or your baseball cards when it's down, you kick yourself for not selling before it went down or for not waiting longer in case it would move back up. If you sell when they're up, you question whether you got enough of the up.

My watching of the calf market is a little less intense as of last week when our calves got on the truck and went down the road. A guy hates to admit it sometimes, but I'm pretty darn satisfied with the price this year.

Don't get me wrong, I'm not apologizing for the price. Once I paid the feed bill, ordered another load of diesel and settled up the operating note and the tractor payment, I figured the good price was justified.

It felt good to pay the bills and have a chunk left over to head into the next year. It's nice to be ahead of the game. I remember lots of years when that wasn't the case. I distinctly remember the 62-cent steers and 56-cent heifers I sold a couple years after I borrowed the money to buy my cows in the mid-1990s. They were maybe 550 pounds and didn't generate many dollars for a highly leveraged young guy just starting out.

So now we need to make it last. We basically get one check, and aside from some cull cows and off-farm income from writing these lucrative columns and such, it has to get us through an entire year. But with this year's prices, I think we can do it.

Family budgets

Every family gets to go through the exercise of making ends meet, whether the paycheck comes once a year or once a month. Sometimes, it's like the poster I saw years ago, "Just when I made ends meet, somebody moved the ends!" The wages might go up, but the apartment rent goes up more. Health insurance, day care, the car payment, it all has to come from somewhere and balance out.

There is satisfaction when the credits and debits come together. Head out the door and head to work each morning, come home to your family in the evening, and know that the sweat or the skill you traded for the day's dollars put supper on the table for the family.

I tried to explain to our kids when we got the cattle check how this all works. I told them there might even be enough to put a little away so they could go to college someday. The 5-year-old told me college was too expensive, he'd rather we buy a toy instead.

He was right about college being expensive, and realizing that at the age of 5 probably means he might do well in college someday, but his cuteness and cleverness wouldn't get me to invest his future in a junky plastic toy today.

Here's hoping the cattle markets and paychecks up and down the line are high enough to even consider putting something away for college. Soon enough, the little beneficiaries will learn it's a better investment than toys and games.

116

Chapter 4
Grease and Grime

Monster trucks
Bigger ain't always better

March 21, 2005

A few years ago, I was lured in by zero percent financing and I bought a new pickup, the first new pickup on the ranch since 1960.

This winter, I made my last payment, which is kind of nice because the pickup isn't even worn out yet. But it does have some wear.

Last week, I filled the tank for a mere $60. It qualified me for a generous $1 discount on a car wash. I usually wash the pickup a couple of times a year whether it needs it or not, so I took advantage of this lucrative deal.

The pickup box was free of barbed wire, fence posts and other things that tend to tangle an automatic car wash brush. There weren't even any feed sacks or pop cans to blow out of the box when it hit the air drier. It was a clean, snag-free operation.

Inspection time

Once the dirt was off, I could see the paint again. Foolishly, I checked it over for chips and scratches.

There was no shortage of rock chips since I live a good 12 miles from the nearest paved road. But the box was in fine shape since I put a liner in it the day I bought it. And it was almost scratch-free since I've been careful to keep it out of the brush.

My dog, however, has been a little tough on the finish.

You can see clearly his claw marks on the front end of the pickup box just behind the driver's door.

Our old dog, Smokey, always has jumped in and ridden in the back of the pickup around the ranch. He's still trying to adjust to the higher profile of today's modern pickups though.

The top of the box on my old 1986 model pickup was a good 10 inches lower than this new rig.

My dog could clear the side of my old pickup in a single bound and land right on the spare tire.

Now we have the dual challenges of an aging dog and a much-higher pickup. He tries to get a run at it, but he usually ends up with his front paws clinging to the edge and his hind legs frantically scratching at the side of the pickup as he tries to propel himself up, over and into the box.

Sometimes he makes it; sometimes he just slides down the side with his front claws dug in deep.

Successful or not, he's left with some blue paint under his claws and I'm left with a little less blue paint on my pickup.

People challenges

Smokey's not the only one having a tough time adjusting to the tall truck.

My wife's a tall gal, but even she needs a little boost to get in the cab. If I'm not around to boost her, she needs to take a little run at it and kind of resembles Smokey

118

with her feet scrambling to get a toehold on the running board.

When I roll down the window to pick up the mail, I barely can reach down far enough to empty the mailbox.

You hardly can visit with a neighbor on the road if they're in a car or a regular height pickup. You don't want the conversation to go over their head.

And, at the fast-food drive-through, I not only have to talk down at the speaker to order my burger, I have to shut the darn motor off so they can hear me. The diesel engine is as loud as the pickup is tall.

But things may get easier for us all. As the tires wear down, the springs start to sag and all the holes start to wear, my new pickup may get closer to the ground all the time.

We can only hope for its age to complement ours.

Learning to share
Tough to go from hoarder to seller
June 27, 2005

Ever since kindergarten, I've been getting comfortable with the idea of sharing.

I like to think I'm getting pretty good at it. I always offer coffee when someone drops in, and I'll give them the last brownie on the serving plate. If someone needs to borrow some wheels, I toss them my keys, and if it's a tool or an implement or anything I've got that someone else doesn't, I tell them to go ahead and help themselves and just bring it back when they're done.

But as I look around the ranch, when it comes to equipment, maybe I should tell the borrowers to just keep it when they're done. I could stand to do a lot more sharing of old haying machinery, dead cars and dying tractors.

No trades

We've never done a lot of business with dealers who want our trade-ins. I guess that says something about the quality of what we've got to trade.

You don't need to be an appraiser or an auctioneer to take a quick look at the old tractors and haying equipment and cars and pickups scattered around our place and correctly figure that none of that stuff owes us much.

Rather than trade in the old or run an ad to sell whatever we've replaced, we just keep everything. We're starting to run out of trees and hills to hide it all.

Dad has 26 cylinders worth of two-cylinder tractors that haven't gone "pop, POP!" for a long time now. Mom has about 28 doors worth of big, old four-door cars parked in a line behind a hill resting in peace.

I think their hoarding of old equipment has something to do with living through the scarcity of the Depression. The 40 acres of scrap iron is their savings account, a rusting financial nest egg to fall back on in hard times.

Me? I'm willing crack that nest egg, or at least convert it to cash.

The highest bidder

Last week, in a radical departure from our usual style of machinery management, I sold my old yellow round baler at a neighborhood auction sale.

I'd become pretty attached to that old baler in the 11 haying seasons we had shared. But after I upgraded balers last year, I just couldn't justify keeping the 26-year-old depreciator around for sentimental reasons.

So I put her on the block and decided to share this piece of vintage haying history with someone else. I thought it was worth $2,500. It brought $1,450. I guess accepting that price is part of learning how to share your old equipment.

I'm going to miss Ol' Yeller, but it's sure nice to have a little extra space in the shop again.

I've got another fella looking at a couple of Mom's old cars for use in a demolition derby. She thinks it's a little mean to intentionally wreck those 30-year-old cars. I think the cars would rather go down in the glory of a derby than suffer a slow death to rust.

Another friend of mine offered to come out with a trailer to load some of Dad's scrap iron for a share of the proceeds.

I'm all for it. I'd like to have the pasture for the cows. Time will tell if the folks are willing to make the shift. Some of our neighbors have big junk collections, um, I mean long lines of retired equipment, too, and one says, "It's just like money in the bank."

Well, call me crazy, but I'd rather have money in the bank. I'm willing to share the steel.

Diggin' it
Equipment-strewn artifacts abound for archaeologists   August 8, 2005

A lot of people like to discover old things and dig them up. So many people are wannabe paleontologists the North Dakota Geological Survey invited them all to take part in a public fossil dig near Medora, N.D., this summer.

The Geological Survey needed some cheap help to retrieve the bones of one of the state's oldest residents. The help was more than affordable; they actually paid to be there.

For nine days, people paid for the chance to dig, dust and brush away dirt from a 60 million-year-old crocodile-like critter called a champsosaurus. They had plenty of takers on this chance to dig for a day, and they put lots of bones in the bag that once framed this prehistoric predator.

Ranch history

I've been discovering a few more recent artifacts out in our hayfield. I discovered a wheel rake tooth stuck in a tire it flattened, I discovered some plastic twine from last year's bales wrapped up in the baler pickup, and I discovered a broken dump rake tooth as it knocked out a guard and a section from my mower sickle.

I wonder if I could get some of those champsosaurus dirt diggers interested in doing a little ranch archaeology and picking up a few of these recent artifacts for me. I wouldn't even charge them for the opportunity to make my fields a little safer for man and machine.

Granted, the metal that busts off of my equipment isn't ancient history, but it's close to the surface and it'd be easy to find with a good metal detector. And you don't need to be nearly as careful as you would with a 60 million-year-old fossil.

People scour old battlefields looking for spent rifle cartridges and uniform buttons. Flint arrowheads, stone tools and assorted implements of the ancient nomads generate a lot of excitement.

I can't help but think that there'd be just as much excitement in the newer things they'd find in our hayfield. It'd be like capturing pieces of history before they get really old and tarnished and, well, historical.

Rakeasaurus Rex

Just as people wonder what prehistoric animal a bone fragment or a tooth could have come from, how big it was and how long ago it wandered the earth, they could ponder the origins of the broken rake teeth they find strewn across my hay field.

"Wow, look at the size of this tooth! I bet it came from a 15–foot-long, nine-wheeled finger rake. From the looks of the paint and the rust on the broken edge, I'd say that rake crossed these fields just last year in search of hay to prey on. What a find!"

Together with the teeth discovered from the stomping grounds of the mammoth 36-foot-long hydraulic dump rake and the many remnants of nomadic hay man's "Plastic Age," they'd have a collection suitable for museum placement, or, perhaps, a sturdy trash barrel.

I don't care where the stuff ends up as long as it isn't flattening my tires or knocking out sickle sections and mower guards.

And if I'm overrun with modern metal digging archaeologists picking up the place, it looks like my equipment is seeding another crop of broken teeth and leaving some machinery messes for next year's dig.

Plugging leaks
Tractor holds oil like a sieve   August 22, 2005

I'm not one of those fiercely loyal guys when it comes to tractor brands.

I remember kids in school getting in fistfights and giving each other bloody noses over arguments about what color tractor their dads drove. Some folks put tractor colors above religion when it comes to their devotion.

Me, I just like my tractors cheap. Green or red or orange or blue, it makes no difference as long as the horsepower comes with the right price tag.

And, these days, along with them being cheap, I admire a tractor that'll run cheap. If it'll make the day on a little less diesel, it'll score a lot of points with me.

Sold, leaks and all

I found what I was looking for in a tractor at an auction earlier this summer. It ran cheap, and compared with similar tractors I'd studied, my final bid seemed reasonable.

The tractor was red with some greasy black accents. The black accent was explained when they said the tractor had a leak. I figured I could stand to fix the leak before taking the tractor to its new home.

A local red paint mechanic came by and replaced a leaky line. All that renewed pressure in the system caused another leaky line. We fixed that one, too, and a few hundred dollars later, I began to drive it home.

Several miles down the road, and I had a third leak and universal fluid pouring from the tractor to mark my trail. Another mechanic, another bill, and we had that one plugged, too.

I drove it the rest of the way home, and, you guessed it, I spotted leak No. 4. I topped off the universal fluid for the fourth time and presented the tractor to my wife as a little haying gift.

The last leak dripped on her foot while she was raking. It wouldn't have bothered me so much in my boots, but my wife wears sandals to the hayfield. Yes, sandals. I guess they go better with the shorts or capris she also wears to the field. I try not to say anything about her work wardrobe; I'm just glad she's out there.

I parked the tractor in the shop to plug up the fourth major leak. I shouldn't have parked it on that concrete floor. I spotted so many leaks I considered dipping the whole outfit in a vat of JB Weld to try to seal her up.

The whole darn leaky tractor seems to be hydraulically driven. If it had a cigarette lighter, the engineers would have run a hydraulic pipe and cylinder up there to help push it out.

Leaky economics

It wouldn't be so bad, but $65 a barrel oil has got motor oil and hydraulic fluid costing so much that you've got to plug the holes to try and keep the stuff in. I used to be able to tolerate a few drips in the days of cheap oil.

I thought about recycling the fluid as it flows out. Maybe wire a bunch of little pails under the drips to catch the fluid, kind of like collecting syrup from a maple tree. That way I could check the pails every third day and pour the drips back into the tractor. I'm afraid our rough ground would spill everything I caught though.

What I really need might be that little Dutch boy who saved his country from flooding by plugging a hole in the dike with a finger. With long arms and legs and 20 toes and fingers. Hans might just be able to save my new tractor and get me through the haying season.

Demo day
A glimpse at how the other half ranches   March 20, 2006

Over the years, I've been pretty good at denying myself the finer things in life. I've driven old vehicles, run used equipment, lived in small houses and steered clear of brand-name merchandise.

Once in a while, though, I like to take a peek at what I've been missing. I'll test drive a new car, visit friends with spacious mansions and buy the occasional $4 cup of coffee.

So when the local equipment salesman swung in the yard and told me he had a brand-new demo tractor and loader in the neighborhood, I jumped at the chance to give it a try.

When he pulled into our yard and saw the old tractors and worn-out equipment, he probably had two thoughts. He either figured we were long overdue for a new tractor and apparently had been saving our money to buy one, or else we were too cheap or too poor to have anything better than what was scattered around the yard.

I guess he opted for the more optimistic of the two conclusions, classified us as a potential sale and put us on the list to get behind the wheel of the new tractor.

Fancy feeding

The tractor was a 95-horsepower, front-wheel-assist with a loader, and it had all the latest bells and whistles. The salesman said it was built for feeding cattle and baling hay. It just so happened that I use a tractor for feeding cattle and baling hay.

The main difference was that I fed cattle and baled hay with a $10,000 outfit for years, and had finally upgraded to a $25,000 outfit just a couple of years ago. My dad fed cattle and stacked hay with a $2,000 outfit, and before that, he used a $3 pitchfork and a $200 team of horses.

This new rig that he drove into the yard had a price tag of $110,000. I tried to hide my shock at the sticker price and take the news in stride. I didn't want him to downgrade my sales potential and leave before I had the chance to try out this deluxe demo.

"That's not too bad a price," I lied like I'd spent my whole life around tractors with six-figure price tags. I showed a little interest in financing programs and trade in values to help justify the test drive.

He tossed me the keys and told me to go ahead and put an hour or two on it. I felt like a kid turned loose in a toy store.

Pushin' buttons

I tried all the buttons and figured out what each of them did by the time I was done feeding the cows. This was an intricate machine. I even had to take off my yellow, fuzzy chore gloves to get a better feel for the buttons that shifted the gears and fine tuned the radio.

A little lever that looked like a blinker switch made the tractor go forward and backward. The seat had four or five levers to adjust its comfort. The digital read-out told you how fast you were going and what gear you were in. I'd never be tempted with the thought of fixing a tractor like this if it ever broke down.

As fun as it was to feed cows like an oil well-rich rancher, I told the salesman that we had to buy diapers and add on to our house before we'd consider making a down payment on a $110,000 tractor.

But I am glad that I got to drive it. At least I'll know how to run the tractor if a neighbor buys one and I have to borrow it sometime.

Winter white
Black oil and drip diagnostics

The snow didn't show up in time for Christmas, but we did get a white New Year's. Now it's shaping up to be a brown Ground Hog's Day.

Luckily, our 10 inches of fluffy, white snow was around long enough for me to diagnose the drips on my loader tractor before it melted.

I suppose some folks have tractors that don't leave a trail to follow, but I don't have that luxury for long when I start owning the tractor. Like Hansel and Gretel's bread crumbs, it's pretty easy to track my tractor. It's real obvious to see where I stopped to open a gate or let it idle awhile.

Oil and universal fluid are getting so expensive I began to contemplate getting the drips fixed. Unfortunately, the hourly shop rate to hire a mechanic who can find the holes and plug the leaks still costs more than the oil that's lost.

So I just watch and fill, monitor and replenish. It takes a lot of drips and drops to make a quart, so I can go quite a while before I need to top off the fluids. Unless, of course, the leak gets worse.

That's where the fresh blanket of snow comes in. I back the tractor out of the shop, off the dirt floor and on to the snow. I let it run a few minutes and see how black the new white snow gets.

If it makes a few spots that are hardly noticeable I just keep on going. If it leaves a couple of big puddles, I make sure to fill up the fluids before doing chores. If it makes a pool so big the tractor can't get any traction to get away from it, I think about bringing on a mechanic.

Other oilers

A friend of mine said he had a neighbor who actually tied a bucket under his tractor to catch the drips. Just like catching maple syrup. When the bucket started filling up, he'd pour it back in the tractor.

He probably thought he was being thrifty, but he could have won an award for environmental sensitivity. Not only did he keep the oil from polluting the ground, he reused and recycled.

Another fella told me about a bush pilot he met up in Alaska on a hunting trip. They were looking over his plane before they jumped in to fly off.

The land-loving plainsman was a little concerned when he looked at the cowling that covered the airplane motor and saw it was covered with oil. The pilot started it up and his passenger could see oil dripping out and streaming back.

The pilot didn't seem to pay it any attention, so his passenger told him in a voice that was a bit frantic and worried about the oil coming out of the airplane motor.

"Oh, don't worry about that, it's really a good thing," the pilot said nonchalantly. "But you keep an eye on it and let me know when the oil quits coming out. That's when the real trouble starts!

Chillin' and gellin'
Frustrations rise as mercury drops   January 22, 2007

Funny things can happen when the temperature gets down to 30 below zero. And when I say funny, I don't mean humorous.

Like most years, I ordered some No. 1 diesel fuel late in the fall to top off my bulk tank of No. 2 diesel. It wasn't quite half and half, but I figured it'd be plenty good for our new globally warmed winters.

When people who don't know diesel ask me what the difference between No. 1 and No. 2 fuel is, I tell them it's a lot like the terms some folks use with their children in reference to the bathroom. "Do you need to do No. 1 or No. 2?" they ask. The same liquid or solid reference is apt when it comes to diesel and cold weather.

The tractor was running nicely all winter until the morning she dropped to 30 below. Of course, I was gone when the cold snap hit, leaving my new hired man on the ranch to fend for himself and feed the cows in my conspicuous absence.

He'd been around enough diesel equipment to know the disappointing sound a tractor makes when its fuel gels up in cold weather. I obviously didn't have enough No. 1 added to keep the fuel from turning the consistency of Jell-O that morning.

I usually like Jell-O, especially the green kind with the mandarin oranges that you find at the potluck dinners. I'm not so fond of the Jell-O-like stuff that plugs your fuel lines and filters on a frosty morning.

Pick your petro

Some days I wonder why I parked Dad's John Deere 60, which ran on cool, clear gasoline, and started feeding with diesel tractors.

I guess I like to have the opportunity to spend an extra 40 cents a gallon for the smelly fuel. And when it's 30 below and calling for more No. 1, it's a special treat to spend another 30 cents beyond that to try and keep everything in a liquid state.

I'm not sure why petroleum refiners and retailers charge so much more for diesel than gas. Or why they charge even more than that for No. 1 diesel. It's probably the old economic rule of big business: "Because they can."

The diesel motors are a lot more efficient in our tractors, but I'm sure I lose a little efficiency by letting those diesel motors run all day and keeping them plugged in all night when it gets so cold.

Feeding cattle and operating a loader doesn't require a lot of horsepower. Dad used to get it done with a 25-horse, gas-powered tractor. Now I use a 140-horse diesel tractor because that's what a crop farmer had used and depreciated so I could afford to buy it.

Lately, ranchers have been known to accept a lot bigger tractor than needed if it means getting a cab, radio and heater. If the package happens to be attached to a super-sized tractor, we just sit in heated comfort and watch the fuel gauge drop as we feed a little hay to the cows.

By the time I got back to the ranch, my tractor was back amongst the living. A couple fuel filters, a jug of conditioner and a few hours of time and travel from the local mechanic put things back on track.

As a backup, I made a trip to town with the service tank to get a little No. 1 fuel for the future.

It always warms up after a cold snap ... but sometimes it takes awhile.

Cashing in the reserves
Stockpiled fuel for the finding   May 28, 2007

Gas hit $3.40 a gallon at my local gas station. Makes me think I should have filled the ranch's bulk tank about 50 cents ago when I couldn't imagine it going any higher.

At least it makes diesel look like a bargain. I complained all winter about the price of diesel being so much higher than gasoline.

I thought my whining would convince the oil cartel to lower the price of diesel back below gas where it belonged. They just raised the price of the gas instead. At least I can feel good about driving my diesel pickup again, or as good as a guy can feel when he's filling up a 35 gallon tank at $2.90 a gallon.

I'm not going to take these increases lying down though.

The escalation in petroleum prices has driven me to take my most drastic step to date as a consumer. Yup, I've decided to tap into the ranch's strategic petroleum reserve.

Finding fuel

Our strategic petroleum reserve wasn't necessarily put in place strategically, but it does amount to a few gallons of stockpiled gas and diesel. It's the closest thing we have to a strategy here on the ranch when it comes to fossil fuel markets.

The strategic petroleum reserve is in the tanks of vehicles and tractors scattered around the ranch in various states of repair.

I just cranked up the 1967 Ford pickup last week. The tires were up, the battery was good and the gas gauge showed three-quarters of a tank! It was like finding an old birthday card from years ago with $40 in it.

I'll drive that pickup around the fenceline and use up that reserve gas. The fenceline may be the only place I can drive it since it doesn't have a current license or insurance.

The 1984 Mercury Grand Marquis still has a license and insurance for some reason. It was retired for the winter, but I got behind the wheel and found a half-tank of gas in that rig to burn up and down the roads while I boycott the retail pumps in town.

A bigger challenge will be the 1951 Chevy pickup of my grandfather's that I fixed up and used while I was in high school. It's been in the pasture for a long time. There's some gas in it, but it may have turned to varnish while the motor was on vacation.

I'm sure I can buy a pint of additive in the automotive aisle at the local discount store that'll rejuvenate the gas, clean the carburetor, increase the fuel mileage, make your hair grow and reduce your waistline all while it's coursing through the fuel lines.

Although we've never had any oil exploration on the ranch, I know there's oil in our hills. Old cars, broken down tractors and retired trucks all have a little gas or diesel or motor oil in them.

The cost of recovery may be prohibitive on some of the units. Some of the motors are stuck, the tires are flat and the transmissions are shot. It might not pay to resurrect those outfits to burn down the fuel left in their tanks.

Some of that fuel just might have to stay in our strategic petroleum reserve. If gas hits $5 a gallon, it may pay to fix the flats and tune up the motors. Or, at the least, go get a siphoning hose.

Out of order
Mechanical frills on the ranch   August 20, 2007

I don't think I could name a single thing with wheels on our hay field that is in perfect working order.

Sometimes it's just a little thing that doesn't function, but, just the same, it's not in tip-top, showroom shape.

Most of the tractors run without working headlights. That gets me home for supper a little earlier. I think my wife may have just unhooked the wires going to the headlights.

Only one has a fuel gauge that works. The rest get checked with an improvised diesel dipstick that looks a lot like a piece of rusty barbed wire.

No temperature gauges. If it's boiling over, it's hot. If the antifreeze is down, you top it off. No ammeters. If the batteries go dead, you just get out the jumper cables.

Getting along

There are a lot of little features on mechanical contraptions that I can get along fine without. Headlights and gauges and such would be nice to have, but it's no deal breaker for anything I own with wheels.

When I got modern with my baling tractor (it's only 25 years old), I jumped into the generation of tight cabs and air conditioning.

I thought I could treat the air conditioning as a frivolous option, like the fuel gauges and headlights on my other machines. I was wrong.

I started the year baling and sweating, hot but not miserable. Then the sun really started to shine.

It hit 103 degrees on the Fahrenheit scale. I opened up the windows trying to find a cooling cross breeze for the tractor cab. The windows on this cab, however, are specially designed to allow only the dust and chaff into the cab from the hay baler and leave any cool air outside.

I brought a thermometer in the cab with me. It registered 122 degrees in no time, with the windows open. It might have gotten hotter, but the thermometer only went up to 122.

I baled a half a day instead of a whole day in my little, green cab greenhouse, broke down and called the dealer to do another couple hundred dollars worth of magic on the A.C. It's clearly extortion, but we pay it and enjoy the coolness.

Ranch reputation

After years of running older-than-average equipment in semi-working order, we've established a bit of a reputation. We even hold our field vehicles to the same low standard.

Old pickups just a rattle or two away from complete disintegration and old four-door cars that might not make it to town but still can make it to the meadow are our motor vehicles of choice for field service.

I remember one time a friend of our family who'd retired from the telephone company was mowing hay for us. It started to rain, so he jumped off the tractor, got in the old four-door field car and headed the several miles back to the ranch.

When he got home, my mother noticed that his head and shoulders were soaking wet. "What happened to you?" she asked.

He replied that he stuck his head out the car window most of the way home in the rain so he could see the road. "Why didn't you just turn on the windshield wipers?" she asked.

You could see the surprise and disgust on his face when he said, "Ohhhhh, no! You mean they work?"

Sometimes our no frills reputation precedes us.

Four wheels or four legs
Depends on gas price   May 12, 2008

It's time for a cowboy confession…I own a four wheeler. Or, as my friends north of the border call it, a quad.

No matter what you call it, it's one of those motorized contraptions that end up replacing a horse on a lot of ranches.

Our ranch went nearly 100 years without a motor bike, three-wheeler or four-wheeler. It was a point of pride for us as a cowboy kind of ranch to say we never owned a four-wheeler.

Then as the 21st century dawned, I broke down and got motorized. I told myself that the new four-wheeler never would replace a horse on our place. I'd use it to save on my old pickup, extending its depreciated-out life by fixing fence, hauling mineral and running out to the hay field with the little all-terrain vehicle.

Horse jobs, quad jobs

I promised I'd still check the cows, move the herd and sort off anything that needed sorting or doctoring by horseback.

Then it happened. Four-wheeler chore creep. Without even meaning to, horseback jobs turned into four-wheeler jobs. It started with checking the cows occasionally during calving with the four-wheeler instead of the four-legger.

I'd use the quad to open a gate and I'd find myself driving around behind the cow herd going back and forth to move the cows to fresh grass in the pasture rotation. Perfectly good jobs for a horse, replaced by a noisy machine.

Finally, I caught myself racing a renegade yearling heifer at top speed to turn her and chase the group into the home corrals. It had gone too far; my horses were standing idle while I hung onto a pair of handlebars like some Sturgis biker.

I wasn't feeling like much of a cowboy when I caught myself revving the motor to turn that heifer. And I didn't feel real safe either.

When I race a ranch horse at breakneck speed in the pasture, it's a slim chance that either of us will break our neck because there's another set of eyes and a brain with the desire not to crash helping me out. I've never heard of a four-wheeler smart enough to jump a bull hole or dodge a cut bank.

More old cowboys are getting hurt on four-wheelers than ever were injured on a horse in their younger, wilder days.

Ridding the guilt

I've been harboring a lot of guilt about the four-wheeled ATV in our yard and the expanding list of jobs I've let it do. Now, I've got more than guilt motivating me to change my ways.

Now I've got $3.70-a-gallon gasoline to make me take action. Granted, the pickup takes a lot more gas than the four-wheeler, but my horse takes even less gas. My fossil-fuel-free horses are low emission, low carbon and have little to no noise pollution.

Nowadays, I'm checking cows and tagging calves horseback. I'll soon be moving cattle by horseback, checking fences horseback and, if I rig up a pack horse, I may even deliver salt and mineral by horseback.

Of course, now that I've recommitted myself to horseback ranching, I'm nearly out of hay, the pastures look dismal and oats just topped $3.50 a bushel.

At the rate things are going, I soon may be walking the range.

Saving gas
Not so easy in the boondocks   June 9, 2008

There're a lot of gas-saving tips floating around these days with the record-high prices for gas being set every week.

I've been trying to figure out if any of the ideas will work on our place. We live 15 gravel road miles from the hometown of 574 people, and 60 miles from the chain restaurant and big box store commerce center with a population of 36,567.

The first gas-saving tip I cross off the list is "use the mass transit system." When you don't have much for human masses, there's not much available in mass transit.

I've checked every approach and intersection between here and town for a bus stop or a set of subway stairs to no avail. The only public transportation I even could consider is hitchhiking. And you can't always count on seeing a car on the 15 miles of road between the ranch and town.

There's the much-touted "change your driving habits" advice to consider. Driving in traffic with jackrabbit starts, sudden stops and extended idling can burn up the gas. In our traffic, we only have to start moving once when we leave and stop once when we get to there. I think we're doing the best we can in that fuel-saving area.

"Build up speed before you get to a hill, then coast down the hill for a free ride." Obviously, not advice written for drivers on the level plains of North Dakota. There's one little hill between our place and town and the hundred feet of coasting probably won't make a big dent in my gas consumption.

"Make lists and buy groceries just once or twice a week," I saw on one list. We've been doing that for years. We've been known to leave the supermarket with eight or 10 cartons of milk, four loaves of bread, the big bag of pancake mix and an entire flat of canned vegetables. People in the aisles look at us like we're survivalists, but we're just stocking up on our big trip to town and feeding two growing boys.

They say tire pressure's important for fuel efficiency. I always considered tires that would hold air all the way to town and back drivable. Forty-five pounds when you leave and 15 pounds when you get back probably doesn't meet the definition of proper inflation.

When it comes to regular pounds, the weighty kind, the advice is to travel as light as possible. It's getting to where we need to unload the posts and the post-hole digger, kick out the dog and jettison the tool box to increase our miles per gallon.

Combine trips and perform as many errands as you can in a single trip is another piece of wisdom. I try to do this, but it's hard to synchronize the breakdowns on the ranch that dictate the need for a trip.

I usually make sure we do at least two things on each trip. When we drive to church, we try to stop at the city park or go visiting. If I go to a meeting somewhere, I try to get a back haul of groceries and diapers.

The other day, my wife took our 4-year-old in to play a little kickball with the other tykes in town. I had her stop and buy some wood corral posts. I'm not sure if I really needed them, but for a couple hundred bucks worth of posts, we justified the drive.

Mostly, though, the only second stop we make on our trips to the big city is at the gas station to fill the car with nearly $4 a gallon gas or top off the pickup with $4.68 diesel.

That full tank of fuel weighs down the car, lightens my wallet and gets us to thinking that the reclusive life of a hermit might not be so bad after all.

Waging war in the wind
Weeds luck out in the breeze   July 7, 2008

When it comes to weather, there's no pleasing everybody. Sometimes you can't even please one person. Especially if he wants two kinds of weather at the same time. I like some wind in the summer to pump the water in two pastures where we use windmills. I really dislike the wind in the summer when I'm trying to spray.

Some farmers in our area are getting big wind generators sited on their land. The checks from the power company are nice enough to make them glad their granddad homesteaded that windy ridge. That is, unless they've got a disappearing window of time to spray the crops in the blustery fields surrounding those wind towers.

Maybe it could just blow at night. Like a lot of thirsty people, my cows could start drinking at 10 p.m. The wind could pump water for the cows all night, then quit in the morning in time for me to spray some weeds.

Nighttime probably isn't the biggest demand time for electrical power, but some cities are fighting the trend. New York, the city that never sleeps, for instance. Las Vegas, where the stuff that happens there is supposed to stay there, usually has a lot happening at night under those big neon signs that need evening electrical current.

Nighttime winds generating nighttime electricity could power those places, leaving calm, still days for spraying fields and killing weeds.

We'll put our order in to mother nature to get those windy hours changed.

Weed wars

As it is, here in the real world, the wind blows during the day and quits at night.

It's a rather poor arrangement for folks who need some still air to get their work done in the daylight hours.

I'd just as soon sleep in, but when it comes to killing my old enemy, leafy spurge, I'll set the alarm for the early hours of morning to go do some spraying before the wind comes up.

If you don't know what leafy spurge is, be thankful. Just pick your least-favorite, local, non-native, introduced perennial noxious weed and you'll get my drift, so to speak.

That was an unintentional pun, but spray drift is what I try to avoid by beating the wind to the pastures.

Cattle ranchers don't have to mess around with chemicals much, and that's fine by me. But leafy spurge has forced me to renew my restricted-use pesticide license, calibrate my sprayer and calculate my gallons per acre.

If I could just get the spray to land on the spurge and choke the life out of that miserable forb. When the wind blows, I get more spray on me than the spurge gets on it. I change clothes, clean up good, and, so far, I haven't shriveled up and expired.

Depending on the wind direction, the spray might just drift over to some of my other spurge or hit troublesome broadleaf plants I hadn't even considered. It might go across the fence to get my neighbor's leafy spurge.

I could bill the neighbor for my unintentional custom spraying work, or, I could just wait for the wind to switch and give him an opportunity to return the favor. Hopefully, it doesn't just blow more weed seeds my way.

Trade-in value
Swapping scrap iron for new iron   August 18, 2008

I've always been close to a lot of scrap iron. Usually, I've been driving the scrap around the field or up and down the road. I never could bring myself to drive it right to the junk yard.

I see a lot of other people driving scrap iron down the road these days. They've got it precariously strapped to trailers and they're off to the junk yard to make a sale.

Metal prices are pretty good right now, and every old car, combine and obsolete implement retired behind the hill and in the shelterbelt is getting drug out and converted to cash.

I watched the market for steel go up, up, up. I decided it was time I join the trend to recycle and make some easy money. By the time I loaded up a couple barrels of my good shop scrap, it had dropped 40 percent.

That's about par for my marketing. I followed through with the sale, though, knowing it might well drop 50 percent by the time I was ready to sell again.

Junk terminology

I grew up using the term "junk yard." If you drove by one, you'd recognize it. "Sanford and Son" had one on television.

The terminology took an upgrade with the word "salvage." It sounded a little better and let you know that something was being saved to be put in use again.

The latest terminology refers to these places as "recycling yards." It's got a nice ring to it, but drive into the recycling yard, and it looks suspiciously like a junk yard.

We don't have a lot of recycling services in our rural area, so I figured selling shop scrap was going to be my opportunity to be conscientious about our planet's resources. I loaded up a couple of barrels of steel and swung by the recycling yard.

I got the higher price for "prepared" steel since the pieces were less than 18 inches long and I got a check for a cool $38.

Buying new

The barrels I sold had things in it like old mower guards that I'd changed out, broken rake teeth, sickle sections and other worn-out widgets.

They were the things that wear out and have to be changed every so often, or that break no matter what. They're the consumables of the haying biz.

I took my $38 check to go buy some new parts to replace the ones I'd just recycled.

The mower guards weighed about 2 pounds apiece, giving them a salvage value of about 12½ cents each. I priced the new ones to replace them; they were $17 a pop.

Needless to say, my $38 check for two barrels of old steel didn't go very far in getting me some nicely painted, new steel parts.

I guess I won't get rich by wearing out metal and selling it back to the scrap dealer. But there are worse investments.

You've maybe seen the email circulating around about the returns made by investing in Enron or Worldcom at one time versus just buying beer or pop and selling the empty cans.

It says a $1,000 invested in Enron when it was $54 a share would have got you about $3 when it had dropped to 16 cents a share.

However, the email says, an even wiser investor could have bought $1,000 worth of beer, drank it and sold the empty cans for a much higher return.

At $38 a trip for my old guards and rake teeth, it'll be a long time before I have a $1,000 to worry about investing.

When I do hit $1,000, maybe I'll invest it in a junk yard.

Avoiding the mechanic
The high cost of self-sufficiency
September 29, 2008

It's been a tough year for the Taylor Ranch tractor fleet. I started the year with five nearly antique outfits in modern running order. I'm limping across the finish line with two still rolling.

No one ever would accuse me of being a mechanic. The trail of crippled tractors is testament to my lack of mechanical skill. I can turn bolts as good as anyone, dismantle machinery and, sometimes, even put it back together. But that doesn't make me a mechanic.

A mechanic's stock in trade is his ability to diagnose a machine's ailment, pinpoint a problem and fix exactly what needs fixing. That's why my local implement dealer dangles the keys to that diagnostic talent in front of me and charges a shop rate of $80 an hour for access to it.

I do whatever I can to avoid those $80 wonder workers.

Repairs by guess

So absent any real knowledge of my own on how to fix things, I start asking friends, neighbors, parts clerks, off-duty mechanics and random people on the street what I could do to get my tractor running again.

After compiling the free advice from my ad hoc committee, I go to the parts counter and fill a box with potential remedies. I buy a few extra parts figuring it costs less than the $80 an hour for a professional, then I go home and start turning bolts.

Sometimes it works. When my starter quit spinning on a 4020, I bought a box full of electrical components and worked my way up from least expensive to most expensive. You have to be careful with the electrical stuff because you can't return the parts once they've been on your tractor. My starter was whirring before I hit the most expensive part, a nice ending when I was able to return the crown jewel of the parts box.

I'm having less luck with the hydraulics on my 656. I've tried this, that and the other thing without any breakthroughs. My main job on the project has been getting a bucket under the outfit to catch the $8 a gallon universal fluid when I'm dismantling things.

Aha, try that

I was nearly ready to give up and take it to a real shop. Then I got one more suggestion from a benevolent mechanic who was generous with his advice.

"Maybe try a relief valve," he said. It was music to my ears because it sounded simple; you spin the old one out and spin a new one in. It gave me goosebumps to think something like that would give me hydraulic cylinders that extend and retract.

We found the valve in the parts bins, it was about as big as my thumb and looked about as high tech as you'd expect for a 40-year-old tractor. I handed over my credit card. He pushed the receipt back to me for my signature when I saw the numbers at the bottom, $242!

I just about spilled my cup of day-old coffee and spit out the free popcorn. I'm usually pretty calloused to the price of parts, but this one caught me by surprise.

They assured me it wasn't a mistake and I gave that famous line of surrender spoken often by guys with old tractors, "Well, I guess I gotta have it."

I wrapped it in crushed velvet, tucked it in a jewelry box, carefully transported it home and put it in the tractor. I was hoping it would have the hydraulics working like new. I started it up and got nothing.

I was devastated. But I did find a reason to smile.

I got to return the valve for a $242 credit on my card.

Cars in crisis
In need of a pull out, not a bailout   December 22, 2008

I'd heard the American auto industry was in trouble, but I didn't know the extent of it until I hit an icy patch of road on the way to town.

That was when my three-quarter-ton Dodge diesel pickup went down the road sideways before it found a little traction, grabbed hold and headed right down into a ditch chock full of snow.

It didn't much matter that it was a big four-wheel-drive with lots of clearance. The snow we drove into was well beyond the clearance. The headlights even were pushing snow. It was stuck.

Anybody home?

In the old days, I would've pulled down my ear lappers, slipped on my mittens and started walking down the road. In these modern times, I turn up the heat in the vehicle, check for cell signal and start dialing the phone.

I called one neighbor in close proximity. No answer, left a message on the machine about my embarrassing mishap. I called a second neighbor. Nobody home, again leaving the story of my subpar driving skills for all to listen to on the answering machine.

Finally, the third neighbor I called was home. I was kind of taken aback by getting a real live voice on the other end of the line. I gathered myself and repeated my story of stuckedness for the third time.

I asked if he could help me out. "You bet," he said. "I'll go plug in the block heater on a tractor. It might start up in an hour or two." I was hoping for more immediate assistance, so he said he'd head right down with his pickup.

To the rescue

He came zipping down the road to the scene of my predicament with a little two-wheel-drive Nissan pickup. While the executives of the "Big Three" auto makers were in Washington asking the government for a bailout, I was in a ditch in McHenry County faced with asking Nissan for a pull out.

I didn't know what to do. My dad, who fought in the Asian theatre of World War II, probably would've refused the pull by a Japanese pickup, even with a kind and patriotic neighbor behind the its wheel.

I was more pragmatic. I'd gladly take the pull, but I didn't think there was anyway on God's snow white earth he'd get me out.

We hooked up a tow rope. He wound up that Nissan and let her rip. We gained about a foot. Again and again he wound that little rig up, sometimes we only gained an inch or two. Between pulls, we'd do a little shoveling around my pickup in the ditch to help it pull a little easier.

Finally, we got some momentum and I started spinning all four of my wheels. I got up and out of that ditch led by a Nissan but gaining on him rapidly as I found traction.

It was a humbling experience for my big American four-wheel-drive diesel truck to be saved by a little fuel-efficient Japanese pickup. I thanked him for the pull, and as I got back into my Dodge, I realized the extent of the auto industry's troubles.

There on the manufacturers tag inside the driver's door of my American pickup it said "Made in Mexico." I wonder if the big three thought about going to the Mexican government to help them get through this tough spot. It couldn't be any more humbling than being pulled out of the ditch by a Nissan.

Equipped for borrowing
With an element of surprise   May 11, 2009

I did what some might consider a strange thing this winter. I had a gooseneck hitch installed on my pickup. Not so strange really, except for the fact that I don't have a single gooseneck-towed implement on the ranch.

And I can't say the financial outlook for the year has me trading up my bumper hitch horse trailer to a gooseneck, or buying a new gooseneck flatbed for the ranch.

But I knew that if I didn't have the gooseneck ball and plate on my pickup I'd be out of the game when the opportunity came to borrow someone else's trailer. The hitch was a necessity to enhance my equipment-borrowing ability and reduce my need to borrow the money to buy a trailer of my own.

A perfectly logical move, I thought, to justify the cost of a hitch to pull something I don't even own.

Undercover hitch

As I shopped the gooseneck hitch market for the gooseneck trailers I didn't have, I considered several options.

I thought about crawling under the pickup with an arc welder to build and secure my own plate and ball. I considered the success of my other projects and welds around the place. I decided I didn't want to be rolling down the highway 65 miles an hour with that wearing on my conscience.

So I started shopping the manufactured hitches. The advantages of a turnover ball, although hidden from plain view, were evident to me.

They market these outfits by extolling the virtues of keeping the bed on your pickup perfectly flat when the ball is turned down and stored. I could see where that would be handy when you're hauling plywood or drywall and didn't want to have that big bump in the middle, a dimple in your plywood or a hole punched through your drywall.

Plus, I liked the covert sneakiness of a gooseneck hitch that's gone underground, or at least under the bed.

Say a neighbor bought a new gooseneck flatbed hay trailer. We could be standing by my pickup visiting and he would have no fear of bragging to me about his purchase because he assumes, incorrectly, that I do not have the hitch necessary to burden him by borrowing it.

I reach into the left rear wheel well, pull a pin, do a little finagling and — Ka-Chow! — I sprout a hitch and I'm fully able to borrow his trailer right out from under his nose.

Part of the success of borrowing other people's stuff hinges on the element of surprise, where you pop the question before they have time to formulate reasons to turn you down. The hidden hitch is perfect in that scenario.

Working well

So far, the new hitch is performing well. I have two brothers-in-law with gooseneck flatbeds, and I've already backed my pickup under one of them and hauled enough hay with it to make my three-quarter-ton diesel gasp for air as we climb small hills.

Now with the advent of green grass and summer pasture turn-out, I'm taking an inventory of the gooseneck stock trailers in the neighborhood in case I need to increase the hauling capacity beyond my little 16-foot bumper trailer.

As I started looking around the yards of my neighbors and relatives for stock trailers, I noticed a couple of fifth-wheel recreational campers. I may need to expand my hitch selection so I can borrow those fifth-wheel campers.

Or maybe I'll just ask to borrow their pickup, too.

Cashed in clunker
Out with the old, in with the new   August 17, 2009

I had to do it. I'd been listening to the urgent radio ads from the local car dealers and I decided it was time for Ol' Gray, the half-ton with more heart than horsepower, to make her last trip to the big city.

It was the "Cash for Clunkers" program from the U.S. government that drove me over the edge on sacrificing my rusty old friend and field pickup.

I don't mind calling it a clunker either. It fit the definition. Clunkers had to be less than 25 years old. Ol' Gray had just turned 23 and had a modest 161,000 miles of pre-owned experience.

Clunkers had to be continuously insured and licensed by the same person for the last year or two. Even though Ol' Gray hardly ventured more than 5 miles from home and stayed on pasture trails and gravel roads in recent years, I kept all her credentials renewed.

It was hard to tell though. Her front license plate had rattled off, and the back plate had a severe case of bumper hitch blight from the horse trailer.

When she was young and tuned up, she might have gotten 14 or 15 miles per gallon. Now, with a leaky intake manifold, some faulty fuel injectors and other assorted motor maladies, it was getting less than 5 miles on 128 ounces of super unleaded.

I was one of those guys who could greatly increase my fuel efficiency by trading in the old pickup. I bought Ol' Gray used in 1993 for $5,500. Her book value appeared to be about $525. The Cash for Clunkers trade in value was $4,500. My rancher math told me to get her into town quick.

That is if she'd make it. I filled the oil and antifreeze, kicked the tires and added enough gas to get to the dealer. I cleaned 16 years worth of stuff I'd collected out from under the seat.

The brake light's been on for a year or two, but the brakes still would bring it to a stop eventually. I checked the turn signals. I had a functioning left signal, but nothing for the right. I considered the journey. At the end of the gravel road, I had to make a left turn onto the highway, hang with that for 40-some miles, drift onto the exit, then make three left-hand turns to the dealership. It seemed like destiny for me and my working left blinker.

When I got to the dealer, the temperature gauge read a little hot and I parked it close to the service shop, just in case. We made the deal and I took him out to get Ol' Gray. I told him I'd start it. She doesn't like to start when she's hot, but I'd perfected the ignition formula of cranking the motor over 17 times, waiting nine seconds, pumping three times, cranking six more, cuss a little then one more pump and two more cranks, and it almost always fires up if the battery is still hanging in there.

The Cash for Clunkers program requires that the clunkers have their motor disabled. I told the dealer that the mere drive to the car crusher might disable Ol' Gray's engine if they wanted to save the cost of adding the motor-seizing acid.

With that, I drove off the lot in a brand-new, four-door sedan that makes 35 miles per gallon. My good diesel pickup will have to take over all of Ol' Gray's duties, but more reliably and efficiently.

And when I head down the highway for anything that doesn't demand a horse trailer or an 8-foot cargo box, I'll be in my little car smiling all the way to the gas pumps.

Zerks in hiding
A lesson in lubrication
September 28, 2009

After walking around my broken-down hay mover all summer, I figured it probably was time to pull it out of the weeds and fix it up when I wanted to move hay the next day. I should've kicked the tires a little earlier in the year.

Last winter wasn't a good season to be a needed piece of ranch equipment in North Dakota. Our hay mover felt the ill effects of 10 feet of snowfall, daily winds and storm stranded hay bales needing some transport to hungry cows.

When I noticed one tire was flat after I had managed to pry the last load of bales out of the snowdrifts and perch them on the mover last winter, I decided to look the other way and run it home. Heck, it had seven other tires to shoulder the load. Bad idea.

My recent inspection showed the flat tire was fairly new. But after a couple miles running flat on the rim, it had aged quickly. Nothing $135 couldn't fix up with a replacement at the local co-op.

Then I noticed the square steel beam that carried the weight of the hay above that flat tire had cracked and broken in several kind of key areas. Nothing $500 couldn't fix in the welding shop.

Then the blacksmith noticed the shaft that carried the beam and pivoted above the four tires had no bearings, no bushings and very little shaft left to do its weight-bearing job. But they'd rebuilt those things before. Another $500 would fix it better than new.

I told him I didn't know there were any bearings there. "Yeah," he said, "and there's a grease zerk, too, but no one knows it's there."

Someone must know it's there, like the engineer who designed it. And a few real thorough managers who don't have to take stuff to town for major repairs. But us guys who drag broken, cracked, worn-out chunks of steel into the welding shop probably haven't found those random grease zerks hidden on implements.

Sure enough, I never had seen this little lubricational lookout. Hidden between two tires, the zerk was attached to a tube that ran a couple feet further in to the shaft and bearings.

I remember wondering about that shaft needing grease, but I didn't see a zerk on the shaft itself and I never thought it'd be fed by a fitting hidden off a couple feet from there. It'd be like looking for the bathroom light switch out on your porch. And when you buy your equipment well used at an auction sale, you don't get an owner's manual outlining these intricate details.

My favorite story about greasing machinery came from a friend whose father had an old combine that he greased religiously. He'd crawl around, reach around and hit every zerk with numerous strokes from his handy pistol grip grease gun.

Some were under shields and out of sight, but he'd reach up, find the zerk and attach his gun.

Finally, for some reason, the machine had a breakdown that required a mechanic to strip down some of the shields and obstacles that had hidden some of the farmer's favorite grease fittings.

The farmer walked up to the stripped-down combine and a look of disgust came over him. All this time, what he thought was a grease zerk was the tip of a quarter-inch bolt.

For 20 years with religious regularity, he'd been greasing the tip of a bolt!

Shrouded in grease, I bet that little bolt looked just like new.

Guilty pleasures
A weak moment, a big payment   January 4, 2010

Most folks who know me know I'm not too concerned about what I drive or the age of the equipment I run. Sure it's nice to have something that's dependable, but I've learned to adapt to regular breakdowns.

Last winter, I had a weak moment in the middle of our daily winds and accumulated 10 feet of snow. Nearing a breakdown — the psychological kind — I called up an implement dealer and had him bring out a nearly new front-wheel-assist loader tractor.

I told myself I'd just try it out for awhile and return it. But I became addicted to not getting stuck and sitting in the comfort of its climate-controlled cab. I tried to put off the inevitable decision, but after a month or so, the dealership either needed the tractor back or needed a check for my down payment.

Just the down payment was six to seven times more than I'd spent on my first tractor, the 460 Farmall diesel. Of course, that tractor required an act of Congress and some divine intervention to start in the winter, so I guess you get what you pay for.

Interest free

One of the promotions that greased the skids on my purchasing decision was the limited-time offer of zero percent interest financing. I noticed after I bought the tractor that the limited time was extended, but I bit the bait to help the company bring in the needed month-end sales.

The zero interest has been a breeze, but the principal is a little tougher to muster. I'm trying to focus on the benefits of not being stuck, being comfortable in the cab when the wind is howling outside and having something dependable to feed the cattle, spray the weeds, make the hay and haul it in.

The boys like the tractor. They can come with me in the new tractor and be a lot safer and more comfortable than they could be in any of our other tractors. And that means my wife likes the tractor, too, if it helps reduce the kid population in our house for awhile.

Ledger losses

The cost of the outfit kind of hit me though when I went in to the accountant's office for a little pre-tax planning at the end of the year. We plugged in all the extra feed and diesel and trucking to get the cattle through last winter, plus the usual high expenses and the unusually low income for the year.

"You could take in a lot more income this year," he advised me. I told him that was a fine idea, and I asked if he had any good ideas on where a guy could find some of that extra ranch income. We didn't really come up with anything, but I'm going to make one more pass between the couch cushions to look for spare change.

The year 2009 was long on expenses and short on income. That nearly-new tractor probably didn't help the ledger out any and it's not nearly wore out enough to fit my broke-down rancher style. But with another couple feet of new snow to mess with, I'm willing to keep my style updated a little.

We'll just run a little harder and hope to catch up with the depreciation in 2010. Here's to the new year.

Warranty woes
The lost attribute of lasting   March 1, 2010

They just don't make 'em like they used to. It seems like I'm becoming more of an old codger making grumpy quotes like that every day, especially every day that something just a few years old quits working.

I've pretty much given up on DVD players. I think we've been through four of them since we started having kids. The last one only made it about two months. You can successfully train kids to not demolish the delicate little movie player, but as soon as we get one trained, we have another little destroyer in that prime 12- to 24-month-old range to take a whack at the latest digital disc investment.

I'm either going to see if I can get a good deal on a dozen of them and dole them out every few months after kid-induced crashes or quit buying them altogether until the youngest enters kindergarten and the player has some chance of survival.

But I guess you can't expect much for $24.99. I get a lot more excited about the big-ticket items that go to heck early in their life.

Timed obsolescence

Warranties from manufacturers give us a little hope that things might last. My diesel pickup had a seven-year, 70,000 mile warranty. I'm too old to cruise Main Street, so the pickup odometer rolled over pretty slowly as I saved it for heavy hauling and bigger jobs.

At the end of seven years, it had 69,000 miles on it. Six months later, it starts running rough and they tell me it needs a new injection pump, a little $2,000 repair that was just hanging on while the warranty lapsed.

The pickup cost plenty when it was bought, but now it's higher yet. $40,000 to replace the pickup, $2,000 to replace the pump — we picked the pump. You'd kind of think a $40,000 machine would at least make 100,000 miles before any major repairs.

In hindsight, I kind of remember the motor having a hiccup before the warranty ran out. I guess I should have hustled it in to the dealer instead of turning the radio up.

Cold storage

The fanciest fridge I ever had breathed its last cool breath at seven years of age, just two years past its warranty when its compressor died.

The ice maker quit a month ago. Then I opened the freezer door for some ice cream and found pure cream, no ice to it at all. The repairman said for the cost of a compressor we'd be better off replacing the fridge.

I'm sure the old one will make a nice thousand-dollar shelf in the shop. I can keep grease cartridges in the condiment shelves and bolts in the vegetable crisper drawer.

So, for now, we're without a refrigerator in the house. We moved everything out of the new fridge and into the "old fridge" in the garage. Our old fridge is the 1975 model that we bought for $75 at a yard sale that probably cost $75 a month in electricity. But at least it works and its 35 years old.

That fridge is a Montgomery Ward, the retailer that closed its department stores in 2001. My parents had a fridge made by International Harvester — the same folks who built tractors — that still was going strong after 40 years when they unplugged it.

You can't get a fridge from either of those outfits anymore. I suppose their appliances lasted so long they never got any repeat sales. That's the harsh business reality of making things that last forever.

But I know at least one guy drinking a warm glass of ice cream who'd give them his business if they were still around. No warranty required.

Loose rocks
And fragile windows
April 12, 2010

"People in glass houses shouldn't throw stones" is the old adage warning folks who are vulnerable not to attack others.

I'd add that ranchers in glass tractors shouldn't pull hay trailers on stony roads. That's more practical advice. It doesn't have anything to do with moral vulnerability and reciprocity, just the fact that replacing windows in tractors is danged expensive.

I give readers this advice having done the hard on-road research. And I write this column in the hope that it'll help pay for part of replacing the back window of my new tractor.

Hay-hauling hazards

It all happened when I got a good deal on some nice hay from a relative. Problem was the hay was 20 miles away. The twine was a little rotten and it was an odd number of bales, so I opted to load it and haul it myself rather than subject a hired semi-truck and trailer to the task.

The trips started out well. Sit in comfort in a nice, tight tractor cab, tune in the radio, sip a little coffee and motor down the road 24.3 miles an hour with my 12 bales on the trailer.

The rear-view mirrors on the new tractor even give me pretty good visibility if someone would happen to get behind me and want to travel a little faster than 24.3 miles an hour. It wasn't an issue though. In my low-traffic locale, I could go the 40 miles round trip without slowing down a single motorist.

On the third trip though, I was cruising for home and — BANG! — I came under attack from behind. It was as loud or louder than a gun shot, and, not having lived in Juarez, Mexico, or the south side of Chicago, I'm not used to that sound while I'm driving.

If I'd been hauling hay in Juarez or Chicago, I'd have dropped to the floor of the cab, but as it was, I figured I wasn't under fire and I'd best keep my hands on the wheel and keep the outfit on the road.

Instant ventilation

The back window shattered into a million pieces. We usually complain that there's not enough gravel on our sandy township roads, so it was quite a surprise that my hay mover tire found a piece of gravel to fire at my window.

It could have been worse. At least the weather was nice, so the fresh spring air felt kind of good. All I could think about, though, as the dust swirled around me in my airy cab was how much money that little rock had just cost me.

It'll probably cost me just a dollar or two less than my high insurance deductible. It may make me want to see how long I can get by with the cloudy clear plastic and duct tape that I stretched over the back of the cab when I got home.

It does add a little cost to the hay I was hauling that day. I suppose another $50 a bale to pay for the broken window.

That's one expense Dad never had to cough up on his no-cab, two-cylinder John Deere. No one said progress and modernization would be cheap.

But I am glad I live a neighborhood where the threat was a rock and not a bullet.

Dragging chain
And a lot of big cable
December 6, 2010

I'm really getting into the Christmas season. Yesterday, I trudged through the snow with a log chain around my neck, just like Jacob Marley in the Charles Dickens classic, "A Christmas Carol."

I wasn't really trying to be the ghost of Christmas Past, I just needed to get some chain hooked up to a tractor to try and pull it out of axle-deep mud and water that my associate and the ghost of Christmas Present thought was frozen. It wasn't. It was quite a predicament.

All four tires were sunk up to the hubs. The temperature was heading toward 20 below zero that night, and as bad as things were, it'd be even worse if that tractor froze into the hole it made for itself.

None of the horsepower I had could budge it. Pulling with my front-wheel-assist gave us a few inches of hope, which just encouraged us to spin it down deeper.

I dug out Dad's triple block and tackle, the pride of the ranch for getting stuck things unstuck. It was half-buried in the sand, and Father Time had not done it any favors.

This was heavier than Marley's chain as we drug the six cables, pulleys and hooks into position. Dad once pulled a big, four-wheel-drive tractor out of the manure pile with our block and tackle. He pulled it out with an A John Deere and didn't even give it full throttle.

I was ready to relive the glory of physics when we hooked it up to our latest mud-bound machine. I don't know the exact formula, but I know six pulleys in a block and tackle gives you exponentially more power than you'd have on a straight out pull.

It didn't really matter because the rusted steel cable in our block and tackle was pretty rotten and broke about as quick as we hooked up to it. Drag it back out of the way, Marley.

We needed a big, long cable. We should be able to locate one. North Dakota is in the midst of one of the hottest oil plays in North America. No drilling here in my county, of course, but plenty of hard, high-paying work for those who'll travel west a ways.

And, when you've got oil activity in an area, ranches have a chance to recycle discarded drill stem pipe, sucker rods and big steel cables. I located 100 feet of that big steel cable. I don't know what it weighed, but dragging that into position was 10 times the burden drug by the ghost of Christmas Past.

Thanks to the goodness of a neighbor with a four-wheel-drive tractor, eight good tires, a couple hundred horsepower and 100 feet of good, strong cable, we got my tractor jerked out of its hole.

Let's quote a little of Dicken's ghost of Jacob Marley. "I wear the chain (cable) I forged in life! I made it (found it in the oil patch) link by link and yard by yard! I girded it on (to my tractor) of my own free will and by my own free will (and a neighbor's really big tractor), I wore it (and got my tractor unstuck)!

That's a little Taylor Ranch version of "A Christmas Carol." Be careful where you drive, and you'll be visited by more cheerful Ghosts of Christmases Yet to Come.

In the words of Tiny Tim Cratchit, "God bless us, every one!"

Giving season
And the occasional taking   January 3, 2011

The holidays are a time to give. I try to reinforce that when I give my kids money in the store, and, before their eyes get too bright and they head for the toy aisle, I tell them to put it in the Salvation Army kettle for people who need it more than we do at Christmas.

It's a good time of year to remember your favorite benevolent causes, give to your church, help serve a free community dinner, think of others and put our own selfish

143

tendencies aside.

It's a fight to remember the higher meaning of the season and the generosity it deserves in the onslaught of crass consumerism that encourages us to want things we don't need to impress people we don't know.

When my wife and I are reading bedtime stories to our children, we're always proud when they pick "Wilbur's Christmas Gift" written by our friend, Rodney Nelson, for us to read. The last page has Wilbur reminiscing about his mother's advice that the greatest gifts he'd ever get were those he'd give away.

There's a lot of agreement on the servant leader philosophy that when you serve others you do serve yourself. It makes us feel good to help others, give of ourselves, teach something to another, extend a little generosity.

I was in such a giving mood this year, I gave even more than I planned.

Hijacked hitch

Two days before Christmas, we left our pickup at a ranch supply store in the "big city," population 36,000 or so. We dropped it there in the morning, so they could hook their gooseneck flatbed to it and load some merchandise on it for me to take home later that day.

Five hours of broad daylight later, I went to retrieve the pickup and trailer, did a walk-around to check the tires and lights and such, and there my receiver hitch was — gone!

Now having your receiver hitch stolen isn't like having someone lift your wallet, take your wedding ring from your nightstand or rustle your cattle, but it really chapped me. It was one of the good hitches, — 4-inch drop, rated for 10,000 pounds of towing, with one of the finest 2 5/16-inch balls you'd ever find.

I'd had that hitch since before I was married, so that when I got hitched, I'd have a hitch to hook to. I felt empty without that hitch riding in its 2-inch steel box channel where it'd been for the last eight years.

Some would say it was my turn. Receiver hitches may be the No. 1-rated item of petty theft in pickup and trailer country. It's probably odd for a guy to keep one for eight years if he never took the precaution of pulling the hitch and throwing it under his seat when it wasn't in use.

I figured since I never took it out it'd be safe. I thought the gravel, rust and corrosion would have it sealed in tight enough to deter the casual, passing thief. Especially one without a hammer and a can of WD-40. I was wrong.

To make the best of the situation I've decided to consider the cowardly Dec. 23 receiver hitch heist an unplanned Christmas gift from me to someone I didn't even know.

So Merry Christmas you scoundrel. Enjoy the hitch or the money you got for it.

I guess I'll be removing the next hitch when I'm not using it and throwing it in the cab of the pickup.

Of course, the doors won't be locked and the keys probably will be in the ignition, in case you need a pickup to go with the hitch.

Chapter 5

Community
Cowboy

The phone tree
A little pruning to keep our identity   September 5, 2005

I've always been proud of my affiliation with the "701 Club."

It's not what you might think. It's not one better than Pat Robertson's "700 Club" of the Christian Broadcasting Network. It's not a batting average fraternity of elite baseball sluggers. It's not a fund-raising scheme to get 701 folks to each chip in $701 toward my retirement. You don't have to buy anything to belong. All you need is the luck of location.

A college friend of mine who left the state told me about his idea for the 701 Club. He figured anyone who lives or used to live in the 701 area code would be granted membership, complete with all rights and privileges.

He hadn't thought out the whole plan, but, at a minimum, it would be a fraternity of familiarity.

We could put that kind of club together because North Dakota is just one big, spread-out community with a single area code, 701.

We're one of only a handful of states united by single set of three digits. Montana, South Dakota, Alaska, Delaware, Hawaii, Idaho, Maine, New Hampshire, New Mexico, Rhode Island, Vermont, West Virginia and Wyoming round out this elite group. Manitoba, Saskatchewan and the Maritime provinces get the job done with one area code each in Canada.

More numbers

But our 701 Club could be sunk before we even get it started. I read that North Dakota may run out of area code 701 phone numbers by the spring of 2012. Our population isn't growing so much, but our use of phone numbers sure is.

Fax lines, second phone lines, data lines, and cell phones are gobbling up our 701 digit combos.

Another area code would really throw a kink in our 701 Club. A new area code could be assigned a certain geographical area of the state and everyone there would get the new area code.

Talk about driving a wedge in the ol' statewide team spirit. There's a little east river/west river division in the state because of the Missouri River and Mountain Standard Time, but it's pretty minor compared to lopping off the Red River Valley and giving all our former brethren a new phone number.

An even more diabolical plan would be what they call an "overlay." Every new number assigned in the state would get a new area code and the whole state could be dialing 10 digits to talk to their friends across the street.

There'd be division and suspicion in every corner of the state. A new family would move into the neighborhood, and longtime residents would wonder if they're one of those new area coders who have forced 10-digit dialing in the old hometown.

Now, I'm all for growing our population, and if that means getting a new area code, so be it. But if we have to get a new area code just to satisfy our phone number gluttony, we ought to start conserving.

I've even made a move toward conservation. We got high-speed Internet out on the ranch, so I dropped the second phone line we had for Internet dial-up.

I'm sure there're a lot of fax machines out there that have become dust catchers. I know some folks who've dropped their land line and just use their cell phone number. Parents might tighten the belt and drop that cell phone for their kids. Drop a line here, save a number there, pretty soon we'll be running a nice tight ship and the 701 Club will be intact.

Who knows? We might even catch up to Wyoming. They're not expected to lose their single area code status until 2022. No matter what, I guess we'll all be exercising our dialing digits someday.

Promoted to protégé
Climbing the lutefisk ladder
November 14, 2005

Like most really big events in one's life, it happened on a seemingly average day. The phone rang. I picked it up and said hello. "Ryan, it's Ernie. Winston can't make the lutefisk dinner. Can you fill in for him and help cook the lutefisk?"

I just about dropped the phone in shock and excitement. I'd been a table waiter at the Zion Lutheran lutefisk supper for years, but I never thought I'd rise to the rank of lutefisk boiling protégé at the tender age of 35.

Ernie, head lutefisk chef, said he thought it was time to start bringing in the younger generation to share in the secrets of cooking the fine and fishy fare. A good plan of succession is just as important in Lutheran fund-raising as it is in Fortune 500 companies. You gotta be thinking about the future and training for tomorrow.

I liked waiting tables for the lutefisk feed — mingling with the hungry public, witnessing firsthand the satisfaction that can come only from a piece of lye-soaked cod brought to a boil and smothered in butter.

Now I was going to see the inner workings of the lutefisk supper. I'd be interning back in the boiler room, the church kitchen. That's where the real machinery of the event puts it all together, from the fish to the meatballs and potatoes, and right down to the freshly cleaned dishes.

"Boiler room" isn't just a catchy metaphor. Everything in that kitchen either was boiling or steaming. At one point, stripped down to my T-shirt and mopping the sweat from my brow, I was wondering if I really had received a promotion.

It must be a step up, though, because a lot of the seniority among the Zion Lutheran men was back there in the kitchen.

Lutefisk is a four-man crew, and I definitely was the neophyte. Ernie and Don each had 40 years under their belt. That seemed like a long time until Clifford the coffeemaker told me he'd been working the supper since 1955. That's a lot of coffee.

They didn't hand me a lot of responsibility on my maiden voyage. I shuffled the lutefisk up to the copper kettles, dunked the fish into their boiling bath, took out the empty containers, drew off a little excess water and anything else I could do to make myself handy.

I spent a little time watching the master practice his craft. Ernie tested the fish with a long, tined fork, standing over the kettles like King Neptune wielding his trident. If the lutefisk grabbed hold of the fork, he kept it boiling, if it slid off smooth and easy, we'd pull it out and serve it up to the hungry masses.

I checked the cooking times with my stopwatch. I thought maybe I could reduce the job to something technical and standardized, kind of like playing the piano with sheet music instead of orchestrating by ear.

The variance told me this was not something that could be plugged into the fast-food assembly line model for some push-button teenager to operate. Lutefisk preparation was a real art, not some paint-by-numbers kind of deal.

The quality was proven by consumption. We served close to 500 people, about the same as last year, but they bellied up to the table and put down 550 pounds of lutefisk, 50 pounds more than a year ago. Many said it was the best they'd had.

Skeptics and non-lutefiskers claim there's no difference between good lutefisk and bad lutefisk. But the real codfish connoisseurs who visited our church the evening before Halloween knew we served only treats, no tricks.

A seasoned crew of chefs, a discriminating fork and one greenhorn pulled it off for another harvest of lutefisk lovers.

In the cards
New news from old friends   January 9, 2006

We made quite a haul on the Christmas cards, photos and letters this year. You'd think we sent one out every year ourselves to be rewarded with such a volume of return correspondence.

These little bits of paper are worth their weight in gold as far as I'm concerned. It's the one time of year where we decide we aren't too busy to bring our friendships back up to date.

When we get a photo card, we grab the Scotch tape and fix it to our friendship wall. We'll keep that wall intact with the holiday greetings clear out to Valentine's Day, or until our toddler son gets a hold of them with his sticky paws — whichever comes first.

The traditional artistic cards and the modern-era, computer-generated letters stay in a basket close to the friendship wall for about the same time span.

We read them all, admire the photos and appreciate the gesture made by each and every greeting, but I have devised an informal three-tiered system of scoring our incoming greetings as they arrive.

Precious metals

Since everyone's a winner who's thoughtful enough to send us a card, I use tiers akin to the Olympic medals of gold, silver and bronze.

An envelope with a card and a signature, or a photo of the kids with names and ages printed on the side in block lettering are mentally cataloged as bronze winners. They're great to get, and they're contenders, but there are higher levels.

Moving into the silver medal round takes a little more effort.

Silver-medal photo greetings have to include the parents. They don't have to print their ages alongside in the standard block lettering, but I want to see how my friends have aged as much, or more, as how their children have grown.

Family pets are a neutral addition to the photo card. Fido and Felix won't score you any higher or any lower on my tally card. However, including a Christmas letter supposedly written by the family pet may take you back down to bronze.

Christmas letters written by human members of the family are a must to earn silver status, especially if you're not including a photo of any kind.

Some folks call these year-end family newsletters the "brag and gag." I don't care so much if the writers are humble or arrogant; it's still interesting to hear what my friends are doing in their lives.

I can even stand a few pretentious paragraphs about the brilliant, athletic, above-average children in their house. I can tolerate the month-by-month memo that assures the recipient reader will not miss out on any of the outstanding fortunes that befell the greeting family throughout the year.

The gold-member winners have to go a little retro, though. They can still use the family photo or the "we're all so outstanding" newsletter, but they have to break out the good, old-fashioned ink pen and handwrite a few sentences to achieve gold-medal status.

There are lower categories in my system — zinc and aluminum. And, in honesty, my family has been mired in the less-than-precious metal designations. We've been aluminum for two years running with no real effort at sending out holiday greetings.

This year, we moved up to zinc with great intentions. We have the letter. We have the photo. We just haven't hit the mailboxes with them yet. As long as it's been this long, I could just as well pick up the pen and go for the gold.

Cowboy cameo
There's no business like show business   February 20, 2006

I finally got my big break into the world of show business.

No, I didn't get summoned to Hollywood to star in the latest blockbuster movie, and I didn't get a casting call from the producers of the newest Broadway show. I did, however, get a small role in a local community theater production.

I made it through the tryouts without even trying out. Of course, trying out for community theater is kind of like trying out for the basketball team in one of our 50 or 100 student Class B high schools. Just show some interest, and they'll find a place on the team, or at least on the bench, for you.

My place on the acting team for a local production of "Will Rogers Follies" was to come off the bench and play the part of "the roper" in the first scene of the second act. Since my character didn't even have a name, you can guess he didn't have a lot of dialogue either.

You could call it a cameo appearance since I had only two scripted lines. By definition, a cameo is a "brief, but dramatic appearance of a prominent actor in a single scene."

It was darn sure brief, and I did a series of Will Rogers' favorite rope tricks including the Texas Skip and a 45-foot giant Wedding Ring, so it probably was plenty dramatic. The other actors who had my rope whizzing a few inches away from their face might have thought it was a little too dramatic.

We'll just have to overlook the prominent actor part, but I like referring to "the roper" role as a cameo. It sounds a little more Hollywood.

Back on stage

It was nice to be back in the thespian limelight. I haven't graced the theatrical stage since my breakout role as Cayo Claiborne in our high school play, "West of Pecos."

Now, a mere 19 years later, I'm 50 miles up the road in Bottineau, N.D., doing community theater. My acting career is on a rocket to stardom.

Stars do shine in towns like Bottineau though. Pulling off a pretty good community theater production of a Broadway musical in a town of 2,300 people is no small feat. When it all comes together, you can't help but smile and clap and swell with small town pride.

My contribution to the show's success was the smallest of the many who were involved. I attended two of the 40 rehearsals and spun rope for five or 10 minutes of the two hours of stage time.

The actors ranged from grade school children to local teachers, lawyers and hair stylists. Whole families took part in the production, and at least a few young people in the area have learned to confront their nerves and perform in front of an audience.

Costumes, lighting, directing, choreographing — every skill they needed was in the community. Even "the roper" lived within 50 miles.

The musical had nice-sized crowds at each of its four performances. "Will Rogers Follies" was an entertaining look at a remarkable man's life, and if anyone stayed home to watch a couple hours of bad television, they made a poor choice.

I wonder what kind of show they'll do next year. Odds are there won't be a roper role, but I'll be glad to do my part as a ticket-buying member of the audience. Live and local, everyone in the market for good entertainment really ought to.

Super, mega, giganza shopping
Something lost in the search for low prices   October 16, 2006

One of the big, new, super-duper, everything-imaginable-all-under-one-roof stores opened in the "city" 60 miles from our ranch this summer.

I told myself I'd never set foot in there. I'd never support their overpowering presence that sucked people out of the small towns and crushed the local independent businesses. I'd scowl as I drove by their storefront on the highway.

But, like Adam and the apple, I had to take a bite.

Super shopper

In search of diapers for our two wee lads one day, I swung the car off the highway and found a parking spot next to the big W. It was the middle of the day, but the parking lot was nearly full.

I walked through the doors into a cavernous structure housing 200,000 square feet of everything under the sun, but there was hardly a window in there to let the sun shine in. I grabbed my cart with the rest of the quiet, expressionless people who all came in search of more stuff and lower prices.

I wandered around wishing for a road map that would tell me which cart highway would take me right to the diapers. Of course, while I was searching, I found some other things to put in the cart that I didn't even know I needed. I think it's by design to force your customers to wander.

I found the diapers and the price wasn't much less than other stores I've been in that were smaller and more personable. From the diaper section, I headed for the grocery aisles to pick up some grub.

Mystery food

I never considered myself a real brand-loyal shopper. I don't mind going generic or picking up the store brand, but there are certain items where I look for the brand-name label.

There were plenty of brands in the super cave, but I'd never heard of a lot of them. I only can imagine the makers of those brands must have swung a heck of a deal with the vice president of cheap procurement and he put them into global distribution to far-flung places like North Dakota where consumers ask, "huh, what's this?"

There's a good North Dakota meat company making an all-beef hot dog that contributes some of its proceeds to the North Dakota Cowboy Hall of Fame. I've watched them make those hot dogs and I have no trouble eating them. I didn't see any Cowboy Hall of Fame hot dogs in the mega meat case.

North Dakota grows a bunch of wheat and has its own flour mill making Dakota Maid flour. The mill's only a couple hundred miles from the store, but there wasn't a single bag of Dakota Maid in the baking aisle.

I was most amused, though, when I went to get some sugar for the ranch pantry. I'd never heard of the sugar brand they had, but it proudly proclaimed "100 percent Pure Cane, contains NO beet sugar."

I don't know if the vice president of cheap procurement did much research on the North Dakota market, but we don't grow a lot of sugar cane this far north. We do grow a lot of sugar beets, and a lot of us like to buy the farmer co-op brand of beet sugar.

I'd had enough of the super shopping experience. I headed out the door to go find my Cowboy Hall of Fame hot dogs, Dakota Maid flour and 100 percent beet sugar.

I needed some sun and I realized there's more to shopping than low prices.

Nice and neighborly
Sometimes it's the little things

We don't have a lot of neighbors in our neighborhood. I guess it's the curse of poor soil and the difficulty of making a living here that makes us few and far between.

When you don't have many neighbors, though, you like to get along with the few you do have.

Good neighbors can make life a lot more enjoyable out in the hinterlands. They come in handy to drink coffee with and help work cattle, and it's hard to pull yourself out when you're stuck bad.

I recently heard a radio advertisement for a towing service that would go out in the country to pull your tractor out for you on the farm. In this age of bigger and bigger farms, it's a sad day when you realize you've bought out so many of your neighbors that you have to call a towing service in town to come yank you out of the mud or snow.

Like they say, I'd rather have my neighbors than my neighbors' land.

Ditch duty

Fall in North Dakota is ditch-mowing time. If you've got township or county roads across your land, it's your duty to mow the grass along the edge to help keep the snow from drifting them shut in the winter.

It's also nice to have the ditches mowed so you can see the deer as they jump out and plow in to the side of your vehicle.

Dad always mowed the ditches with a B John Deere and a No. 5 mower. He'd mow the three miles up to the mailbox and back even though it wasn't all our land. I think the neighbors appreciated the gesture.

This year, my neighbor got a new disc mower and he mowed just about every ditch I was supposed to mow. It was sure nice to drive out of the yard one day and see he'd already mowed my ditches ahead of the commissioner's deadline.

That's how it should work. Without even being asked, we help each other out, and we'd never think of charging anything.

I did hear of a couple neighboring landowners in the area who had gotten in a squabble over a land purchase or leasing and one mowed the other's ditches as the fall deadline neared and sent him a bill for $100 a mile. I didn't hear if it ever got paid.

We could all use a favor once in a while, and the favor usually does get returned.

Stray cows

Fall is also the time when we bring in the roaming cattle herds and get a handle on the number of calves we have to sell and the number of cows we have to feed through the winter.

I've had three of my neighbor's cows in with mine all summer. I tried to get them out a couple times but they were too ornery and I didn't want to take the time to put the whole herd in the corral to sort them off. Grass was tight, but I figured I'd catch them in the fall.

Some days, I'd look at those three extra cows I was grazing and feel a little sore about it. Then my bulls and the neighbor's bulls got into a scrap, took down some fence, and pretty soon I had 10 cows and calves over in my neighbor's pasture.

He said not to worry about it, we'd sort them off in a couple weeks when they brought the herd in.

Someone said good fences make good neighbors, but, when the fences go down, good neighbors still are good neighbors.

Queen for a year
A special person her whole life through   December 11, 2006

Every once in awhile, good things happen to good people, and when they do you can't help but feel good yourself.

That was the case when I heard that Miss Rodeo North Dakota, Ashley Andrews of Bowman, N.D., was crowned Miss Rodeo America at the National Finals Rodeo in Las Vegas. I think every North Dakotan's chest swelled up with pride.

It's not often that prairie folks end up at the top of the list in the pageant business. It seems like there's always someone from a more populated state with a little more clout that takes the titles. Even in rodeo, it's only happened twice now.

I can't help but feel a little connected to the new first lady of professional rodeo. I was one of the judges several years ago when she was crowned Miss High School Rodeo North Dakota.

I'm not quite sure how a fella like me got asked to be a judge in a rodeo queen pageant, but I was there and one thing I knew for sure was that the rancher's daughter from Bowman, N.D., we crowned that day was going to go far in life. I just didn't know how far.

So now that I helped judge the pageant that crowned the young gal who went on to be Miss Rodeo America, I think I'll retire from the queen judging business while I'm at the top of my game.

Genuine determination

I ended up getting to know Miss Rodeo pretty well since then. North Dakota is a pretty small state, people wise and even though her family's ranch is 300 miles from ours they feel like neighbors.

Her folks are ranchers. The real kind. Not the kind who are just enjoying a rural address while they make their money in town or the kind looking for a tax deductible way to spend some family fortune. No, they depend on their calf check like the rest of us.

I always liked the idea that rodeo was a professional sport with its roots in the business of ranching. Granted, not many of the athletes who make it to the National Finals Rodeo can stay home enough to still be real ranchers, but some start out as ranchers and some retire from the sport as ranchers.

I like the idea that our Miss Rodeo America knows what it's like to have chores that need doing on the ranch. Not every queen has a pair of insulated overalls in her wardrobe. It's a nice touch.

I'm sure her upbringing helped her win the personality contest in the pageant. Her education and her intelligence helped her win the speech contest and the written test. But it was her determination that helped her win a contest that wasn't even a part of the pageant.

Earlier this year, our Miss Rodeo America faced a contest more daunting than anything in a scholarship pageant. The doctors told her she had Hodgkin's Lymphoma, a cancer of the lymphatic system.

Now, I can't put myself in her shoes, but I can only imagine that when you're getting ready to compete for a national title as a big-haired rodeo queen, getting diagnosed with cancer and learning about the months of cancer treatments ahead, that would be pretty hard news to accept.

But she took it in stride, she blossomed in her faith, and now her cancer is in remission and she's Miss Rodeo America. It couldn't have happened to a nicer person.

Congratulations, Ashley.

Everything you need
And a few things you just want
June 25, 2007

Some people like shopping malls. Others get their pleasure in the urban boutique districts of our big cities. Not me though. I'm happiest simply walking the aisles of most any farm supply store.

It's prime purchasing time for me and my farm supply store habit. Fencing, spraying, haying, working cattle. Seems like everything I do creates a little shopping list of pieces and parts that I need to complete the task.

I don't get to town a lot, but when I do, I'm ready to shop. I'm always amazed at how much neat, useful stuff you can find in these places. They have stuff I didn't even realize I needed until I saw it on their shelf.

I run a high risk of straying from the confines of my shopping list when I go to these stores. It doesn't take long, and I've filled my cart with items off the list.

Sometimes I'm just taking inventory off their shelves to build up the inventory on my shelves. I may not use those bolts and fasteners for a year or two or ever, but it makes me feel good to know I've got them on hand when I need them.

There're projects I never even thought about tackling until I saw all the handy tools and gadgets made to get the job done. My imagination runs wild and my ambition overflows when projects are strictly in the shopping cart stage.

I invent projects right there in the store and start collecting the things I need for the project as I go. For some reason, the projects never are quite as satisfying in reality as they are when I'm imagining them in the store aisles.

The softer side

I suppose folks can tell by the way I look that I do most of my clothes shopping at farm supply stores. It's a fine place to outfit your wardrobe as long as you like denim and reinforced-wear points.

I often gauge my lifestyle by the rate of my blue jean purchases at the farm supply store. If I buy a new pair of jeans and put them right on when I get home to go do some greasy, dirty task, I've entered the realm of truly hard workers.

A person is the real deal when it comes to hard work if they don't have enough soft work to break in the new blue jeans before they hit the field.

As it is, I still have enough town tasks, church attendance and white-collar work to wash the blue from my jeans before they're graduated to the work drawer. Sometimes the cycle is a little faster and I feel guilty putting on my "good" jeans for work to replace the torn, patched and shredded ones I've tossed aside.

Most farm supply stores have a good selection of toy tractors for the youngsters, a few food provisions for the kitchen and a rack of greeting cards so you can wish your mother a happy birthday.

They're pretty much a one-stop-shop. The downside is that last stop at the cash register before they let you exit with your cart full of ambitions.

The only thing you can't get in bulk at the farm store is money. For that, you have to go down the street to the bank. And that's not near as fun as the farm store.

When the going gets tough
People get helpful   March 30, 2009

My home state is in the national news this week. Nope, it's not the nation's cold spot, it's the nation's flooding spot.

And it's not just the usual river, the Red, that defies good sense by flowing north into colder, icier climates. Rivers and creeks all over the state are flooding cities, farms and homes. Lots of snow, a cold winter and a sudden melt has made a lot of water flow in very little time.

Our ranch is far from a river and sandy enough to soak up lots of melting snow, but every other year, I head to Bismarck, N.D., for four months of part-time public service as a state senator.

Bismarck is a Missouri River town. It doesn't cause much concern usually with a major dam upstream that keeps the flow under control.

This spring brought unusual concern. A huge ice jam formed just south of the capital city and the river started backing up.

Then another smaller ice jam formed to the north of town. That was a good thing, but it put the city in the precarious position of having an ice jam to the south that would be there quite a while and an ice jam to the north that, if it broke, would push all kinds of water right into the cities and housing developments of Bismarck and Mandan.

A retired couple that heads south for the winter is kind enough to rent their home to my family for the few months I hang my hat at the Capitol. Guess where it's at. Yup, right on the river, between those two ice jams.

This week, we were kept a close eye on the backyard river. It kept on rising. Soon, the city was telling us to prepare for a flood. Everyone went to work to fill and distribute a million sandbags.

My Bismarck neighbors and I got a couple loads of sandbags for a small dike around the first level walk-in on our landlord's split level home.

In the scope of flood fighting, it was a small project to build a little dike and start moving things up off the first level of the house. But it gave this dry land cowboy a little look into a community's effort to hold back a river.

It did my heart good to see volunteers walking toward the civic center in Bismarck with shovels in hand to help fill sandbags as we drove up. When we drove inside, hundreds of people, a lot of them teenagers and college students, were filling bags and then filling the pickups and trailers that were coming through. It was a snappy operation.

Kids are kids, and although the work was hard it looked like they were having fun. They offered to send people out to help us unload the bags and build the dike. Another fella with an empty pickup offered to haul another load if we needed.

The Missouri River is receding as the engineer's work to clear the ice jam seems to be working. But the old nemesis of eastern North Dakota, the Red River, is breaking a 100-year record for crest height and the residents of Fargo are working around the clock to save their city.

It's bringing out the best in people as they do everything that needs doing. A single cause focuses everyone as they put any differences aside and stand shoulder to shoulder to fight a flood. It's a place where thousands of heroes emerge.

As I write this, we don't know who will win the fight with the Red River. But I know it won't be lost for lack of effort.

Stand strong, Fargo.

Our sense of place
Summer celebrations make it shine
July 6, 2009

As I write this column, we're a day or two ahead of our Independence Day celebrations on the Fourth of July. My friends in Canada just finished their Canada Day activities. These are the high points of summer for a lot of folks in the little towns where this column is read.

Last week, I was at the induction ceremony for the North Dakota Cowboy Hall of Fame in Medora, N.D., to give the keynote address as the latest round of inductees was welcomed.

One of the points I made in that speech dealt with our "sense of place." I talked mostly of our sense of place here in North Dakota, but I'm sure other places and locales have that same sense.

"Sense of place" may sound like some funky, new age term, but us not-so-funky, old age kinds can understand what it is. Most of us who live in places that have it, though, often are too busy just doing what we do to realize we're helping create that sense. It usually takes someone from the outside to tell us how strong and identifiable our sense of place is.

Sense of place is what makes your spot in the world unique and different from any other place on the globe, different from any other gathering of people with the same strip malls and big box stores and a mobile work force that moves from one job to another, one house or apartment to another, one city to another.

A sense of place cannot be created overnight, or recreated by an ad agency. You can't make it up, or fake it, or simulate it and sell tickets to it like an amusement park. Our "sense of place" is built over generations of time by people like the cowboys, cowgirls, ranchers and others we've inducted into our state's Cowboy Hall of Fame.

It's built in every community when they take the initiative to put together that summer gathering of friends and neighbors. In my hometown, we're having an all-school reunion for a school that's been graduating students for 100 years. We're celebrating 50 continuous years of hosting a Fourth of July rodeo in the big arena that local ranchers built on the north edge of town.

Those seemingly little things build up our sense of place. When we embrace our history, tell our stories, keep up our old buildings, maintain our institutions and events, and recognize the heroes, the characters and even the crazy old codgers in our midst, we make our place different than those faceless places with the same stores that sell the same stuff, host the same big concerts and serve the same Happy Meals.

Folks who live where there's a sense of place wake up every morning feeling pretty well rooted. We step out of bed and head out the door to do the chores on the same ranches and farms that our ancestors homesteaded, bought or built generations before us.

Granted, everyone can't stay on the home place or take over the family business. But a few of us need to so our classmates who've moved on and pursued careers elsewhere have something to come home to when it's time for the school reunion.

And if you come across those people who helped organize the school reunion, put on the rodeo, lined up the parade entries, judged the seedless watermelon seed spitting contest or just stood on the street and welcomed our former residents back home, tell them thanks.

It's because of them that we have our sense of place and have not slipped into geographic anonymity.

Love that lutefisk!
Chairing the church supper   November 9, 2009

'Tis the season here in the land of immigrant Norwegians to partake in the annual lutefisk suppers.

Some would say the immigrant descendants eat the gelatinous lye-soaked codfish to remind themselves how much better off they are than their ancestors who left the old country and its lutefisk for a fresh start, and some fresh food, in America.

Lutefisk was the food of the poor people in Norway I've been told. Those who left Norway 100 years ago or more generally were pretty poor. Makes sense I guess. If they were rich, they'd have had no reason to leave. Our poor ancestors brought their food and their eating habits with them when they crossed the Atlantic.

Funny thing is this poor folk's fare costs upwards of $15 a plate these days. If it didn't cost so much, maybe people would eat it more than once a year. Or, maybe not.

I'll admit I like lutefisk. Not so much that I could eat it every week, but come fall,

I kind of crave the odiferous stuff.

I guess that's why I felt compelled to step up when the longstanding chairmen of our Lutheran men's lutefisk supper announced they were retiring from their duties. If no one took over the reins, the annual lutefisk supper would perish in our parish.

I found a couple of partners and we took on the job of chairing the supper to give the community its annual fish fix.

A new day

I used to think holding elected office was kind of challenging until I became a church supper chairman. Chairing our men's lutefisk supper is way harder.

Not knowing any better, we suggested some changes for the supper. We proposed a move to a modified buffet style of serving the supper. It was kind of like proposing national health care reform or a reduction in carbon emissions. It raised a lot of eyebrows.

But the members gave us a chance and said we could give it a try. We had to reconfigure the flow of the fish and fixin's from the kitchen to the masses, but we got a system figured out.

Various crews got all the preparations made ahead of the supper — cutting up the lutefisk, peeling the potatoes, making the meatballs. The women of the church took on the task of making most of the lefse and the apple pies for the supper.

Everyone took to their jobs with youthful enthusiasm, but the crews weren't necessarily youthful. The average age of our potato-peeling crew was 80.2 years old. No wonder they call them the greatest generation. We did have a 44-year-old join the crew later in the peeling session, so maybe there's hope for a younger generation to help take up the paring knife.

The day of the supper brought out an abundance of help though — both young and old. We had a forty-something protégé dunking the cod into the copper boilers under the tutelage of the master chef. We had the usual crews doing the usual fine job of washing dishes, making coffee, cutting up pies and boiling potatoes. We had an attentive group of waiters seeing to the needs of the tables, and some fine youngsters lending a hand to anyone who needed a little help with their plates. The new buffet line was a hit.

We had fathers and sons working together and men of the church from age 8 to 80 enjoying the fellowship and the fun of the effort. We raised some money for church projects, and we carried on a longstanding tradition involving the lowly lutefisk of our ancestors.

When the day was done we'd served some 420 people. Therein lies the main point — we served others. And serving others is good thing to do in a church, or anywhere for that matter. Even if it was lutefisk we were serving.

March madness
The small-town, donkey ball bracket

No one would ever accuse me of being much of a sports guy. I don't watch a lot of sports and I haven't played many organized sports, but I'm always game for unorganized sporting events.

I used to play a little hay mow barn basketball when I was younger, and what I lacked in talent, I partially made up for with height. Still I was at a severe disadvantage to guys who actually knew how to play the game.

This March, however, I discovered the equalizer that put me at par with real basketball players. Play the game on donkeys and you even things up a bit. It changes the dynamics of the game completely.

First-round pick

Most folks don't volunteer to play donkey basketball. You're drafted, coerced or shamed into playing the game for the benefit of a laudable local charity.

Local luminaries usually fill the roster of players. Like the song says, everybody's famous in a small town. As a local legislator, I was an easy target. I graced the court with the grocer, the mayor of a neighboring town, a representative of the local media and some good-hearted students.

The goal was to pack the stands from far and wide to raise money for our Dollars for Scholars chapter and fund student scholarships. We did. You couldn't have fit many more in the school gymnasium. Parking spots were at a premium all around the school.

It was go time for a little donkey b-ball. It was as close as you get to March Madness in a town of 574 people. We only had four teams, so there wasn't a lot of extensive bracketing as fans prognosticated on advancers to the championship round.

I played for the much feared "Ba Donka Donks." It was a riveting game against the "Honky Tonky Donkeys." After 15 minutes of play, the score was 2 to 0, with the Honky Tonkers leading. It wasn't a high-scoring match, but we took a lot of shots at the hoop to keep the crowd engaged.

With just seconds left on the clock, I galloped my cranky donkey up the zone — maybe it was trot — OK, it was slow but steady walk to the basket as I banked one in to tie the game.

The crowd went wild! Well, they did clap quite loudly and some leaned ahead in their seats. In the sudden death round, our team emerged victorious to go on to the championship round against "Eeyore's Delights," who'd beaten the "Beasts of Burden."

Advanced bracket

The championship game scored slightly higher than our defensive first round, which we won 4 to 2. The grocer canned a three-pointer, probably because it was easier than persuading the donkey to get any closer to the net. I made a couple of slow-motion layups atop my long-eared friend.

We tromped Eeyore's Delights and won glory, admiration and hometown bragging rights.

I'm not sure where my Ba Donka Donks go from here. As the Towner conference champs, I assume we're in a "sweet sixteen" of the donkey kind to get in some more tournament play.

I reckon I'll just wait for the call while I practice shooting hoops from the back of my kid's rocking horse.

The road to the four-legged final four takes determination — and stubbornness.

Going to court
With an auctioneer, not a judge
October 11, 2010

I was back in the courtroom again last week. No, not what you might think. No judge, jury, lawyers or witnesses. Just a bunch of uncomfortable ranchers and an auctioneer gathered to renew the leases on some pasture and hayland owned by the state.

The auction was held in our county courthouse in the old courtroom on the second floor. The courtroom is one of my favorite places in my little hometown with its 102 years of history; its old, dark wooden seats; high ceiling; and its painting of Themis, the goddess of justice, behind the judge's bench.

I can look on the back wall of the courtroom and find a framed composite of photographs taken of the first jury called to sit and hear cases in the new courthouse after it was built in 1908. My great-grandfather sat on that jury, and I usually look up at his picture and let him know his name still carries on in our county with a fifth generation making little law-abiding footprints on his ranch south of town.

His son, my grandfather, could have sat in the same seat I did to bid on the same piece of pasture I did that day. It was Section 36 in Gorman Township, the "school land" left in state ownership in every township in the state, along with Section 16, to help fund the education of the next generation out on the prairie.

I have the receipt my grandfather got in 1915. He rented the whole section for $72. The market is a little more now.

I like knowing that a part of the cost of education for our children comes from something as real and old fashioned as ranchers sitting in a courthouse writing checks to rent land for their cattle to graze. Not much different than they did in 1915.

Peaceful neighborhoods

The reason I said the courtroom was full of uncomfortable ranchers wasn't because of the hard, wooden seats. The lack of comfort comes from wondering if you'll get the pasture back you've come to depend on.

Auctions in general make most bidders kind of queasy. It's just heightened a little when it's about a quarter-section of grazing or haying land and not just a ball of used barbed wire at a farm auction.

A lot of the land had been rented by the same family for generations, so there's kind of a personal attachment to the parcels of property.

The minimum bids were based on the local market for similar land, so they weren't giving the land away. But still it's a free market and anyone can bid on the land for themselves, and as outfits rush to get bigger and run more cows and cover more land, there's bound to be more bidders.

Most of the tracts in our little courtroom auction didn't get run up to two or three times what they were worth to satisfy anyone's greed or growth. Brothers and cousins and neighbors left on good terms mostly. Renters maintained fair land for a fair price and the state can rest assured it'll be well cared for.

Ranchers in the neighborhoods of the school sections still will wave at each other when they meet on the gravel road, help each other out when it's time to work cattle and be there if someone gets sick or gets in a bind and needs a hand.

As I left the old courtroom, it was nice to know that, even today, a lot of folks still would rather have their neighbors than have their neighbors' land.

Water, water, everywhere
And problems go with the flow   June 6, 2011

A neighbor called me from his cell phone the other day, wondering if I could come pull his pickup out of the water and mud he'd driven in to. "Sure thing," I told him, "I'll be there as quick as I can."

I kidded him a little about his thinking he could drive through the newly formed rain-made lake where his pickup sat. But, after a wet fall, a heavy snow year, and a big spring rain, a person can get stuck most anywhere, including the graded roads that lead to town.

I went to help a friend work his calves in the opposite end of our county, and getting to his place was like running a maze. There were more roads closed because of water flowing across them than there were roads open. The chance to rope calves and eat the big meal at the end was plenty of incentive to complete the maze, though.

Likewise, there are no direct routes on the ranch for checking fence or checking cows unless you're riding horse. I've even had to turn the horse around when the mud has gotten past his hocks.

I knew I shouldn't have chastised my neighbor about getting stuck with his pickup in the pasture, because that very same day, I got stuck with the four-wheeler in our pasture.

When they say "all-terrain vehicle," they didn't mean all that terrain I attempted crossing. I didn't call anyone to pull me out though. I was soaked from the hips down from my attempt to get it out of the bog, and I kind of needed the cool-down time as I walked home for the tractor, water sloshing in my boots with each reflective step.

Water reflections

I decided one thing while I was walking home in a swarm of mosquitoes to get myself pulled out. I figured my problems with water were pretty darn minor in the big scope of things, here in North Dakota and elsewhere around the globe.

I might be getting stuck and pumping water from our little cellar, but my house doesn't have a ring dike of sandbags around it. I haven't had to haul everything out of the house and move machinery from the yard to higher ground because a river is rising to new highs.

My friends in Bismarck and Mandan have had to do just that because the Missouri River is showing its mightiness. In Minot, N.D., and nearby communities, the Mouse River is proving it's not as meek as its name might imply. Sure these rivers have dams on them, but they can only hold so much water, and then it's got to go.

My friends and relatives in Devils Lake, N.D., have watched water come in to their closed lake basin for 18 years gobbling up land and homes and roads. My cousin and his wife put on life jackets to jump in their old pickup and drive in to their newly created island home with water coming in the bottom of the pickup doors.

Every once in a while, Mother Nature steps in and reminds us who's in charge I guess. All around this state and others, folks will pull together to save as much of their property as they can while the waters rise.

Stay safe, flood fighters. This, too, will pass. Let's not let it take us with it.

Chapter 6
Going domestic

Pesky varmints
Squirrels, gophers and prairie dogs   November 1, 2004

Sometimes little critters can make for some big problems.

Just a couple of weeks ago, a local varmint in Bismarck, N.D., was credited with 4,000 residents losing their electricity for an hour or so. The utility spokesman said a certain squirrel squirreled his way into a substation and triggered the outage.

I didn't get any details on exactly what the squirrel did to take out the power — or if he lived to brag about the dastardly deed he did. I have this picture in my my mind of a rather charred squirrel being taken from the scene of the crime, leaving behind nothing but a little squirrel chalk line in the substation.

I did not doubt the ability of this little mammal to do such harm to the advances of modern mankind. I've seen similar critters do similar damage to some of my own technology.

Cold floors

When I built my little concrete-floored ranch abode, I thought it'd be nice to have a warm floor under my feet when I hopped out of bed in the morning. So I installed some electric heat cable in the sand before we poured the cement.

It was pretty nice. Turn up the thermostat and enjoy the toasty current as it coursed beneath my toes all winter long.

When last winter began, I noticed the floor in half my house seemed pretty cold.

Then I remembered seeing some gophers digging alongside my house the summer before. An electrician tested the continuity of the cable and confirmed my suspicions of gopher blight on my floor heat. He said he'd seen those little rascals chew through underground wires before.

So now I have to cold foot it 10 or 15 feet to the warm half of my house when I get up every winter morning.

The gopher damage to my electrical circuitry is pretty permanent. The folks in Bismarck should feel lucky that the squirrel short only cost them an hour off of the power grid.

I guess there's a chance we can do some high-tech search and rescue of my severed heat cable. If we can locate the chew spot, all we need to do is start busting concrete and make a splice. I think I'll buy a few rugs and tough it out for awhile.

Could be worse

As disgusted as I am with my gopher-cold floors and as inconvenienced as Bismarckians were by their squirrel-caused blackout, it could be worse.

I heard another recent story about yet another small varmint doing destruction in Santa Fe, N.M. Prairie dogs there were scattering the bones of the dead at one of the town's most historic and honored cemeteries.

I guess I'd rather be bothered with resetting my electric alarm clock in the blackout or getting a pair of fuzzy slippers to combat my cold floors, than having my ancestors exhumed by a bunch of prairie dogs.

The cemetery's caretaker isn't allowed to fire a rifle in the city and take out the prairie dogs Old West-style, even though it is Santa Fe.

He's tried stuffing dry ice down the holes and then plugging the holes with newspapers. I reckon they just threw on a sweater and pulled down their little prairie dog earlappers.

If I was him, I'd put a couple of electrically charged squirrels and gophers on the job, send them down the hole with a wire and watch the sparks fly.

Roughing it
Back to heating basics
October 31, 2005

Seems like a lot of people have had to go without power lately. Some of the folks down in hurricane country haven't had electricity in their homes and businesses for a long time.

We had our own little storm-related power outage here on the Taylor Ranch, but it was pretty minor in the world scheme of things.

An early snowstorm left a foot to a foot-and-a-half of heavy wet snow around here in early October.

On the bright side, it was good precipitation for the pastures and we needed the fall moisture. On the dim to dark side, the lights were out for nearly three days.

That snow was sticky. It could hang onto an electric high line wire like a fourth-generation trapeze artist. Then the wind started swinging those ice and snow laden wires and the sparks really flew. Breakers broke, poles snapped and meters quit metering all around the neighborhood.

My family and I were down in sunny Huron, S.D., for a speaking job and drove home to a cold, dark house the day after the storm.

We heat our house with electricity. I feel really smart about that choice when heating fuel and propane prices are skyrocketing. It's clean, convenient and affordable. It just needs one thing: electrical current.

Without any juice coming through the meter, I decided I needed something a little lower tech to heat the homestead, like a wood fire.

I scavenged around the ranch and rounded up a cast-iron box stove that would do the trick to cozy up the cabin. I had a steel chimney in the house going unused and, after a little work with a tin snips and some stovepipe, I was ready to start a controlled burn in our shack.

First, I had to get something to burn. My wife figured I could clean out my office and create enough fuel to get us through the week. Instead, I started up the chainsaw and headed for my collection of old, oak fence posts.

I knew the day would come when I'd need those broken-off posts I'd salvaged and piled up over the years. Burning those twisted, old, knotty posts that bent fencing staples their whole life was going to be real satisfying.

Burning the refuse of my fence-fixing chores must match the satisfaction of the mechanic who heats his shop with waste oil, or the corn farmer who saves the hassle of marketing his crop by running it through a corn furnace.

I got a nice jag of firewood out of my post pile. Luckily, I didn't run out of gas for my chainsaw since we need electricity to pump the gas out of the tank to fill it.

I was caveman proud when I got a fire going with the wood I cut in the stove I installed with the stovepipe I fit. I stepped outside and admired the smoke coming out of our chimney with pride.

I was feeling like the backwoods hero of the house when the smoke alarms began to wail and scream. There was an awful-smelling haze in the house, and I began to think that new stovepipe probably needs a little open air when you first fire them up. So we opened the doors and windows and let the cold wind reclaim our once cozy cabin.

I let the fire burn out, we piled on some extra covers and, somewhere under all those blankets, I think I heard my wife's muffled voice giving thanks for her somewhat self-sufficient husband but earnestly praying that the power would come back on soon.

O Christmas Tree
Bringing in the holiday forestry   December 26, 2005

In North Dakota, trees are pretty prized possessions. We don't have a lot to spare.

We need a pretty good reason to go out and sacrifice one of the few woody species tough enough to survive life on our grassy plain. Not even the Christmas tree tradition will send us out to the grove with an axe until we've really weighed the need.

Most years, my family has decided to let someone else, somewhere else, sacrifice their trees. Let 'em grow in conducive climates on fertile tree farms in places like Oregon and Michigan. We'd just drop a check at the local dealer and haul our tannenbaum in the trunk to the Taylor Ranch.

My folks even strayed to the dark side at one point and bought an artificial tree to decorate our home for the holidays. Sure, it might have saved us the hassle of buying a tree every year and cleaning up a few needles, but how much Christmas spirit can you find in a hunk of imported steel and plastic?

When I established my own household, I knew I wanted to go "au naturale" for the annual tree tradition. Of course, I preferred not to spend any money.

Low-cost conifers

I decided to go deciduous the first year, bringing in a spindly little poplar tree to string a few lights on and stack some presents under. Luckily, I was a bachelor back then.

Then I started eyeing the pride of the ranch, our nice straight rows of Ponderosa Pine planted back in 1979. The Ponderosas are one of the few successful tree projects ever to survive in our sand.

One of the women on the planting crew figured it was the dumbest thing she'd ever done when she was sitting on the tree planter, sticking perfectly good pine seedlings into that dry, sandy trench.

Now, 25 years later, we're all amazed by the 40-foot trees that took root from her efforts. In hindsight, they were planted awfully close together. Of course, we didn't expect them to grow!

We never had the nerve to cut any down when they were 6 feet tall. Believing strongly in the power of low expectations, we were sure most of them still might die and we didn't want to chop down a possible survivor.

When I built a house next to the Ponderosas, I considered decorating one of them right where it stood, live and green. But I needed the extension cord to plug my tractor in at night, and I wasn't sure the glass ornaments could handle the wind.

This year, finally, I decided to saw one down. Since our house has 8-foot, not 40-foot ceilings, I shimmied up 35 feet of branches, Swede saw in hand, to cut a nice little 5-footer to adorn our cabin.

The saw cut nice, the little tree top fell nicely, and I didn't.

If you go tree shopping, you'll notice that people who grow Christmas trees don't grow Ponderosas. There's a reason.

But since this tree was free for the taking, I didn't mind that it only had about three branches and a bushy top that no star or angel could straddle.

No sir, Charlie Brown and his pathetic little tree on the Peanuts cartoon have nothing on Ryan Taylor and his sparse Ponderosa. But, as Linus Van Pelt told Charlie, it's not about the tree anyway.

"… glory to God in the Highest, and on Earth peace, and good will toward men. That's what Christmas is all about Charlie Brown."

Well put, Linus. And Merry Christmas everybody.

Big, heavy gifts
Keeping the homestead happy
May 1, 2006

I received some advice from a friend once who said that women most appreciate "very small, very expensive" gifts. I think she was referring to things like diamond engagement rings.

But once a ranch wife has gotten the very small, very expensive diamond ring gift, it seems like her desires become a little more practical, especially if she likes to garden.

Last week, my wife said she'd really like to have a few loads of manure for her vegetable garden and the flower gardens by the house.

It's not like she was asking for string of pearls or a remodeled bathroom, this was a desire I actually could satisfy! I ran right out the door to start up the loader tractor to go scoop the poop.

I didn't want to disappoint her in what is one of the most practical requests she's made of me. I looked for the best manure the ranch had to offer.

Only the finest

I found some manure in a pile that'd been rotting for a good 10 years. I think more advanced folks call that a compost pile. At any rate, after a few years of decay, it was beginning to look a little more like dirt and a lot less like cow manure.

I scooped it up and headed for home. She was standing in the yard, rake in hand, and smiling like I'd just come home with a dozen roses. Sometimes being a good husband is so easy, I wonder why I didn't start the job a little earlier in life.

She guided me in and showed me right where to sprinkle it. I was precise in my placement and I didn't even run over the garden tiller. I wonder what husbands in the big cities do to please their wives when they don't have so much as a garden plot or a yard to plant flowers in?

It's a mile between our best manure pile and our house, but it felt so good to see my wife smile I made the trip several times. Nothing makes our nearly infertile yellow sand grow a few plants like some well-placed organic matter.

Similar satisfaction

I know how she feels when she sees that tractor come down the driveway with a big scoop of dirt-like manure.

I felt the same way when I was a little tyke and Dad would bring me a loader bucket full of our fine native sand for my sand pile. We had so much sand on the ranch that I never considered confining myself to a box. I preferred a pile.

The fresh sand with a little moisture left in it was ideal for digging, piling and building roads with my rusty fleet of Tonkas. Our little guy has taken to sand piles, construction and destruction, too, and with a few of the same old wounded trucks and dozers I had.

Somehow, I always needed more sand every year or two. And my wife puts in an order for more garden manure every now and then. I guess a little erosion, wear and tear and some hot, dry wind takes us back to base level eventually.

As happy as my wife and son are with the gifts of manure and sand, I'd be even happier if the county would put a few loads of gravel and clay on our soft, sandy roads.

I guess we all appreciate gifts hauled in with heavy equipment.

Half finished
And sometimes never started   May 29, 2006

I don't think I'm lazy, but that might be the conclusion if someone counted all the well-intentioned, half-finished projects around my place.

I'd suggest the tally relates more to my shortage of time than my lack of motivation. It may be that I have too much motivation, planning tasks and starting jobs that languish for what seems like eternity.

I know a lot of husbands get accused of never finishing household projects that they've started. I've seen unfinished basements waiting for sheetrock, front doors lacking a porch and bathroom floors tiled halfway across. It can go for years.

I have my share of those household halfways, but I'm an equal-opportunity slacker with just as many good intentions and projects in the pipeline around the ranch.

Confessions

I have a new interior door for the house that's been stored in my exterior shop since the day I bought it, but I also have the paint I purchased for the barn that has yet to see the outside of the can.

I've been meaning to varnish and nail up the trim boards around the closet that I built a few years ago, but I've also been storing quite a few rolls of fiberglass insulation and particle board with the intent of insulating and sealing off a corner of my cold shop.

I plowed in some electrical cable to my horse stalls, but haven't quite wired any lights or outlets yet. I have a new flapper for the toilet-flushing lever, but, so far, the "temporary" fix has kept it flushing.

No, if my wife claims I'm ignoring only the house, I can come back with just as many projects being ignored around the ranch. We're all sharing in the pain of my procrastination.

I do have to admit that I've finished a lot of projects, too. My batting average of completed to uncompleted tasks probably is better than most. But it's the unfinished ones staring me in the face that always come to mind.

I have seen examples of others who've put things off even longer than me. I remember driving by a fella's gray-weathered house where he had the scaffolding up and everything ready for painting for at least 20 years.

I've driven by pole barn timbers that got put in the ground but nothing ever got nailed to them. I've seen houses spend years defending themselves from the elements with nothing but a thin layer of Tyvek house wrap. I suppose the longer the house went without siding, the less he figured he needed it.

Big eyes

If my projects were food, an observer would say my eyes are bigger than my stomach. When I'm walking through the lumber yard, farm supply shop or home improvement store, I think my eyes are bigger than my calendar and the timepiece that dictates what gets finished.

But, now, the prices are even bigger than my eyes. With the fuel-induced, hurricane-fearing inflation in building materials, I'm making a resolution — no new projects until I use up the materials I've got on hand.

By the time I work through the stuff on hand, my appetite for projects should be pretty well diminished. And when I get done with it all, I'll probably be too gray, stiff and sore to start anymore.

Don't try this at home
Home improvement needs lots of improvement   July 10, 2006

I know "you can't beat a man at his own trade." But, in my ignorance, I convince myself that I can do a job close to it and do it a lot cheaper.

The big box home improvement stores count on suckers like me with a miser's desire to do-it-ourself. They've got everything you need right there including the instructional video with the annoyingly handy couple who can do everything from tile a floor to shingle a barn.

That in itself is a good reason to shop at your local little lumberyard. They don't tempt you with aisles of stuff for projects that you shouldn't be trying to do yourself.

What little retail space they have is dedicated to the simple things like nails and screws, a few tools and maybe some paint and brushes. All the stuff for the hard projects is hidden out back for guys who know what they're doing.

But when you walk into the big box store you become transformed. You're right there within reach of things you have no business touching. You're sure that your ability to see and buy things like drywall tape and joint compound means you actually can tape and texture a wall in your house.

I know. It happened to me.

Slinging mud

I don't know how long it would take someone who knew what they were doing to tape and texture a room 13 feet wide and 20 feet long. It took me forever and then some.

I suppose the fact that I was completely clueless played a factor in the excruciating tedium of the job.

It would have been easy to quit halfway through and hire a professional. But after my naïve do-it-yourself confidence played out, sheer stubbornness took hold.

I'm convinced there's a plot to trap people into doing their own drywall projects to increase the sales numbers at the home improvement stores. They sell more tools that get used once, more mud and tape that sits unused after people give up in disgust and then sell even more stuff to the guys who know what they're doing that go out to take over the job.

By the time I got done with my 260-square-foot grudge match, I was ready to put my mud hopper and taping knife in the collection of things to be sold in a rummage sale for two cents on the dollar. And I'd be willing to negotiate on the price.

Stop me, please

Generally, I like picking up a few new skills. But drywalling is a skill I'd just as soon leave lay.

I finished the room, and the only good thing I can say about it is that it's done. The wall is full of hills and valleys. The texture is gobby and uneven. The only possible compliment one could give my deviating drywall is in the area of artistic acoustics.

All I can think to do is find more pictures and furniture, anything to cover up as much of those walls as possible.

I don't know what my next big home improvement project might be, but I'm a little gun shy about the prospects.

As a matter of fact, I'm granting permission to anyone who sees me in one of those stores eyeing the materials for any project more complex than pounding a nail in a corral rail to tackle me, render me unconscious and drag me out of there.

You'd be doing me, my family and our house a big favor.

Unwanted guests
Trying to find the unlocked door

Like most country folks, my wife and I enjoy being close to nature. But we do appreciate a sturdy wall of separation between us and the creatures of the great outdoors.

Lately, that border seems a little porous. When I built my little bachelor shack, I was pretty proud of its ability to seal out furry little creatures. The bachelor shack soon became a newlywed bungalow and my bride was happy, too, with the structure's mouse-free status.

Now, after eight years, the little vermin have somehow found a way in to enjoy the luxuries of indoor living.

The first time I saw the little rodent scurrying along the base of the kitchen counter, I debated even telling my wife about it. I decided it probably would be better if I told her, rather than have her make the discovery on her own.

We went to town and bought some supplies to run our little rodent trapline — two kinds of traps (assuming one would be the "better mousetrap" we've heard so much about) and a medieval mouse torture device called a glue board.

We caught one in the old-style trap and stopped one dead in his tracks on the sticky board. The better mousetrap has yet to yield. It'll be awhile before we get enough for a fur coat, but it's coming along.

I'm in charge of emptying the trapline. It was a day or two before I got under the sink to throw out the glue board. It was a big board, and I thought the unlucky one might serve as a decoy to bring in another one to share the cost of the board. No such luck.

It did remind me of the time I was visiting one of my bachelor rancher friends in his trailer house though. His mobile home was far from mouse-proof and, like us, he took action.

But putting out the glue boards is kind of where his efforts stopped. I was sitting on his couch once and thought I smelled something a little more peculiar than the normally peculiar bachelor home smells.

Sure enough, we looked behind the couch and there's one of those sticky boards with a fully decomposed mouse skeleton stuck spread eagle in the middle. "I guess I'll have to check those a little more often," he concluded as he plugged his nose and carted off the bones.

Limited entry

I've tried to become more proactive in the mouse battle and keep them from coming in the house to start with, but I can't find their entry.

I guess they can squeeze though the smallest of holes. I'll have to keep looking.

Neighbors have told me the only animal more capable than a mouse in squeezing through tight spots is a bat. I think I'd rather have a mouse scurrying along the baseboard than a bat flying through my living room.

Another one of my bachelor friends had to move in with his parents for a week or two while he tried to solve a bat infestation. I don't know if he was more bothered by the bats, or more fond of his mother's cooking, but he just plain moved out when a colony of bats moved in.

If it ain't one thing it's another with mother nature. If I get the mouse problem fixed, my wife says I can start working on repelling the squirrels who jump on her window screens, the wild turkeys that walk across the patio every day and the deer and raccoons who get first pick of whatever they want from the garden.

Oh well, it's still better than some of the neighbors you can end up with in the city!

Heated comfort
Keepin' up with the Joneses   February 19, 2007

"Four-car garage and we're still adding on," is the line Waylon Jennings used in his song, Luchenbach Texas, as he lamented the rat race of acquisition and the yearning for simpler times.

There's no one in our neighborhood with a four-car garage, but there're a few two car models and some steel pole barns that neighbors park their cars in.

So, to keep up appearances with our neighbors, and because we really thought it'd be nice to have, we began pondering some car storage.

I suggested an 80-by-160 pole barn structure with a small patch of concrete and an overhead door in one corner for parking the car. As long as we were building, we could just as well overbuild a little and have an indoor roping arena or a place to work cattle or store some equipment away from the elements.

My wife suggested a two-car garage attached to the house. I told her we could attach the roping arena — I mean big garage — to the house, too, but she wasn't buying what I was selling. I put away my bar napkin blueprint for the arena and we settled on a two-car garage.

Extended completion

Like most projects, the jobs we hired professionals to do, like pour concrete and frame up the structure, didn't take too long. The jobs we left for ourselves to do — insulating, drywalling and finishing — is yet to be done.

In an effort to stimulate my winter ambition and finish the garage, we hooked up the heat for it. Actually, I was going to do that myself, too, but after looking at the box full of copper fittings, pumps and valves I'd bought for the electric boiler, I caved in and called a plumber.

So now we have a heated, unfinished garage, a year after the carpenters left, but I've given myself a quota of hanging two pieces of drywall each week. It won't be long, and I'll actually be able to park a car where I've had that dry wall stacked for the last year.

The garage has been extremely useful in helping us get the stuff out of our house that we didn't really need anymore, but we didn't want to throw away either. Most folks have a basement for that kind of stuff, but we built our house on the surface above our high water table.

I've had friends complement us on the idea of taking the money saved by not digging a basement and building a garage instead. That way you don't have the wasted effort of climbing up and down a flight of stairs with the boxes of stuff you should've thrown away but chose to store in your basement for a couple years before finally throwing it away. Storing those same boxes in a garage keeps you on the same level without the strain of the stairs.

I can see the biggest challenge of garage ownership will be to keep the boxes to a manageable level so the cars don't get squeezed back out into the cold. We have grown fond of heated indoor parking.

No ice to scrape off the windshield, no block heater to plug in, a warm car to get into when its 30 below outside and a warm garage to pull the sleeping baby and toddler into as we move them to their beds without waking.

It's almost as good as an attached roping arena with a car corner.

Conservation to consumption
Letting it run free and full   April 2, 2007

I was ready for spring to spring on us this year. I yearned for that time of year when the ice breaks up and the rivers flow, and, likewise, the ice melts in my pipes and my house regains the modern convenience of running water.

It got a little cold on the ranch this winter. A couple weeks of below zero temperatures combined with a week's absence from our house combined with too much rancher plumbing in our water system made for a big disappointment when we returned.

I turned the faucet wide open. Nothing. Nada. Zilch. Our water was froze up, and it wasn't something I could fix without hiring a backhoe.

So I rounded up a few 5-gallon buckets with lids and started hauling water to the house for my bride and family.

You learn a lot about water conservation when you're bringing it in five gallons at a time. Hand washing was practically done with a finger bowl. We realized that certain foods can be eaten without silverware. We strayed from our manners and did some of our dining right out of the cookware.

I don't need to share a lot of details on changes made in our bathroom water conservation plan, but I can admit that there wasn't a lot of needless flushing going on with the commode.

We were thankful for baby wipes and disposable diapers. And glad that my parents had running water and were just a mile down the road.

It was frozen for a long time. Then one sunny day, it happened. The faucet still was open and I heard a "drip, drip, drip." Within minutes, it was gushing and burping as the air and ice and a nice collection of rust was purged from the water line.

The whole family was beaming like we'd just won the lottery.

Off the wagon

When the water started running, I fell off the conservation wagon. I opened up every spigot in the house and let it run. Just the sound of it brought me joy.

I flushed the toilet every chance I got, and my wife took two showers just because she could. I ran a big sink of water to wash the dishes and let the hot water run liberally as I rinsed the suds off.

Of course, we don't live in a desert, so I didn't feel too guilty. Our water is easy to get, when it isn't frozen, and plentiful in our water-bearing sands. Punch a pipe 15 feet in the ground, and you can have all you want.

Still, a guy shouldn't waste something as important to the survival of the human race as water. In the long run, it's even more important than oil. And more expensive as everyone points out when they calculate the per-gallon cost of convenience store bottled water.

Although gas and oil won't freeze solid like the water in the pipeline between my house and the well, the recent 35 percent rise in our gas prices does give me a chilly feeling. If it goes much higher, it could get to be like my frozen water — a little too hard to get. It might even, gulp, make me think about using a little less.

Of course, when it drops back down to a mere $2 a gallon, I'll probably go wild and revert from careful conservation to carefree consumption just like I did with my rejuvenated water pressure.

In the dog house
Rainy days improve puppy housing   June 11, 2007

Rainy days are true blessings. Obviously, it's a blessing anytime you get some moisture when you're in the business of growing and grazing grass. Less obviously, rain takes away any excuses you might have not to complete a few projects that had been put off for the proverbial "rainy day."

Rainy day projects don't need to be important. If they were really important, we wouldn't have been able to wait for a rainy day to do them.

As luck would have it, we got two or three rainy days in a row. A good, long wet spell like that should get our pastures off to glorious green start, and it assured the completion of projects that could have been started and suspended with the passing of a quick cloudburst.

I considered my list of rainy day projects carefully when it looked like the precipitation was going to set in for awhile. There were lots of overdue projects that could have made the ranch more profitable, my life more efficient or our household more organized. I studied them all and picked number 112, "build a doghouse."

Puppy protection

We recently acquired a haphazardly bred puppy to torment and entertain our youngsters. Mostly black Lab, partly border collie, I'm hoping he has the genetics to stay home from the neighbors and stay away from me when I'm trying to work cattle.

The ranch yard has some dog housing, but the yard where my wife and I have our home has a bit of a dog housing shortage. There's plenty of place for a pet to take shelter like a small pole building and a plastic storage shed, but nothing that would fit the traditional definition of dog house.

I decided to build the little fella his very own humble abode. I hadn't built a dog house since I was 8 or 10 years old. It was a lot easier back then when I didn't know much about carpentry.

This time around I had the benefit of some spare parts left over from one of our other building projects — short two-by-fours, scraps of particleboard, leftover siding and some surplus shingles.

I allowed generous measurements (nearly 12 square feet of doggie luxury), engineered an innovative removable top and decided to shingle and side the mutt's quarters to match our own house. Nothing but the finest for our canine.

I had no idea I could spend so much time on a single, relatively unimportant task. Three partial days into the project, I figured I better wrap it up.

It was time to get the dog house out of the garage and into the rain to see if it would shed water and keep our pup high and dry.

Even with the removable roof, it barely budged when I put my back into it. I was about to go rent a forklift when my wife volunteered to give me a hand with the house moving. Pound for pound, I doubt there's a stouter dog house in the entire neighborhood.

The puppy moved right in and gave it his approval. The cat seems to like the bonus room on the second story.

And now I know where to go when tornadoes or severe weather approaches. Find a small, sturdy room in your home to seek shelter? I'm heading for the dog house.

Taylor taters
Gardening without the green thumb   April 28, 2008

My family is a gardening family. Every member has a job. Some are so talented they have several jobs.

My wife does the tilling, planting, weeding, watering, harvesting, canning and cooking of 15 or 20 varieties of vegetables grown in our garden patch.

Our two little boys are in charge of challenging the garden's vigor with semi selective plant pulling, row trampling and occasional early harvest.

Me, I'm a specialist. I have a single vegetable in my garden portfolio. I am the sole caretaker of the potato patch.

It's a family tradition. Dad was always the chief of spud production when I was growing up. I grew up believing that growing the noble potato was man's work.

I think the real gardeners in the family figure the taters are the one vegetable on their list of things to grow that is so hardy it can withstand the abuse and neglect handed out by a husband.

I've proved they're not quite hardy enough.

Sacrificial spuds

Despite the challenges of the dog, deer, raccoons, kids and poor soil, my wife has pretty good luck with her vegetables. My potato patch has yet to see a winning season.

I'm not Irish, but we've had a miniature potato famine here on the ranch for two years running. My family got to eat though since the failure wasn't widespread and I had the cash to go to town and buy potatoes from more successful growers.

Last year, I planted a couple dozen hills of potatoes and harvested about an ice cream pail full. It wasn't blight like in old Ireland. There really weren't enough potatoes to even attract a decent fungus or any other self-respecting pest.

It may have been my seed treatment. When you cut the seed potatoes and ready them for planting, you're supposed to leave them awhile to let the cut side heal up before you stick them in the ground.

Last year, my potato cuts spent a few weeks laid out on a cement driveway. The dog drug them around the yard, and by the time I planted them, the cuts were healed, but the dog's teeth marks were still pretty fresh.

I don't think it improved the rooting ability.

Occasional care

I'd always heard you're supposed to plant your spuds on Good Friday. I suppose the success of that plan depends on when Good Friday falls and if you live in an area where you have to clear snow to get to the dirt or chip through frozen ground.

I figure the best time to plant is when you can. Where to plant is a whole different decision.

Dad used to put a few potatoes in the garden and then planted the rest of the seed off site. Biosecurity I suppose. He'd plant spuds out in the hay field or try his luck in the bed of a dried-up slough. Those potatoes had to look out for themselves.

I plant my potatoes pretty close to our house and garden, but they still have to make it on their own without the meddling intervention of my watering and weeding them.

This year's crop went in on April 12. The ground was powder dry, but my seed was in better shape than last year.

I'm optimistic that this will be my year for potato production. With a little luck, I might just get my seed back.

Up, up, up
Goes the house and the prices   June 23, 2008

The best line I heard from a guy trying to sell me something this year was, "It's expensive, but everything is." It was an honest admission given in a matter of fact, better get used to it kind of way. I appreciated the sincerity, but I still didn't buy what he was selling.

He was right, of course. Everything is expensive, and it's getting higher every day it seems.

Home improvement

We're in the middle of the biggest building project on the ranch since 1927 when our barn was moved out from town where it was the city livery stable.

With baby No. 3 on the way, we've well outgrown the one-bedroom, one-closet, high-efficiency home built for my bachelorhood.

We're adding four bedrooms, numerous closets, a couple bathrooms and enough floor space to keep three kids under the age of 5 pretty well tuckered out if they run circles in the house for an hour straight.

It's been exhausting, and I'm not even swinging a hammer. We actually hired a real carpenter for that work. Just paying the bills and making decisions, or at least agreeing with my wife's decisions, has me worn down to the nub.

There are about 300 styles of faucets to pick from. They all turn the water on and off. There're some 400 styles of lighting fixtures to choose between. Basically, they all make dark places brighter.

There must be 50 shades of white paint and another 500 other colors of interior paint to consider.

The differences in all these things are subtle. After looking at catalogs an inch thick, stacks of pamphlets and reams of color swatches, my eyes begin to cross and I don't see any difference at all.

But you have to pick, or, at the least, smile and say, "Oh, that looks nice," and "Yes dear," once your wife has made up her mind.

Time is money

The best part about paying for a project like this is that you paid today and not a month from now. Anything that comes on a truck or takes some energy to create, which is pretty much everything, is going up on a regular basis.

I feel pretty smart that we poured our concrete two years ago, bought our shingles last year and got the copper wire and anything steel priced several months ago. Unfortunately, there's a lot of expensive stuff left to go.

My wife doesn't seem to notice the prices when she's paging through the catalogs with the thousands of decisions to be made. Whether its doors, carpets or kitchen cupboards, she'll look and look to find something she likes. I'll quickly look for the dollar sign and inform her, "You should like it, it's the most expensive one they have!"

"That just proves I have good taste," she counters. "Well I can pick out the high-selling bulls at every bull sale, but it doesn't mean I buy them and bring them home," I tell her.

I'm sure a $10,000 bull would do the ranch good, but if the budget says $3,000 or less, that's where the bidding stops. Of course, anything selling today for $3,000 might cost $10,000 next year the way things are going.

With that line of thinking, we should get the higher-priced options today because next year the crappy stuff probably will cost the same as today's premium.

I hope we finish this house soon, I hear there's another round of price increases at the end of the month.

Big backyards
Sometimes too big

June 8, 2009

Before we added on to my 896-square-foot bachelor built ranch house, I'd always say, "The house is small, but the yard is big — about 3,000 acres big."

I wasn't bragging, but I had to find some advantage to our living space, especially when my wife would look longingly at people's 4,000- or 5,000-foot mini mansions in the big city. "Yeah, it's nice," I'd tell her, "but look at the lot, that yard ain't even a half an acre."

Some of those half acre yards probably could grow more grass than 10 of our rangeland acres. But without a horse or a couple yearlings grazing that production, it's a waste of good growing conditions.

Our two boys are glad our yard isn't covered with thick turf grass. On our place, wherever the grass isn't growing, the sand is blowing. And little boys love that yellow sand we call our soil.

Ranchyard boundaries

Now that summer's here, it's nice to have the great outdoors just outside our door for the little tykes to run and play. They may want to stay inside to watch cartoons or play on the computer, but we put on their shoes and tell them to go and out and use their imaginations a little.

They play pretty well, too, and realize that not all entertainment comes from a video screen.

We're not always right next to them outside though, so we try to establish some boundaries.

The fence that runs between our house and some planted ponderosas is kinda kidproof. It once was fenced for sheep and has six strands of barbed wire. Not exactly a chain link playground fence, but they don't challenge it.

There's a two wire electric fence where our horses graze along the road. That's a "big ouchie" we instruct them and we tell them never to touch it. If curiosity gets the best of them, it doesn't take long for them to learn that Mom and Dad were right in their caution.

Otherwise it's three barbed wires along some pasture, an open driveway and some steel cattle panels. Easy stuff to get around, through or over — name your favorite preposition for a wandering kid.

Keeping track

The horizon is pretty open in our country, so you can spot a kid for a long ways if they wander off. Just to amplify our kid's spottability, we've been known to dress them in a little blaze orange, and not just during deer hunting season.

We got a dog, thinking that it would stay with the boys and if we find the dog, we'd find the boys. As it turns out, all we find if we find the dog is his dog dish or the best shade on a hot day.

178

Our cat is better about following the kids, but he doesn't always come when you call him and it's hard to spot a brown tabby tomcat in the grass. Maybe he should wear a little blaze orange, too.

For the most part, the kids are predictable. They're usually playing in the sand pile, making mud with the garden hose, picking grass and petting a horse or terrorizing their mother's vegetable garden.

We doubt that they'll pick up and walk to the neighbor's place. And that's a good thing since the closest one is three miles away.

But if they're wearing their orange caps, we can watch them go most of the way.

Oh Tannenbaum!
Looks like it's been bombed   December 21, 2009

With three little tykes in the house, you have to exhibit a little holiday spirit. You darn sure have to put up a tree so old Santy Claus knows where to stack the presents for Christmas morn.

We've had a variety of Christmas forestry in our house, but lately, we've been harvesting a short-needled spruce in a nearby tree lot that the landowner lets us do for a modest charge.

It takes some effort to get a tree from there. These aren't manicured 5- to 10-footers ready to saw. They're mostly 30-foot or higher waiting for someone brave enough to scale their branches and drop the top down to get that familiar Christmas pine scent.

Invariably, the best candidates always seem to be on the tallest trees. Or maybe they just look better because they're so high up we can't see them that well.

With a crosscut carpenter's saw in one hand, I shimmy up the branches. When the tree starts swaying back and forth from my weight, I start thinking about making the cut.

"Are you OK up there, Dad?" a little voice chirps from down below. "Yup, everything's fine, just stand back when I drop this tree," I tell my son. He has no idea that other kids go to the parking lot at Kmart and pick out their tree with no risk to Dad's life and limb.

The cursed conifer

This year, I found a nice 12-footer about 20 feet up, sawed it off and let gravity bring it down to earth. My 5-year-old and I drug it a long way to get it to the pickup, or maybe it just seemed like a long way because he was riding the tree that I was dragging.

We loaded up and headed down the road. Then I looked back and I realized we weren't loaded up anymore.

We retraced our route and found the unlucky rider on the gravel road where it landed after skidding about 40 feet. There were a lot of little branches and needles scraped off that one side. There'd be no wondering which side we'd put against the wall this year.

The tree looked tough and had lost a lot of sap, but we figured he'd come back around once we got him in a nice warm house.

My wife was kind of wondering what happened to those branches that were stripped clean of needles, but she was a pretty good sport about it as we stood the tree up and let the short people in our house plaster the first 4 feet of it with decorations and tinsel. After the kids were in bed, we finished the decorating, sat down and decided, despite its problems, the tree looked pretty good.

The next day was a different story. I got the cell phone call while I was feeding cows to come home. The tree had fallen down not once, but twice.

Every glass ornament but one was smashed to pieces on the floor. Even the tree top angel had cracked her skull. There was water on the floor and wet presents around the base.

My wife was trying to clean up the glass fragments and our three little elves were right in the middle of it. To say she wasn't exhibiting a lot of Christmas spirit at that moment would be a real understatement.

But the tree hasn't tipped again since then. It's been redecorated with the remaining unbreakable ornaments, a little thicker on the bottom where the kids do their work.

And it's doing what it's supposed to do, needles or no needles. It reminds us that it is Christmas, and the realization of the season, and its meaning, is a lot more important than any broken branches or shattered ornaments.

Chapter 7
Taylored Technology

Cow chips
Computerized cattle counting

February 7, 2005

There's a lot of talk about identifying our animals these days.

I've always been able to identify my cattle. There's the one with the short tail, the one with the long toe, the skunk-faced cow, the crooked-horned heifer. Beyond that, there's a whole bunch of rather non-descript solid black cows that I know only by their ear tag or a freeze brand.

Now we want to expand on identification so that complete strangers can recognize our cattle, too. It's hard to imagine that folks who've never even met my cows would be able to identify them.

The prospect of a U.S. National Animal Identification System is being bantered about in cattle-producing states from coast to coast. A lot of people have to sit down and take a few deep breaths at the thought of individually identifying 100 million cows and calves across the country.

Canada's a step ahead. They've known the name, rank and serial number of their cattle for a few years now. It's catch-up time for the Yanks down south.

The big question for most? "How?"

Head count

Most of the discussion on "how" is centered on putting a radio frequency chip in an ear tag.

I saw these tags in action at a big calf sale last week. A calf would jump off the trailer, walk down an alley, walk between a couple of electronic readers, and the computer says "Yup, No. 701445598904521 is present and accounted for." The cowboy unloading the trailer just says, "Yup, a red baldy heifer is here."

The trick is to make sure the computer counts as good as the cowboy. The computer count's not a 100 percent deal yet. Sometimes the reader would only count eight calves when 10 of them trotted past.

That's why they had bib overall backup. A guy in bib overalls would stand by the gate wagging a finger at the critters and correct the computer when it was off. A sale barn cowboy often could out count the computer, but the machine could out remember the cowboy when it came to the calves' individual ID.

I wonder sometimes if it'll be like scanning groceries at the supermarket. Whenever a supermarket scanner makes a mistake on a price or a sale item, it always benefits the store, the seller.

I guess as long as I'm always a seller that'd be all right. I just want to make sure there's cowboy backup to give me credit for 10 head instead of eight when I unload the trailer.

Experience

My personal experience with RFID is limited. I put some of the tags in our calves at branding one year with the idea of tracking them all the way to slaughter. The guy

I sold them to cut them out. So much for advancing technology.

My two other experiences with high-tech tagging had nothing to do with cattle. When I ran the marathons in Chicago and New York City, we were given an RFID tag to lace onto our running shoe to track our time and progress.

We got scanned at the starting line, at a couple of midpoints and at the finish line. At each race, a pack of 30,000 runners ran across mats embedded with scanners and it would beep, beep, beep until everyone was accounted for.

As near as I could tell, everyone in the race got counted and clocked. If we can read 100 percent of chipped full-speed marathoners and only 80 or 90 percent of chipped high-speed cattle, the solution to animal ID might be to put the chip on their hoof and install the same scanning mats from the marathons in the cattle alleys.

Either that or strap a marathon runner onto every cow.

On the paper trail
Keeping up or catching up   April 18, 2005

Pay now or pay later. That little adage can refer to money or time or most anything of value that requires a little steady discipline.

For years, I've tried to become a better record keeper. You can either do a little every day or you can do a whole lot at the end of the year. And doing a whole lot at once always is harder than doing a little every once in awhile.

Dad used to do the whole-lot-at-once method with his income taxes. A week or two before his tax appointment, he'd set up the folding card table and haul out the shoe boxes full of receipts, bank statements and canceled checks.

It was a year-end reconciliation of all the accounts. During the year, the checkbook balancing was aided by overdrafts.

When I came back to the ranch, I took over the taxes and the bookkeeping. Dad didn't fight me much on that transfer of responsibilities.

I computerized the outfit. I began entering checks, assigning accounts and reconciling statements every month. At tax time, I left the card table in the closet, hit a button on the computer and printed out the year-end report for the tax man.

It was a lot easier to get an appointment with the tax preparer because I could take one of the early time slots. It was as easy as getting the front pew in church. There aren't many takers for the front seats of the church or the front end of the tax calendar.

Calf tally

With the taxes and finances in order, I began to think about computerizing the cattle records. I've been thinking about it for at least 10 years. I even bought the software.

But it seems like I never have a computer when I need one. No desktop by the cattle chute, no laptop in the pickup, not so much as a Palm Pilot in my snap front pocket when I'm riding the range.

The technology amounts to a tally book, a piece of paper torn from a mineral sack

183

or the dust on the dash of the pickup. With a little luck, all the odds and ends make it into my tally book, but the bits of data have yet to be converted to bytes.

By rights, I should be entering new calves into the computer every evening during calving season. What I end up doing is entering all of last year's data in one fell swoop before the start of the new calving season.

I'm just now entering the calves born last spring and the calf weights taken last October, and those calves are long gone from the ranch. It makes me more of a historian than a visionary manager.

I'm taking cows out of the database that became hamburger long ago. Next year, I'll probably add last year's replacement heifers to the digital herd.

Of course, if hind sight's 20-20, my vision for the herd should be real clear. It's like I've got eyes in the back of my head.

But just like the ranch's switch to computerized finance, I hope to get caught up and get ahead with the cattle data. Either that, or like Dad, I'll wait it out for the next generation.

Of course, if I have to wait for my 11-month-old son to take over the responsibility, it's going to be awhile. I'll make sure and save all my tally books and scraps of feed sacks so he can get everything up to date.

Who am I, anyway?
Trying to remember my cyber aliases   December 12, 2005

I learned my name at an early age. Parents and teachers taught me how to spell it. They put it on my driver's license lest I forget it in a nervous panic.

I never had a nickname that really stuck, although a few people in college knew me as "RT" to differentiate me from another Ryan who they knew.

Now, I must have about 50 new nicknames — they call them user names — that the cyber world knows me by. I bet I can't remember 49 of them. Along with those 50 user names, there're 50 pass codes to recall. I doubt I'd pass the test on remembering my pass codes either.

I don't know how I ended up with so many aliases to forget. I guess it all started when I rolled onto the information superhighway and I was asked to create a user name and pass code, a login, for my first email account. I've been stacking up the logins ever since.

If I wanted to buy something or bid on something or book an air ticket or get my phone bill or do some online banking, they'd all ask for another user name and pass code.

It doesn't have to be a high-level transaction to warrant the special super-secret clearance system. I can't even read most newspapers on line without being asked to set up another user name and pass code.

Somewhere along the line, I was told not to use the same name and pass code for every account. It should be easy for you to remember, but not so easy for someone else to guess, they advise.

If some hacker got a hold of your one name and code they could roll through every account you had on line. Before you knew what happened, the scoundrel would be reading your newspaper and paying your phone bill.

So I got creative with my secret identities. Capital letters, lower-case letters, the occasional numeral, all three to 10 characters in length.

Cracking the code

When I go back to a website and I can't remember my name and code, I'll take a shot in the dark and see if I can crack the login. Hacking into my own account allows me to experience some of the same thrills a real computer hacker must get when they're on the job.

Cracking the code, even if it's for your own account, is pretty exciting. Given some of the obscure pieces of personal information I've incorporated into my logins, it's a real accomplishment when I can take a guess and get in.

Sometimes you can get a helpful hint about the pass code if you set one up with the site's webmaster. I hate it when I have to use one of these "life lines" and have them clue me in with an email that whispers, "Pssst ... what's your mother's maiden name and what city were you born in?"

When all else fails, I just set up another account. I must have a half-dozen accounts and logins set up with some outfits.

I reckon that's how some e-commerce companies post such impressive growth. When they say they have 50 percent more customers shopping online with them, I wouldn't take that as a valid reason to rush out and buy shares of their stock.

Chances are, they could have lost customers and just kept a handful of really forgetful ones.

With guys like me out in cyber country, they should have good account growth every year, but probably not much for sales. I hope they don't start charging a toll on failed attempts to log in.

Out of range
New phone returns me to the old days   February 5, 2007

I took an old friend to town the other day and left her there. The old friend was my trusty bag phone. I left her there and brought home a sleek little handheld model.

I had my bag phone a long time. Twelve years ago, I was an early adapter, a man on the cutting edge of mobile phone technology. Sure, the phone was the size of a shoe box, but it was relatively portable.

I remember walking in the shopping mall with my trusty bag phone slung over my shoulder as I waited for a phone call. If that ain't the definition of cool, I don't know what is.

That phone was a good piece of equipment. It took a licking and kept on ticking. It had a hard life, but it outlasted every other piece of plastic electronics I ever owned.

This year, though, it started showing its age. The buttons quit working, the screen went on the fritz, and it would turn itself on and off like a phantom.

My analog phone and I had avoided the world of digital communications for a long time, but our time was up.

Trading up?

One reason I stuck with my bag phone when the rest of the world was going to phones the size of a wallet, was the reception I got.

Sure, the cellular provider's map of our state shows a solid block of coverage, but that's only the case if you're packing the big black bag phone with 3 watts of power. Trade up to the new digital handheld and you get a strong signal in the cities and a few major highways. The rest of the time, you'll be more than a little frustrated.

When you're driving in the outback that I call home, the signal is spotty at best. You can try to use the little phone with all the nifty features, but the only feature you really notice is the dropped call message.

Sometimes I drive up a hill and try again, but once you've dropped the same call three or four times, you feel like throwing that phone as far as it'll go. I guess you can buy insurance for that if you lose your phone in the frenzy of frustration.

There are options for us folks in the cellular hinterlands. You can get a booster and an outdoor antenna for another $400. I'm about at my spending cap for extra communications though.

Ten years ago, who'd have thought a husband and wife could justify spending another $1,000 a year to have a couple phones so they could track each other down at the shopping mall?

The phones have eliminated my need for a grocery list. I can walk through the grocery store with a phone to my ear and my wife can talk me through the needs of the ranch pantry aisle by aisle.

I do miss my old bag phone and its power, but I think there may be a positive side to my newer poorer signal. In today's world, we may be too accessible. It may be all right to drive down the isolated highways, tune in the radio and tell the callers, "sorry, but I'm out of range. Feel free to leave a message."

Wireless and clueless
Where'd I put that thing?   September 17, 2007

Going wireless was supposed to be a big advance for modern society.

I think I liked it better when things were wired at our place.

Used to be, when I wanted to find the phone I just walked over to where it was nailed to the wall and there it was. If it wasn't hanging on the receiver, I'd just follow the curly cord a little ways and find it.

Now that we've gone wireless and cordless, it takes five minutes to find the phone so I can make a two-minute call. Seldom is it on the charger. You can't even count on it being in the house. With 5.8 gigahertz of range, it could have been left in the barn or a half-mile down the driveway where we last used it.

That old phone that was nailed to the wall would last forever. I'm sure my parents had the same one for 20 years, and it always worked. Their only investment was one of those shoulder cradle add-ons that let them use both hands for something else while they were talking.

Our cordless phones, if we don't lose them or drop them in the sink, make it about a year, maybe two tops. That's when the battery goes dead and you realize it's cheaper to get a whole new phone than a replacement battery.

Kid blight

The phones might last longer in a house without little kids. Cordless phones are more popular than lead-painted Chinese toys with the toddlers in our house.

They're really drawn to the beeping sounds, the lights, the recorded message on the other end of the line asking if they really meant to place a call to Singapore. Mostly, they like the reaction they get from their parents when we find them using the phone for a hammer on the floor.

Sometimes I just give up on finding the house phone. I could use my cell phone to make a call if I wanted to go outside, walk up the hill and climb a tree. Of course, I can't find my cell phone. No cord on that thing to help me locate it, and it could be in one of several vehicles, a tractor or maybe in the kids' toy box.

Rather than get frustrated, I take the opportunity to forget about work, people I should call and phone message I should return. I plop down in the chair to watch a movie. The only problem is that I can't seem to find the remote control for the DVD player, the remote for the VCR or the remote for the television itself.

I'd listen to some soothing classical music to calm my nerves, but the remote control for the stereo is missing, too.

Tag reader

Finally, I pick up a cattle magazine and read about the benefits of using some electronic ear tags in our calves this fall. To make full use of the technology, the ranch ought to have its own wand to read and scan the tags while the calves are being weighed and worked.

Ranchers have a chute side choice between wired or wireless wands. The wireless wands even have something called Bluetooth that's supposed to make them more valuable.

After spending half my day looking for wireless gadgets in the house, I'm not so interested in whether a tag scanner has Bluetooth.

Forget the blue stuff, just dip my reader in extra-bright blaze-orange paint. And, to save a little time, attach a long, curly cord to the thing so I can find it when I need it.

Button bidding
Mouse buys a bull   March 3, 2008

Boot me up and call me a high-tech redneck. I just bought my first bull electronically through an online auction.

With the click of a mouse, I spent a chunk of change that makes my other online purchases of EBay rummage look pretty paltry.

Blame it on too many time commitments or the high cost of diesel to fill my pickup, but it just wasn't in the cards for me to make a 300-mile roundtrip to go sit in a sale barn and bid on a bull.

The catalog said I could log on to the Internet, watch the auction and make purchases from the comfort of home. With a new user name, password and bidding number I was all set.

Auction time

I missed the social aspect of going to the sale in person to visit, eat and drink coffee, but the computer screen version of the sale had some advantages.

You didn't have to drive anywhere, shave or find a clean pair of jeans. Not everyone cleans up to go to a bull sale, but a fella wants to at least look half as good as the auctioneer and a fourth as good as the freshly pressed ring men.

When I logged on and started watching the sale, I was impressed with how quiet it was. Then I realized I wasn't getting any sound. Even after I turned on the speakers, it was fairly quiet because the only audio was the auctioneer. No ring men screaming through the computer.

Dad always contended that there was nothing worse than a highly vocal ring man in close proximity taking bids when you were trying to have a nice conversation and enjoy a sale. All that noisy bidding can really ruin a good auction.

Online bidding didn't have near the pressure to purchase as being there in person. When you're sitting in the crowd, you feel kind of obligated to buy something, especially if there is a free lunch.

I have to really work at avoiding the eyes of the ring man and the auctioneer when I hit my limit and quit bidding. I just stare at my shoes until they've sold the bull to someone else and it's safe to look up again.

When you look at a computer screen, it doesn't look back.

Phantom buyer

I watched my first bull sale on the Internet for quite a while as my favorite bulls sold out of my price range. Soon enough, though, a bull came on the screen that was in my budget.

I intensely examined the bull on the 3-inch-by-4-inch streaming video, or as intensely as I could study a 1,300-pound bull crammed into a corner of my monitor.

His performance numbers looked all right, so when the cry for bids bottomed out, I moved my mouse over to the words "bid now" and pushed the button.

I couldn't see my opposing bidder in the seats at the sale; they must have thought I was a ghost just raising the price.

I always like to know who's jacking my price up when I'm bidding on a bull. I'll be hot after a genetic bargain when the auctioneer will look to the rafters, find a bid and ask me for $500 more than my last bid. I'll look over at the same spot and all I see is rafters.

I could imagine the suspicion when the auctioneer looked at a computer monitor on the auction block and asked someone in the stands to bid $250 more than my offer.

When the gavel came down, I got a bull with two clicks of a mouse. Now all I have to do is wait for delivery and find out why he sold in my price range.

Going digital
And going without

We've been hearing the warning for months — get your digital converter box or your television will go black on Feb. 17.

It scared me enough to hustle right over to my computer, go online and get the $40 coupon. I bought the analog-to-digital converter box and prepared myself to enter the age of digital television.

Little did I know this big step forward in television technology would take our ranch reception back in time.

Channel surfing

We never have had cable TV out in the boondocks where our ranch is located. We've never broke down and spent the little net income we earn on a satellite dish and its monthly entertainment ransom.

Our little warm glowing box has depended on the low-tech hardware of an outdoor antennae mounted on a pole out in the yard with a string of wire going to the house.

In the early days of entertainment, we got two channels, NBC and CBS. Then public television, PBS, broadened our minds and our choices. Eventually, we began pulling in the UHF channels and we got ABC and Fox broadcasting. Wow, five channels — I figured it couldn't get any better.

Sure, my pals in town with cable and those who paid for dish programming could get 50 or 150 channels. Of course, only four or five are worth watching. The rest of their time is spent flipping through the other 100-some channels to realize that.

I was pretty happy with the five channels we could pull in from the antennae mounted atop the 16-foot pine corral rail nailed to a post in my backyard.

Channel 13 always was great, and 6 was pretty good, 10 was a little snowy like our weather outside, 14 didn't always have sound, and 24 didn't always have anything you wanted to hear. But it was tolerable.

Digital search

Then we entered the new age, the digital broadcast revolution. My analog channels started dropping off as they went digital. Channel 13 and 24 hung tough, but the rest were gone.

I hooked my new signal-converting contraption. Shazam! The reception was crystal clear. It was amazing reception, and even more amazing was the fact that I now had only one channel. One darn clear, but lonely, channel.

No local news and weather on my screen. Just one fine public television station.

Don't get me wrong, I love public television. I even send them a little money during their fund drive. I like the smart programming and the lack of commercials. The kids love the children's programs. Big Bird, Curious George and Super Why are staples of our day.

But I'd kind of like to see the local news and weather that I used to get on my broadcast channels.

I guess for the next few months until my strongest analog broadcaster goes digital, my "channel surfing" will require pulling the television away from the wall, unscrewing the coaxial cable from the TV and the VCR and the digital converter, and hooking the antennae wire back directly to the TV. Not quite as handy as pushing a button on the remote.

It looks like this will be our family's opportunity to make good on the old resolution to watch less TV and read more books and newspapers.

Thanks to all the advances in television technology, we're one family who'll spend less time in front of it.

Always lost
Sometimes found
August 3, 2009

Whoever decided to issue small, delicate, expensive electronic devices to farmers and ranchers should be taken out and whipped with a curly car phone recharging cord. That is if you can find the cord when you need it.

I first experienced the expensive electronic-ranching revolution when I got one of those electronic fence testers. I was tiring of testing the strength of the ranch's electronic fences by grabbing the wire with my hand and determining its voltage by whether it tickled, caused me to yelp, stood my hair on end, or put me down on the grass rolling in convulsions.

It was about as big as an oversized remote control with a digital readout. I paid $70 for the little wonder of technology.

It was carried and mixed with the other high-tech stuff in the back of the pickup, the cab of the pickup, the crate on the four-wheeler, the saddle bags on the horse. It often was lost but usually found.

The last time I misplaced it, it didn't turn up again. The one I found to replace it at the farm store included a fault finder and cost $120. I was pretty mad about losing the $70 fence tester. Now I'm practically paranoid about the thought of forgetting where I left the $120 fencer's friend.

Where's my phone?

"Honey, where's my phone?" is a pretty common exchange between my spouse and me. Most times, when the loss is seeming more real, it's more like, "Where is my $#@$*&% phone!" The measured response to the frantic plea is usually, "I don't know, I suppose it's right where you left it."

For all the time savings made possible by cell phones and mobile communication, I think it's all eaten up by the time spent looking for the darn phones when they're missing.

I didn't have the problem back when I had my old bag phone. Never did lose that 10 pounds of technology, not even once.

The march of miniaturization has marched right to the point where the cell phones are the size of the palm of your hand and impossible to find when they're not in the palm of your hand.

Farmers and ranchers, if they're close enough to a tower, feel like they have to have their phone with them all the time.

We need to be connected. So our wife can call and find out where we are. Used to be they just had to guess. Now they can confirm that we're on the tractor, in the shop, out in the barn. ...

I lost my first phone last winter feeding cows. It was done in by a loose holster and probably still is lying out there in the pasture. I had insurance and got it replaced for a $50 deductible. I figured the insurance had done its job, so I dropped it. What were the odds of losing it again?

Two months later, I lost it again. Now we're talking a couple hundred dollars for a new one. I thought it was in the yard, but it could be in the hay field. It wasn't a needle in a haystack, but its chances for discovery were about the same.

A week later, walking from one hayfield to the next to move some machinery, I happened to look down at the ground, and there it was. I'd been searching for it a couple miles from there.

The key may be to tie the little phone to a big concrete block and paint it neon orange, kind of along the theory of a key chain. It'll be a little less portable and folks won't always know where I am or what I'm doing, but at least I'll know where my phone is.

Socially networked
With new digital copies of old friends September 14, 2009

Seems like the old 3-pound coffee can is lasting a little longer these days. Sure, we still make a pot every morning, but we hardly ever have to brew another pot later in the day to share with friends that might drop by.

Growing up, I often remember there being a friend or neighbor stopping by to park their feet under our kitchen table and wrap their fingers around a hot cup of my mother's famous boiled coffee. They'd visit awhile, catching up on the latest news, the rain report, who was doing what where and sometimes something a little deeper about our existence here on earth.

That doesn't seem to happen much anymore. People are busier I guess. You can drop in on folks, but chances are nobody's home. Jobs in town to support the smaller farms and ranches, or bigger farms and ranches that don't allow folks to slow down the work long enough to visit. When work's done, the child chasing to all their sports and activities begins.

Still, people are social critters, so there needs to be an outlet somewhere. Usher in the computer, the Internet and something called Facebook.

Adding virtual friends

If the term Facebook leaves you blank, you're obviously not one of the 250 million active users the social network lays claim to.

It used to be a college age thing, but now the fastest-growing demographic of

Facebookers is age 35 and older. The fastest-growing group is women over the age of 55. Grandma wants to see pictures of those grandkids … now!

I'm not sure how I got hooked. Drawn in by all of the buzz, I guess. My wife got on the site more when her 20-year high school reunion was being organized, mostly via Facebook.

So, even though we're all too busy to visit people in person, or write a letter, or even call them on the phone, we find a half-hour or an hour each day to stare at Facebook walls on the computer screen.

It's not all bad. In my older years, my stack of birthday cards in the mailbox was down to one or two from my sister and a dedicated aunt. This year, on Facebook, I got 43 greetings on my birthday. I don't think I've ever had that many well-wishers of my aging process, even when I was 5 and birthdays were a big deal.

But, if you Google "Facebook addiction," you get more than 17 million links, so I guess that's an issue. Students are updating their Facebook pages during class, employees are logging in on the job when they're supposed to be working, kids are going hungry while moms check the profiles of old boyfriends. Like everything, a little moderation is in order.

Maybe letter writing was considered an addiction years ago. Kids probably were writing long, cursive notes and addressing envelopes in the middle of class. Addicts were spending their egg money on postage stamps and ink for their fountain pens.

It has been fun to catch up with old friends and distant relatives thanks to the Internet age. It's nice to see the photos of their families, find out their favorite quote and 25 obscure things about themselves.

But, if someone's in the neighborhood, I'd still like to brew a pot of coffee and have a good, old-fashioned offline chat.

The new West
Reach for the phone, pardner   Fall, 2009

Back in the day, a cowboy in the West made his way with a holster on his hip, packing a six-shooter to keep him safe and to administer a little justice from time to time.

These days, a cowboy in the West still makes his way with a holster on his hip, but now he's packing a cell phone. A lot lighter, a little higher tech, but still ready for the quick draw.

I have to smile when I see the 21st-century ranchers out and about with a shiny, hand-tooled leather holster. It takes a lot less cowhide for a phone holster than a revolver holster, but the plastic and silicon inside of it probably eats up any savings in leather.

The ranchers with the nicest holsters must have ranches that are darn close to a cell phone tower. Us folks who have to drive up the road and over the hill, climb a windmill or stand on top of the barn to get a phone signal aren't nearly as likely to have a fancy holster. We're just not that attached to the phones we can't always use.

Our place is a ways from the closest cell tower, but we're able to pick up a couple of bars of signal strength in a few key places in the pastures and hay fields. Of course, there's absolutely no signal in the house or the yard. That would make it too easy to cut the long distance bill on our land line.

My wife and I are informally mapping out the good spots. The pen behind the barn, the east pasture, the hill out west. A few other places might pop a signal if the atmospheric conditions are just right and you stand on your tiptoes with the little dummy antenna on the phone full extended.

For some reason or another, I lose a phone once in awhile. I try my best to lose them in an area where there's a good signal. That way I can take my wife's phone, walk around the area where I think I lost mine, call my phone and try to hear it ring.

The phone is real hard to find if I left the ring option on vibrate. Then I have to try and feel the ground shaking when I dial it up. With luck, I track down the missing phone before the battery goes dead.

Cell phones on the ranch have added another dimension to our colt training. Along with getting a young horse used to saddle and bridle, it's a good idea to get them used to your cell phone, too. A good way to lose a cell phone is to have it ring while you're riding a green colt.

If there's a chance your phone might ring while you're riding a young horse, it's a good idea to pick out a nice, easy-listening ring tone. Stay away from anything too loud, shrill or out of the ordinary. Maybe the sound of birds singing or a bucket full of oats being shaken would be a good choice.

If the six-gun and holster helped settle the West, the cell phone and its holster is helping to keep it settled. Ranchers always have lived in isolated places, but we don't have as much affection for isolation as we used to.

And our spouses may have even less appreciation for the nail-biting solitude we're granted out here. But with the husband packing a phone in his holster, a wife can call and let him know that being home alone with a house full of preschool aged curtain climbers is beginning to grate on her.

If you've got a phone signal and receive her call, technology will allow you to cheer her up a little. With the phone, you can tell her not to worry about the kids drawing on the walls and drawing blood as they fight with each other. You can assure her that after you fix the fence, chase in the bull that's out and haul in a few bales, you'll be right home.

Hopefully, her holster won't have the old West in it by the time you get there.

Packin' the berry
Ready to communicate, kind of   January 18, 2010

I merged a little farther onto the information superhighway recently. But I've still got my hazard lights on to warn traffic about the high tech redneck on the road.

When our cell phones had breathed the last of their useful lives, my wife and I headed to the big city to get a couple of new ones. Who'd have guessed, they were having a big promotion at the time.

Produce sale

We'd been thinking about an upgrade and they had these Blackberries on sale for $50 a pint. I guess the berries were in season and they'd had a good crop.

These units were much more than a phone, the salesman informed us. You could text, email, browse the Web, take photos, listen to music, play games, and do 49 other things you never thought you needed to do on a telephone.

And, our salesman added, he was at a meeting where the speaker said these little gems could save the owner an hour a day. I'm not sure where that hour came from but I think it had something to do with answering your email when you shouldn't instead of when you're sitting safely at home at your desk.

The phones were cheap, two for $50, after the mail in rebate, of course. But there was one other detail: We'd have to upgrade our monthly cell phone plan. Another $40 a month for the two of us. The potential profit margin from another five calves per year I figured. Hmmmm.

We took the bait and got the phones. We "needed" them. I figured the communication and time savings could make our calves more valuable, allow us to run a bigger herd, or, at the least, make it possible for me post my status and a photo on Facebook from remote ranch locations that could pull a phone signal.

Accessorize

The cost didn't stop with the phones and the plan, however. Before we left the store, we needed $75 worth of other stuff.

We got a couple of chargers for the car, one to have and one to look for. Since the $25 phone would cost $300 to replace, and given the rough treatment on the ranch, I spent the extra money to have my phone wrapped in rubber and plastic, waterproofed and synthetically rawhided. It didn't look so sleek anymore, but it was nearly bulletproof.

I'm still waiting to start saving an hour a day with the new-fangled gadget. I can't get it synchronized with our computer and I haven't scratched the surface of figuring out how to use all its applications. I can make a phone call with it, though. Sometimes it won't even get cut short for lack of a signal.

Right now, I call my Blackberry my chokecherry, the sour prairie fruit with the big pit in the middle, not nearly as sweet or tasty as its blackberry cousin but useful.

I still may figure things out and move it up from a chokecherry to Blackberry, but I'm not there yet.

It wouldn't be so bad if they had a cheaper monthly plan for us chokecherry users, but I won't hold my breath for that.

All this talk is making me hungry for some jam and toast. Maybe I can check my email while the bread is toasting.

Texting while tractoring
Reaching full utilization
July 18, 2011

I'm starting to feel like I'm reaching full productivity here on the ranch now that I've got a smart phone buzzing and chiming in my pocket.

A lot of modern agriculture is about driving, and even in cattle ranching, or North Dakota ranching, you have to spend a lot of time hanging on to a steering wheel. Making hay, spraying invasive weeds, hauling salt and mineral to the cows — it all has you behind the wheel driving 3 to 4 mph across the landscape for hours on end.

Now with my smart phone and its full Internet and email capabilities, I can do two or three things at once. The things I used to have to go back to the house to do now can be done while I'm doing other jobs that also needed doing.

It's one thing to be gawking at your phone and typing text when you're going a turtle's speed across an endless sea of grass, and quite another to be one of those who think they should do it when they're hurtling down a highway 70 mph on a road they're sharing with others and their families. So I don't advocate texting while driving, but texting while tractoring, in a field and not on road mind you, is changing the way I operate.

I've also seen some texting while horseback, or, at the least, cell phone answering while riding horse across the open range if it's within reach of a cell tower. But an annoying ring tone on the wrong green broke colt is a good way to find yourself walking home and picking grass out of your ear.

High and low tech

I reckon there are lots of farmers with global positioning and auto steer technology who can do a lot of Web surfing and communicating while they're out in the field. My smart phone finds its best utilization on my dumb equipment.

Now that I'm baling, I'm sure glad I didn't spend several thousand dollars extra for my baler to have the super-quick Net wrap option. By using good old-fashioned twine to tie my bales, I'm allowed about 60 seconds to email someone from my phone while the bale is tying.

And sometimes I continue typing after I've kicked the bale out and I drive on to make the next bale. My distraction kind of helps the tractor weave back and forth to find each edge of the windrow to fill the baler, hopefully evenly.

Otherwise I pick up on the typing when it's time to tie the next bale. I'm one of those guys who likes to use whole words and correct spelling, even when I'm typing with my thumbs. Old habit I guess. I still write "you" instead of "u," and "are" instead of "r." So sometimes it takes several bales to complete a dictionary perfect and grammatically correct outgoing message.

My old spraying rig and the terrain and leafy spurge I'm spraying doesn't allow for straight lines, and that's OK, because I'm doing important stuff like monitoring Facebook on my phone to see who just did something really important on Farmville that had to be shared with everyone, or I'm checking the weather to see how stiff the breeze is or how soon it's going to rain again.

And sometimes, when I can't catch a signal from our distant cell tower, I just … pay attention to my work and my surroundings. Maybe the smartest thing I can do with the addictive smart phone is shut it off and put it away. Right after I respond to one last message.

Driving with confidence
Country boy becomes a city driver   February 27, 2012

When I was learning how to drive, Dad started me out with the pickup in the hay field. Keep it in first gear until you get the hang of it, he told me. The only obstacles were some duck sloughs and hay stacks. Just stay out of the sloughs and don't hit the stacks, he said, although the hay stacks were a somewhat soft, fairly forgiving bumper.

Before you knew it, I was trying my steering hand in pastures, on prairie trails and on seldom-traveled gravel roads. All before the age of getting a formal permit. However, the licensing process forced me to learn another whole vehicular environment — one with other cars and other drivers.

Instead of maneuvering around hay stacks and cows, I had to look out for cars that were right there on the same road as me! Crazy stuff.

But in a small town with no stoplights and just several hundred people, a new driver could survive as long as he could handle the one four-way stop and parallel park. Sometimes it was hard to find two cars parked close enough together to practice parallel parking, so the driver's ed instructor would have to give you another landmark like a light pole and tell you to pretend that was where the second car was.

The challenges kept coming. To pass the "behind the wheel" portion of driver's ed, we'd have to go to the big city of Minot, N.D., population about 30,000 or so with unhurried and courteous drivers back then. The trip would expose me to traffic lights, that one one-way street there and some "who has the right of way here" exercises with drivers you didn't even recognize at the intersection.

I got my driver's license, so I guess everything worked out OK.

Big city driving

The driving skills have had to step it up a notch since I've gotten older. As a North Dakotan, it's kind of inevitable that I've had do some driving in Minneapolis and Denver. I've gotten behind the wheel in Dallas/Fort Worth, Seattle, San Francisco, Los Angeles and a few others. Not that I lacked the courage, but I did just take a cab and let someone else drive when I was in New York.

Most times when I'm driving in a big city, I'm in a rental car, so it's not like I have to worry about wrecking my own vehicle when I'm out learning the local traffic patterns. I should take out the extra insurance at the rental counter, but I always heard that was a rip-off, so I never do.

My big-city driving experiences haven't been too traumatic. But I've missed a few exits, driven past my destination and remember finding myself in the "bad part of town" at night where the stores have bars on their windows and I wondered if my rental car still would have hub caps when the light turned green.

Now, I can cruise the cities with complete confidence, thanks to my Blackberry global positioning application. A blinking red dot tells me exactly where I am at any given moment. I miss fewer exits. I know when to abandon course and regroup.

I drive with confidence. And when you got your first driving lessons on a North Dakota hay field and you find yourself careening down a Los Angeles freeway in a rental car, you need to have confidence.

For me, the GPS navigator is the great equalizer. Helping hesitant country boys become confident city drivers around the globe. Thanks, technology.

Chapter 8
All the rest

Left-handed living
Four weeks of forced ambidextrousness
September 20, 2004

Ranching can be a dangerous occupation.

The work has some inherent risks that come with cattle and machinery and such. But sometimes it's not so much the work that'll hurt you, it's the play.

Recreation got the best of me a couple of weeks ago when we were doing a little team roping in our arena. I started the evening with two good hands. I finished the night with one, and my left one at that.

No, I didn't fall to the usual team roper's fate and smoke off the end of my thumb in the dally of the rope. I did something much more difficult and probably impossible to repeat.

Somehow, when I was going down to take a dally, I managed to rap my hand down on the metal-capped saddle horn hard enough to break a bone in my right hand.

I roped another half -dozen steers after it broke just for good measure. I waited three days before seeing a doctor. We've all got to do our part to stem this health care crisis, and stubborn, stoic cowboys do all they can to cut down on frivolous clinic calls. I finally succumbed to the idea of a professional opinion.

Doctor's orders

They took some X-rays and told me I had a fracture. Then they commenced to splinting, binding and more or less making worthless my steer-roping, pencil-handling, coffee-drinking, wrench-turning, face-shaving, diaper-changing, gear-shifting hand.

They called it a boxer's fracture, and a lot of times it takes surgery and pins to fix. The nurse told me that most boxer fractures come from fella's who get mad and punch a wall.

Now, I felt a little silly about hurting my hand while doing some recreational roping, but I can't imagine how silly you'd feel heading to the doctor after losing a fight with a wall.

I'm trying life out as a southpaw now. I figured ranching was getting so easy with our modern conveniences, I'd try doing it with one hand tied behind my back.

I've always considered myself a little more ambidextrous than most after having my right wrist in a cast for 12 weeks when I was a lad. Regardless of prior practice, it's still darn tough for a right-hander to go left.

Unhandy

It's the little things that are the biggest challenge. When I'm reaching up to comb my hair with my left hand, I'm lucky to do anything but hook an ear or curry an eyebrow. My left hand doesn't just brush my teeth, it brushes my lips, my chin and a bit of my nose.

My table manners aren't so good as a lefty. But I just hang in there and take my time. Skinny cowboys can't afford to get even skinnier.

The bolts that I once tightened with my right hand, now need to be broken loose with my left hand. I'm getting better at using my foot in these delicate mechanical operations.

Working in the grease and grime hasn't made my half cast and bandages anymore attractive. I've solved this soiled dilemma by keeping a set of dirty work bandages and a clean set of "goin' to town" bandages for special occasions.

I am starting to get used to my temporary handicap. I've even wondered if I should keep with the left-handedness after my right hand has healed. I'd be in good company with other lefties like Albert Einstein, Mark Twain and Beethoven. Some say lefties tend to be gifted and more creative.

No, I think I'll try to use both of my hands a little more equally. That way, I'll be equally prepared for my next big break.

Poor pen pal
But thanks for the letters
October 4, 2004

Letter writing, they say, is becoming a lost art.

But I'm proud to say there's a stack of letters from readers on my desk to disprove that claim.

However, that claim probably is supported by the fact that I haven't answered those letters. I'm ashamed to admit how far behind this writer is on writing back to people.

This may be a cheap way of getting around it, but I was kind of hoping this column would qualify as return correspondence.

I've been writing this column for 10 years and, like many ambitious upstarts, I answered every piece of mail I got those first several years. Then I started getting a little behind. Before long, I was so far behind I was too embarrassed to sit down and write a letter beginning with, "Thanks so much for your letter written five years ago."

Lately, I may not have answered every letter, but I guarantee that I have read and appreciated every letter. So, to everyone who's ever written to me, thank you.

Far and wide

I've heard from folks 100 miles into the Alaska wilderness who say my column can make them smile even when they're, "having a bad hay day or a heavy wolf day." I consider cheering a rancher up on a "heavy wolf day" to be quite a compliment.

I got a real nice three-page letter and a picture from a couple living on the Deadman River in British Columbia, Canada. That ranch sounded like the kind of place I'd like to visit.

Canadian culture has produced good letter writers. My longest letter, and one well worth reading, was a five-pager from Kenaston, Saskatchewan.

I heard from a U.S. Army soldier in Afghanistan who read my book and shared it with his fellow servicemen to help explain life in the Dakotas.

I found out my columns often were read aloud to the senior creative writing class at the Visalia Adult School in Visalia, Calif. I also found out my column was a favorite for a couple of inmates in the California prison system.

I hear from a lot of retired farmers and ranchers and others who are getting on in years. They always have good stories to share.

One story I enjoyed reading was from Emil, whose father had a two-cylinder Hart Parr tractor. It was a hand cranker and hard to start. His Dad got tired of cranking it by hand, so he took a long rope, wrapped it around the belt pulley, pulled the rope with his car and started that tractor with a lot less sweat.

A few readers have written to me more than once. I've gotten Christmas cards, wedding cards and notes of congratulation on the birth of our son. They all brighten my day.

I have a reader in Brocket, N.D., who cuts my articles out and saves them. She asks me to greet my parents when she writes. We both share the challenge of a family member with Parkinson's disease.

Some people handwrite their letters, others type them. One 83-year-old reader and former stockyards man closed with, "This type pounder is old and so am I so better quit."

I always knew plains people appreciated self-deprecating humor, but none put it as well as Omer who raised sheep for 60 years in South Dakota. He wrote, "Your humor and all the things you tell on yourself — the more you tell and the lower you put yourself down—the more we read and like you." Thanks, Omer … I think.

My best advice came from a reader in Wimbledon, N.D., when I started working a corporate job off the ranch several years ago. He wrote, "Don't leave us with nothing to read out here because they will try to kick you upstairs in some big town. Life is more than money."

Yes, it is. Life is also good people who take the time to write some columnist a letter. To everyone whose done that for me, I thank you.

Wine snob
Rancher turns vintner   October 18, 2004

I've always been a do-it-yourselfer. I guess that's how I ended up buying a wine-making kit on impulse.

I'm better at buying do-it-myself projects than I am at actually doing them. I walked around that wine-making kit in our house for nearly two years. I know wine is supposed to age, but I doubt that's how you're supposed to do it.

It reminded me of the pole barn building package I once bought. The truck unloaded the rafters, poles, lumber and steel in the yard, and I walked around that pile of materials for a good year before I even dug the holes for it. I finally hoisted the rafters up just before they rotted into the ground

I've always had more plans than I've had time.

Patient persistence

Time is a key ingredient in the wine-making business. My kit would produce a batch of wine ready to bottle in 28 days. The first seven days required some close monitoring.

I know I'd never cut it as a dairy farmer because I had a tough time looking at the calendar and finding 28 days in a row when I'd be home to perform all the needed steps to create the perfect vintage.

The opportunity to be a homebody came with the birth of our son. When little Bud came home to the ranch, it looked like we'd be spending a lot more time on the homestead.

The wine kit came with its own plastic 5-gallon pail. Somehow I kept that pail out of the feed bin and kept it clean enough for human consumption. I mixed up the grape juice concentrate, water, bentonite and yeast the day after we came back from the hospital.

From then on, it was like checking heifers or milking cows or taking care of a baby — I had to be there. I checked the temperature, dunked the hydrometer and calculated its specific gravity every day at the same time as things began to bubble. It was quite a chemistry experiment.

In seven days, it was siphoned from the feed pail into a big glass jug that us vintners call a carboy. Another 10 days and I stirred in some metabisulphite, sorbate and chitosan, which they referred to as packets two, three and four for us beginners.

My kit came with its own bung and airlock. Most of the bungs on this ranch don't come with an airlock. But it's good engineering for winemaking because it keeps the carboy from exploding without letting outside air in.

My mother used an improvised airlock when she used to make chokecherry wine. Her airlock was a balloon stretched over the neck of the bottle. When that balloon inflated you knew the wine was doing something. When it deflated it was close to done. Not as professional as my new setup, but effective.

Cork and bottle

The end result of my 28 days of winemaking was 30 bottles of Taylor Ranch Merlot corked and laid into my wine rack for about $2 a bottle.

After a few months of aging, my taste buds would have to say that 2004 was a very good year for our ranch winery. Not so good for haying but pretty good for winemaking.

Guests have drank it and figured it was worth at least $4 or $5 a bottle. It's a good thing that I don't charge for my time. In true rancher style, I get the most satisfaction from just giving our wine away.

A friend of ours said she was surprised that I was such an oenophile. I took a couple of steps back and told her I didn't appreciate name-calling.

I guess it's an oenological wine thing. I have a ways to go before I'm a real wine snob.

Going to the dogs
New Thanksgiving tradition
November 29, 2004

My family had the usual Thanksgiving traditions this year. Gather a few relatives, founder ourselves on a feast and retire to the living room for some rumination.

This year, we added another tradition. We watched a little of the National Dog Show, taped in Philadelphia and broadcast for our holiday pleasure on Thanksgiving Day.

It was quite a spectacle. More than 1,900 dogs of 150 breeds were all prettied up and put on parade for the judges to ponder.

These dogs were cleaner and better groomed than all of my bachelor friends and most of my married friends. They were better behaved than any kid or adult I know.

After watching the professionals, I stepped out my front door to size up the two uncoddled canines that grace our porch.

Worlds apart

Laid out on the front yard of the Taylor Ranch were Jesse, our border collie, and Smokey, our borderline border collie.

They weren't real well groomed. Jesse smelled like a skunk. She has yet to learn not to chase those black-and-white-striped cats.

Smokey's aroma was more reminiscent of the ranch's dead pile where the less fortunate livestock awaits burial. He really prefers home-raised carrion to any brand of store-bought dog chow.

Dogs in the National Dog Show put up with a lot of poking and prodding by the judge. Judges check out their teeth, stroke their coat and feel up their limbs.

Smokey won't even let me put that drop of dope between his shoulder blades to fend off the wood ticks without snapping at me.

Smokey's training has been minimal. He's learned how to jump in the pickup, ride in the tractor and stay in his dog house when we work cattle. He's a pretty ideal ranch dog.

His only fault is a marginal vertical lift when he's jumping into my new pickup. For some reason, new pickups are a foot taller than the old pickups. I've got Smokey's claw marks on the side of my new pickup to prove the difference. His weary bones prefer the box height of my old field pickup.

Some would say he's no good, but I prefer no good over nuisance.

Hyper help

Our other dog, Jesse, falls firmly into the nuisance category. She is a papered border collie, so she's always looking for a job.

She does chase cattle — whenever she wants and for as long as she cares to. On good days, she'll settle for herding the cats around the yard. On bad days, she'll try chasing your horse just as you put your foot in the stirrup.

She was a trained herder at one time in her former life. But she was trained to bring livestock to you, while I like to go out and move livestock away from me. This gets a little frustrating with me and my horse herding cattle from behind and the dog out front chasing them back at us.

Although her name is Jesse, the casual observer would swear her name was "Dammit Jesse," by listening in on our discourse. I could reduce my cussing considerably by just calling her DJ for short.

One of the real drawbacks with this dog is that our veterinarian's name also is Jesse. Once when he was pregnancy checking the cows, our hard working cow dog was lying in front of the headgate doing her nuisance best to keep the cows out of the chute.

"Dammit Jesse," I said, "get out of here!" My veterinarian was halfway back to his pickup before I smoothed things over and convinced him to come back.

Ever since, I tie up Jesse the dog before Jesse the vet comes out to work cows. Veterinarians are just too hard to find in our neighborhood to insult them every time a dog does something wrong.

Idle time
Cold starts and warm cars   January 10, 2005

I don't mind winter so much, but one thing I don't like is a cold car and an icy windshield. I guess that's why some people have garages.

People with heated garages don't get the whole icy experience. They jump into their warm cars with their clean windshields, pop open the garage door and drive off into the frosty tundra without a care.

As for me, I sprint out into the cold, sweep off the snow, scrape the ice off the windshield, start 'er up, plunk my warm butt down on that hard cold seat and drive away.

If it's really cold, I'll start it and sprint back to plunk my warm butt down in the house while the car burns a little high-priced gas to create a little highly valued heat.

I'm not sure who invented the idea of winter idling, but I bet they were tied in with the petroleum marketing business. It's got to be a real sales boost for them.

I know folks who'll let their car idle for an hour with the defroster on full blast rather than scrape so much as a speck of ice off their windshied.

I've had neighbors who'd stop for a visit and let their pickup idle half the morning rather than sit in a cold cab when they left.

I've seen cars parked and idling just to keep the heat going for dogs they left inside. I hope my dogs never find out that other dogs get to spend the winter indoors and in warm cars left idling with the heater blowing.

Start your engines

Thanks to modern technology, it's gotten even easier to have your car idling, burning gas and blowing heat. Remote car starting has revolutionized the winter warm-up.

I was a little frightened the first time I walked through a parking lot and saw cars with no one inside start up all of a sudden. It was like they were possessed with a poltergeist. I picked up my step thinking the ghost car's next move might be to put the shifter in gear and run me over.

Eventually, I learned that the possessed cars cranking their engines were having their buttons pushed hundreds of feet away by their owners.

That's the kind of progress we've made in northern climates. You can start your car while you're in the shopping mall, keep on shopping and walk out to a warm, locked, idling car.

I thought it was quite an advance when I got one of those little key chains that pulled apart so I could leave the ignition key in and the car idling, lock her up and have the car door key in my pocket.

Of course, I don't go to many places where I'm not comfortable with just letting the car run without being locked. Maybe I just don't drive anything worth stealing. Car thieves are picky enough to pass over my cars even if they are unlocked and idling.

I don't think the new remote auto start would work on some of my vehicles anyway. It takes more than a signal and a crank to get their motor started. Many mornings it takes a little prayer, a few synchronized pumps of the foot feed and, sometimes, a pair of jumper cables. You can't put all that on a switch in your pocket.

My wife is pretty envious of the cars with auto start. Granted, it would be a nice feature when you're toting a baby around in the winter.

But I told her as long as she had me around, I'd be her auto start. So while others are pushing buttons to start their car, my wife is just pushing me out the door to start hers.

Considering the couple hundred dollars it costs to get an auto start installed, she never can say her husband is worthless.

Speed bumps
Up and over, down and out   January 24, 2005

It's about 16 miles between our house and town. We like to call it a 20-minute drive.

At least we did before the speed bumps were installed.

No, there's not a big push from the county law enforcement to slow traffic in our neighborhood. There's not a single speed limit sign between the ranch and town, and I've never seen a police officer on our road unless he was off duty and hunting geese or something.

The speed bumps installed on our road were put there by a higher power than the highway patrol.

With a 60-mph wind, the good Lord turned white, fluffy snow into rock hard drifts, effectively putting the brakes on our thoughts of driving as fast as that wind blew.

Pillows?

We call these little fingers of snow sifting across our road "pillow drifts."

I've never seen a pillow as hard as our most recent pillow drifts, not even in the cheapest motel I've ever tossed and turned in.

I could handle a few pillow drifts if they were more the consistency of the down pillows that my wife puts on our bed. It'd be fine if they were more like the cheaper synthetic or poly-fill pillows I used to sleep on.

No, there's no give or cushion at all when you drive across our newest pillow drifts.

I hadn't checked out the hardness of those drifts when I drove my wife and baby to church last Sunday.

We hit that first pillow drift doing 50 mph. The impact crumpled down the 5-inch crown on my cowboy hat until it resembled a 2-inch accordion.

My wife had spent 20 minutes with a curling iron and hair spray to get her hair to defy gravity. We were both defying gravity after hitting that bump. The hair, however, was as flat as the car ceiling when we landed.

The baby was just happy to be strapped into his car seat. His only concern was the toys that flew up in the air. Luckily, he caught most of them in his lap when they came back down. He just giggled after the landing.

The way everything in the vehicle was suspended in mid-air, we got the feeling of space travel without the expense. Luckily, I had the spill proof lid on my coffee mug.

Slow down

The speed bumps worked just like they would in town. I had to slow down until I was just barely moving and roll over the drifts that were hard enough to support the weight of the vehicle.

Then, also like city speed bump zones, I would accelerate to pick up as much speed as possible before slamming on the brakes for the next one. It was a pretty jerky drive to town.

Like all smartly constructed speed bump zones, I couldn't even find a way to drive around the bumps to make a little better time.

We barely made it to church on time that day. Fortunately, but completely out of character for us, we had gotten an early start.

If we had walked in late, we'd just have to explain to the preacher our run-in with God's new speed bumps on our road. Apparently, the Drift-maker would like us to slow down a little and enjoy the drive.

Cash, credit or crap?
Save the premium, take the money   February 21, 2005

It's ag show season again. Time to walk the rows of booths and gather up what I affectionately call "free crap."

Pens, notebooks, calculators, rulers and calendars are free for the picking if you show even a mild interest in the products being promoted at the booths. A lot of this stuff gets carried out of the show and lives out the rest of its useful life on the dashboard of the pickup.

One of the free premium items I got even helped me make more room on my dashboard for more stuff. It was a little pad about 6 inches square, with the company's name and logo on it of course, that you'd affix to the steep side of your dash.

Then — voila! — stuff that normally would slide off the dashboard could be stuck to this little sticky spot.

It looked pretty handy, but why stop with a little 6-inch square area? I was more interested in getting a big roll of this adhesive material.

Imagine how much stuff you could stick on your dash if the whole area was covered. You could roll it out on the roof, seat and sides as a safety feature to keep you and your stuff in place in the event of an accident.

Double stuff

Vendors try to be original with their premium items. They're starting to realize that farmers and ranchers have about all the baseball caps they could use in two lifetimes. Some companies are moving to logo-imprinted, leather fencing gloves. It's a good move because I'll always need more gloves.

Coffee cups and travel mugs also have gained commodity status. You can lose and misplace a lot of travel mugs to create some demand for new ones, but I've still got more cups than my wife cares to keep in the cupboard.

Somehow I also ended up with a slug of soft-sided company imprinted briefcases and nylon bags, too. I figure briefcases should hold important documents. I now have important documents scattered amongst a half-dozen bags. It can make for some frantic searching when you really want to find something.

I guess premiums and free stuff always have been a part of making the sale, but I think the pace has picked up lately. Thanks to China and other cheap labor countries, you can get most of this stuff for pennies.

Someone buys $1,000 worth of cattle vaccine, give 'em an 89-cent calculator. Get $10,000 worth of feed and mineral, and they throw in a 99-cent coffee mug. Buy a $25,000 baler, and get yourself a couple of $3 caps.

Another option

I don't think I need any more $10,000 coffee mugs. The next time someone tries to pawn off their logo goods and advertising premiums on me, I'm going to tell them to just give me the money instead.

We can even do it electronically. Swipe my credit card and add the pennies and dollars to my account. Keep the pen, keep the baseball cap; just swipe my card.

If they're not set up for electronic crap option credits, they always can give crap option cash. It makes no difference to me.

At the end of the year, my dashboard will be cleaner, my house will have less clutter, and I'll be able to buy something I can really use.

That kind of program really could make for a loyal customer.

Nesting season
Downy birds, hay-filled beds
April 4, 2005

Spring has sprung on the Taylor Ranch. At least that's what the geese are telling us.

The honkers are heading north again, although as mild as our winter was they could have saved the wear and tear on their wings and skipped heading south for Christmas this year.

It's reassuring to see them each spring and fall, a sure sign of the changing seasons just in case you don't have a pocket calendar or a Palm Pilot. I appreciate the passers-through, and I like the stay-arounders, too.

We always have several pairs of giant Canada geese who put down roots on the ranch in the spring and summer to raise a family. Actually, since they mate for life, these ganders and gooses may well be annual tenants of the meadows and lakes on the ranch.

They're a pretty impressive bird. They like to honk and talk back and forth, they can run on water, and they can fly and flap a 6-foot set of wings without bumping into each other. Since I don't have any delicate crops that they can damage or a golf course that I'm worried about them soiling, I truly can say I enjoy their company on my piece of the prairie.

Nesting sites

I'm so supportive of our feathered visitors, I once had the local wildlife professionals put up a predator-proof goose nest on one of our pasture lakes.

It was pretty high tech. It had a composite nesting tub attached to a sturdy steel pipe driven deep into the lake bed. It was virtually varmint proof, sure to discourage assorted egg stealers from shimmying up the pole for a snack.

A young goose family would be hard pressed to find better accommodations.

But, as deluxe as it was, word of the new nest must not have made its way to the goose or her gander. It never has had a tenant.

Geese continued nesting around the lake, taking their chances and building their own humble abodes.

Occasionally, I leave a little slough hay or part of a windrow for them to work with. This winter, I left a whole bale for them to perch on.

It wasn't a completely conscious and benevolent gift for the local wildlife. I was going to pick the bale up and take it home, but when I felt the loader tractor sinking in the mud around the bale, I aborted the effort and chalked it up to environmental stewardship.

Unintentional conservation

I get to drive by my favorite example of a rancher's forced generosity with nesting geese every time I go to town.

During one rather dry haying season, I noticed my neighbor's tractor and baler along the road parked in the middle of this slough. He was making the best of the drought by haying his sloughs, but this one wasn't as dry as he thought. His baling outfit wasn't quite as nimble and light as his cutter, and there it sat mired and immobile in the gray, greasy mud.

The next time I drove by, there was a telltale set of tracks where they pulled it out and a nice, big, round bale sitting there where they lifted the baler gate and lightened the load before the pull.

The following year, the rains came back and that bale found itself in the middle of a water-filled lake. And, sure enough, a goose built her nest on my neighbor's ill-fated forage.

Proof positive that ranchers are environmentalists, even when they don't plan it.

Polo, anyone?
The sport of royalty and one peasant
September 19, 2005

When you say polo, the first image for most people is a line of fashionable clothes or expensive cologne and a guy named Ralph.

Me? I think about galloping horses, smacking a ball with a stick and a couple of guys named Roberto and Esteban down in Argentina.

Earlier this year, I was chosen to be part of a small delegation of young people from across the U.S. to go to Argentina and Uruguay as part of a leadership exchange. So, a couple of weeks ago, I wrapped the twine on my last hay bale, put the cattle on fresh pasture, kissed my family goodbye and struck out for the southern side of our hemisphere.

We kept a hectic, busy schedule on the trip, but one weekend allowed for a couple of hours of free time in Buenos Aires, Argentina. Most of the crew opted to go shopping. I asked if I could catch a game of polo.

Somewhere in my years of reading horse magazines and National Geographic and a few travel articles, I knew that Argentina was a polo-playing country.

As it turns out, Argentina isn't just any old polo-playing country, it is *the* polo playing country of the world. They dominate the professional play of the sport and most of the world's top 10 polo players consistently are Argentine.

One of our Argentine hosts, Esteban, went to work on my request for some polo, and, before you could say "the oldest ball game in the world," he was driving three of our delegation out of the big city toward the La Sofia equestrian center to try a little polo.

At La Sofia, I met Roberto, my new polo coach. I had learned about 50 words of Spanish since I landed in Argentina, Roberto didn't know much more English than I knew Spanish. But once we were horseback, we could communicate.

I always thought roping a steer or cutting a cow from the herd was as much fun as one could have on horseback. But galloping down a grassy field and whacking a little white ball with a polo mallet may have it beat.

Roberto would pass me the ball, and when I'd get a good stick on it he'd yell, "Muy bien, muy bien!" It felt very fine, very fine indeed. I was hooked in a matter of minutes.

Fully equipped

If I was going to keep up with my newfound sport, I needed some equipment. I struck a deal with Roberto for a couple of balls and a polo mallet.

When I was a teenager, I pondered the sport of polo but gave it up when I found out the mallet alone cost $100.

When I converted the pesos and discovered I could get an Argentine mallet for $50, I handed over the cash. But now I had to get it home. The freight to ship my new mallet to the U.S. was about $46. I decided to cart it around South America and back to the U.S. and save the money.

If you think it's hard to board an airplane with a fingernail clipper, try getting on with a polo mallet. Trying to take it as a carry-on nearly caused an international incident, then getting it through customs as checked luggage nearly put me on the most wanted list as some kind of polo playing terrorist.

In the end, I got it home without snapping it in two to fit inside a suitcase and without paying an extra $80 to declare a third piece of luggage.

Polo may be the game of kings and royalty and people of privilege, but this polo player's on a ranching budget.

Poco bilingual
Picking up a little Spanish   October 3, 2005

In my neighborhood, being bilingual means knowing a few Norwegian niceties taught by your grandmother or maybe a couple of German cuss words occasionally slipped by a great-uncle.

I never did learn a second language beyond a couple of those Norwegian terms for "thank you." I once took the initiative to buy a set of "Learn to speak Spanish" cassette tapes about 10 years ago, but that's as far as the initiative went. The whole set is still in mint condition.

I was going to give them a listen before my trip to South America this summer, but things got busy on the ranch and time didn't allow for the luxury of lingual learning. I was going to have to learn the language of the locals in Argentina and Uruguay by way of immersion.

Immersion, as the term suggests, is the "sink or swim" way to learn the lingo. Drop an English speaking cowboy into a sea of Spanish speakers and watch him paddle and flail. I like learning new things, so I worked hard to tread a little of this wordy water.

Sign language

The first thing I tried to do in the two Spanish-speaking countries I visited was get the locals to speak English. The typical egocentric traveler, I figured they would want to adopt my language.

I learned that there are a couple things we like to do to make others understand us. If the person we're addressing doesn't speak English, we try again louder and slower. In reality, if a fella doesn't know a lick of English, he doesn't understand it any better if you shout it and methodically enunciate every syllable.

Another tactic that's slightly more effective is to add some hand signals and impromptu sign language to help pantomime the message we're trying to get across. This is real entertaining for awhile. But like any other mime, it soon can become annoying.

Sometimes it's a little embarrassing to work a word into sign language. For instance, "May I use your bathroom?" can bring out some nearly vulgar gestures as you do the charades-style explanation of your query.

So I began to learn some Spanish. Simply say "baño?" and they'll point you toward the bathroom. A little bit of language can go a long way in providing comfort while you travel.

It's also important to be able to order food to sustain you. "Carne de vaca" will get you some beef, "ensalada" and "patata" and "cerveza" will get you some greens and spuds and suds to go with it.

Before long, I was walking the streets and giving folks a tip of the hat and a little native "buenos dias" in greeting.

At meetings, I learned enough of the language to introduce myself in Spanish. "Hola, mi nombre es Ryan Taylor y soy ranchero de los ganados de Dakota del norte." Hello, my name is Ryan Taylor and I am a cattle rancher from North Dakota.

Then they really thought I knew the language and they'd come back at me with a high-speed string of Spanish words that went right over the top of my head. So I'd give them my fall back phrase, "No hablo español."

I'm not sure what they thought when I told them I didn't speak Spanish in Spanish after I just greeted them and introduced myself to them in Spanish.

But, on one occasion, when I told my new Argentine friend, "no hablo espanol," she smiled and said, "That's OK. Can you speak English?" I guess she'd learned more from her English tapes than I'd learned from the Spanish cassettes gathering dust on my shelf.

"Bueno," I said. It'd be good to speak some English. Even an immersion learner needs to come up for air once in awhile.

No-show Taylor
And feeling awful about it   October 17, 2005

It's a high compliment to say a man's word is good. Unfortunately, sometimes our word might be good but our memory is bad, or just overly dependent on notes not put into high-tech electronic calendars.

The ranching lifestyle doesn't really require much for appointments and calendars and needing to be anywhere but the ranch day in and day out. But along with my ranching, I've fallen into the business of being an after-dinner speaker and entertainer. It means I need to keep a pretty accurate calendar of where I need to be and when.

That's why my heart sunk clear to my boots when I got a phone call on Saturday night saying I was supposed to be 225 miles southwest of where I was at that very moment to speak to 250 farmers and ranchers and other good people who had assembled to eat a pancake supper and hear me speak.

In all my years — even in my old dating days — I'd never stood anybody up like that.

I've given 171 presentations of rope spinning cowboy logic since I started leaving the ranch to try to entertain others. The only two times I failed to show up had me stuck in a blizzard or home with the flu. Even then I was able to call ahead and let them I know I couldn't make it and help find a replacement.

On 171 occasions my word was as good as gold. I'd talk to someone doing the organizing, they'd give me a date, I'd say "yup, I'll be there," and when the date rolled around, I was there with no further reminders. Then there was that 172nd speaking job that I didn't get transferred from the notepad where I scribble things to the calendar that tells me where I need to be.

In baseball, I'd be batting .995, 171 hits out of 172 at bats. The folks waiting for me that Saturday night needed someone batting 1.000 though. They deserved a guy who'd remember to show up when he was supposed to. It still makes me sick just thinking about it. It's really not like me to miss a free supper and a paying job.

Reputation reconciliation

Dad told me once, it didn't matter so much if you were poor, as long as you were honest and had a good reputation. My mistake was an honest one, but I don't reckon my reputation is too good in one small North Dakota town.

Reputations are built over years and destroyed in moments, they say. I guess the reputation rebuilding starts with an honest apology. I'm sure extending that along with an offer to make things right somehow down the road.

Of course, there might have been a few folks at the supper who were kind of glad I didn't show up. Nothing spoils a good supper like having to listen to some yahoo talk and spin ropes for up to an hour.

Those final door prizes were handed out a little quicker without some speaker dragging things out. And everyone got home a little faster to let their supper ruminate before watching the evening news.

But to those folks who really wanted to hear me, boy am I sorry. From now on, I'll be hanging yellow Post-It notes from the brim of my hat and requesting wake-up calls a day ahead of the events to help me keep my word.

Daylight lost
But I'm still saving
November 28, 2005

I guess we were supposed to quit saving daylight on Oct. 30, according to the daylight saving time enforcers.

Not me, I'm still saving daylight. No, it's not so much because I've bought into the idea of extra energy savings or that I yearn for an extra hour to play early winter golf. I just can't remember how to reset all the clocks that still are staring at me in DST.

I don't remember being surrounded by as many clocks as I am now. One watch on the wrist and one in the kitchen used to be the extent of the domestic timepieces. Now they're truly ubiquitous, which is kind of like omnipresent, or if I didn't have a computer thesaurus I'd just say they were everywhere.

I've got two wristwatches, one for beating up and losing and one for keeping clean and going to town. The work watch cost a fraction of what the dress-up watch did, but it's equally hard to reset.

I don't often keep the instruction book or warranties on $8 watches, figuring they'll quit working before I need to refer to them again. When I got the cheap watch that I wear for work, the instructions for it were printed in six different languages. Really.

I got the initial setup on the watch done after intensely studying and rereading what appeared to be the English directions. I probably could have cut the time in half with a Chinese friend to translate one of the other sets of instructions written in Mandarin.

But when daylight saving time ends, I wish I still had those instructions, well written or not.

I still have the paperwork for my good watch, so if I dedicate an hour or two to deciphering them, I can have that watch reset without messing up its settings for the month and leap year and the varying tilt of the earth.

Then there're the vehicles to consider. The car clocks have more technology and complexity built into them than my father's entire pickup did when he was my age. Back to the cubby hole (known as a glove box in some local dialects) to try and find the car manual to get it all figured out.

The house is a veritable minefield of digital clocks that need setting whenever the time changes or the power goes out. The microwave tells me what time it is, as does the stove and the VCR and the stereo and the two alarm clocks and the two wall clocks and a couple more that hang around for the sake of decoration.

I do hand it to the computer engineers who made it possible for my computer to change itself automatically. I wonder what the computers in Saskatchewan, Arizona, Hawaii and parts of Indiana do when daylight saving time rolls around? I suppose they're either customized for local time or simply ignored.

Ignoring the clocks is what I've tried to do for the last month or so, but my math skills are wearing thin from the constant subtraction in my head. I may have to just bear down, find the owner's manuals and get the clocks set back to standard time.

If don't do it pretty soon, I could just as well ride it out until the first Sunday in April and be right back in sync.

On the ice
Fishing and fraternizing   March 6, 2006

I've never been much of a fisherman. I've been even less of an ice fisherman.

I like catching fish and I like eating fish, I just never made the time to do a lot of fishing. I might go once or twice a summer if someone who really likes it invites me or offers a spot on their boat.

I'd never set foot in an ice house or gathered around a hole in the ice with the heartiest of fish seekers, the great northern ice fisherman.

That is until this winter.

Enter the realm

I've driven by lakes in the winter dotted with these little wooden shacks on the ice and I always wondered what went on in those recreational cubicles. I figured it had to be pretty special for what they spent on their portable houses and the value of the pickups that they'd occasionally sink to the bottom of the lake.

This winter, I had an invitation to not only enter one of these luxuriously heated ice houses and wet a line, but to sit in there next to a couple of seasoned Minnesota ice fishermen.

It's one thing to go ice fishing, it's another to go ice fishing with a Minnesotan. Minnesotans are to ice fishing what Kenyans are to running marathons or the Chinese are to playing ping pong. All three sports take about the same amount of perseverance and tolerance for tedium.

I was in good company as we cut the holes in the early morn, fished out the ice chunks (hence the name ice fishing?), dropped our lines and pulled up a chair to stare into the icy depths. After a couple hours of that and a thermos of coffee, it was time to switch into "auto fish" mode and set up the card table for some pinochle.

Between hands, we'd check our bobber function and pull up the minnow to make sure he was still wiggling. After a couple hours of card playing, we'd worked up enough appetite for lunch. But the fish hadn't worked up enough appetite to bite on our minnows and hooks.

We bobbed the lines up and down a little after lunch, bobbed our heads up and down in something as close to a state of sleep as you can get sitting upright. When we woke up, we shuffled the cards and played pinochle for a few more hours.

One single fish

For 12 hours of good hard fishing and card playing and eating and drinking, we had but one fish to show for our party's seven lines dropped in seven ice holes.

We had some visitors from the neighboring ice houses. We'd talk about the dearth of fish beneath our ice houses and make a little chit chat. I never saw a woman that whole day on the lake. They must know enough to buy their fish in the store when they get a hankering for fish and chips.

Meager fishing aside, I did get to win a couple of hands of pinochle. I got to know the friends and relatives in the ice house a little better. And I got away from the stress of the usual daily chores.

But I think next time we go we'll just pull the ice house down the road a mile or two and park it alongside the road. That way we can save the work of drilling holes. The card playing and lunch should be just as satisfying.

If we really need some fish to show for our efforts when we get back home, I say we just filet a couple of the minnows from the bait bucket and tell them about the ones that got away.

North to Alaska
A taste of life on the last frontier   April 3, 2006

There aren't many places in the U.S. where I can go and have the people refer to me as being from "down south." But that's what they say to a guy from North Dakota when he's in Alaska.

My Canadian friends don't say down south when they reference my home. I'm just from "the states." I reckon to them, "down south" would be tropical climes like Estevan, Saskatchewan, or Morden, Manitoba. They do have a densely populated piece of geography called "down east," but that's something else entirely.

In Alaska, though, I'm from down south and, by their definition, that can mean anything from Washington state to the Dakotas or Florida. It kind of made me want to drawl my syllables a little while I was there.

After visiting our state up north, I can lay claim to visiting 31 of the 50 states in the U.S.

I had lots of good reasons to visit Alaska, like an aunt and uncle and five cousins who've made the last frontier their home.

I had a little time to travel before calving started, a neighbor who said he'd feed the cows and a mother-in-law who said she'd take care of our toddler.

Plus, I had a bunch of airline miles saved with one of our bankrupt airlines. I figured if they go completely belly up, my loss of airline miles and free travel would be the least of their concerns, so I'd best start using them up.

So my wife and I headed north, which, in the world of air travel, meant going east, then west, then north.

A different world

In my part of the world, which happens to be the exact middle of the continent, if you want to go anywhere, there are thousands of miles of road going each direction. Just jump in the car and take your pick.

In southeast Alaska, the island and coastal towns don't have much for highway miles. Some of the local taxpayers seem to like it that way. As one bumper sticker said, "If you want more roads, move down south." You know, south, like North Dakota.

So, in places like Juneau or Petersburg, if you want to get there from here or here from there, you better be ready to hop on a boat or jump in an airplane.

My wife and I got plenty of both, from ferry boats to skiffs, jet planes to personal aircraft.

It helped that I have bush pilots, fishermen and tug boaters swinging from the branches of my Alaskan family tree.

We got to do things that we don't do a lot of on a prairie ranch, like fish for salmon, trap crabs, dig clams and see bald eagles fly around as thick as blackbirds. The seafood we ate couldn't have been much fresher. The ice in our drinks floated in on a glacial iceberg.

But, deep down, a fishing town up north isn't much different than a ranching town down south. People still depend on the whims of the market and hope for a profit. When it's time to sell, you have to sell.

They watch the weather and know that it can make their job a little easier or a heck of a lot harder. The things they need are bought at retail, and the things they sell are sold at wholesale.

When times are tough, they're sure it'll get better. And when times are good, they get nervous.

The folks up north are good people. And I'd say that even if I wasn't related to a bunch of them.

216

Leisure time
And hobbies I don't have

I'm not sure if I've ever had much leisure time. Whatever I had, I have less now.

Right now, I'm writing this column instead of roping steers over at my neighbor's arena. I don't want my editors to take this the wrong way because I love writing this column, but I think I'd rather be roping.

I'm not a very good roper. Some would say I'm not a very good writer either. So I could be at my computer, or in the arena, doing my mediocre best in either case.

The nice thing about our neighborhood team roping is that it's pretty low pressure. There're no entry fees, no prize money, no screaming fans expecting us to catch 'em quick on every run. A guy needs some stress- free fun in his life.

At times when I'm roping especially poorly, I always can justify the run for the good it's done my horse.

My horses aren't high-dollar, seasoned mounts bought and brought to the ranch ready to use. They're mostly home raised and home trained. I can take the blame for all their good and bad habits.

One thing I really like about horses is that they have an appreciation schedule instead of a depreciation schedule. The more miles you put on a pickup or a four-wheeler, the less they're worth. The more miles and hours you put on a horse, the more they're worth. It looks good on paper at least, because I've never sold a good horse.

So, as I tell my wife, roping steers with the neighbors does have some financial benefits. It makes my $2,000 horse worth $4,000, even though we never test that net increase on the cash market.

Diminishing hobbies

Several years and obligations ago, it was a lot easier for me to list my hobbies. I'd say things like roping, running, skiing and the like. Now, in light of my limited leisure time, I'd have to answer the question by saying my hobbies are "not roping, not running, not skiing."

I've still got all the gear, I just don't get as much use out of it. When it comes to unused equipment, another non-hobby I've picked up is "not golfing."

I have a fine set of clubs that I got in a swap with a hired hand for a worn-out garden tiller. I pick them up religiously once or twice a year and hit the links. If you saw me swing, you'd agree that "not golfing" more accurately describes the hobby for me than "golfing."

I've also developed some expertise in "not hunting" and "not fishing." I put in a solid day or two of hunting every fall. Some years, I don't even get time to sight in my rifle, which kind of limits my success. One day on the lake usually will prove that I'm definitely "not a fisherman," but it's another minor source of limited recreation for me.

My wife has gotten into the act, too, with old non-hobbies like "not playing softball, not playing basketball and not going to the lake."

I guess the nice thing about hobbies is you can limit them to whatever time you have available.

And if the lion's share of my time goes to things like being a father and husband, a rancher and writer and a pretty active community guy, I guess it's all right that I'm a pretty mediocre roper and a darn poor golfer.

Rain dancing
It's always worth a try   July 24, 2006

It's been a dry summer on the Taylor Ranch. Not as dry as some places, but a lot drier than we're used to.

Like they say, it always rains after a drought, and each day without rain gets you closer to a day with rain. But despite that power of positive thinking, I was starting to get a little depressed.

We had gone about a month since our last big rain, which was a whopping tenth of an inch. It just about evaporated before it hit the ground. When it came, I ran out to our tin-roofed pole barn to listen to it in amplification, and even that didn't make it sound like much of a shower.

So after a month or more of passing clouds and fond memories of the last ten-hundredths, I took action. I got ready to do my rain dance.

Rituals for rain

I don't actually dance, but I do have a ritual of different little things I do to try to bring on some precipitation.

I've known people in town who think that washing their car will bring on a rain. I wouldn't know much about that since I rarely ever wash a vehicle. They just get dirty again anyway when you live 12 miles from pavement.

No, my rain-attracting rituals are a lot more practical. I start by leaving the windows rolled down in my pickup when I park it outside for the night. I mean every window from the slider in the back to the triangular vent windows in the front.

I leave my good saddle out hanging on the corral overnight. I don't cheat by throwing the saddle blankets over the top of it either. It's out there, bare and vulnerable.

I think about cutting down a nice field of premium alfalfa and leaving it lay there to tempt the rain. Then I remember that I don't have a nice field of premium alfalfa. It was a thought anyway.

My wife tries to leave our clothes out on the line and waters the garden knowing that those two things almost always bring a cloudburst.

When I'm really getting serious, I put a couple of $20 bags of cattle mineral in the back of the pickup and throw in a paper-clad sack of cow cubes for good measure.

Real results

I did all those things to try to break our last worst dry spell, and I'm pleased — and pretty darn surprised — to report it actually worked.

This year, whenever a good thunderstorm is predicted, we just get the wind or the thunder and lightning or the chance of a tornado. Last week, though, when a nasty storm was forecast and my pickup windows were rolled down and the paper mineral sacks were laying in the pickup bed it actually rained, and hard.

We got an inch and eighty hundredths in about a half an hour. And our dry, sandy pastures and hay fields sucked it in as fast as it came. The only puddle on the place was on the driver's side seat of my pickup.

After the storm quit, I plopped down on that wet seat and went out to the pasture to put out some mineral. The water-soaked paper bag broke before I could get the mineral to the feeder, but it didn't bother me a bit. That rain was worth an awful lot more than a $20 bag of mineral.

As proud as I am of my rancher's rain dance, I do have to disclose that timing has a lot to do with the success of any rain dance.

Cowboy Yogi
Trying to bend but not break   March 5, 2007

I always thought yogi was the cartoon bear with an appetite for picnic baskets at Jellystone Park, or the Hall of Fame baseball manager named Berra who said "when you get to a fork in the road, take it."

Actually, it turns out a yogi is someone who does yoga. Most serious yogis probably don't spend a lot of time watching cartoons or quoting Berra in the midst of their transcendental meditation. They do spend a lot of time in twisted positions connecting with their inner spirit though.

My wife was interested in taking a yoga class while we were living in the big city of Bismarck for North Dakota's legislative session. When you've been married awhile and have young children, experts say you ought to take some time to do something as a couple. Learn a new skill, try something different.

For me, yoga would darn sure be new and different. I told her I'd cowboy up and take the beginner's yoga class with her.

I've been twisted into some pretty uncomfortable positions on the ranch. I figured yoga would be a walk in the park for a lean, limber rancher.

Class time

We went to the class, grabbed a mat and got ourselves spread out on the floor, ready to stretch and meditate. The instructor walked in. She looked innocent enough, rather healthy and hip.

The music was steady and trance-like and the lights were low as we got into our asanas (that's yoga talk for poses).

It wasn't long and I realized that peaceful instructor was tougher than rawhide and could stretch like a rubber band. She could bend herself around like a toy action figure. Gumby had nothing over on her. As for myself, I felt about as flexible as a stick horse.

Although I couldn't actually get into the positions she was showing us, I could relate to the names of the poses. Cat, cow, camel, dog, eagle. Like ranching, yoga seems to be a lot about animals.

I could do the cow pose where you get on all fours and see how far you can sag your back. I've done an even better cow pose in the past when I've been run over by a cow. It's amazing how far you can sag your back when there're hoof prints on your spine.

The downward facing dog was a pose I'd never seen my hyperactive border collie do. She'd never stand still that long. In case you're curious, the dog pose had nothing to do with lifting your leg in fire hydrant fashion.

I didn't find a horse pose, but I've bought horses that've resembled camels. I didn't notice any similarities by looking at the pose. It bends you backward as you reach back to grab your ankles. If riding a camel puts you in that kind of shape, I'll keep riding horses.

I followed along as best I could on most of the animal poses and even made an effort on the non-animal poses like "warrior" and "child." The one I liked best, though, was at the end of the session where you lie on your back, arms out, palms up, eyes closed listening to the soothing yoga tunes.

When they woke me up, it was the best I'd felt during the whole class.

Sunday smash
Daylight deer crossing does some damage   November 12, 2007

Deer season started a couple weeks early for me this year.

I got a doe, but it cost a bit more to bag than the average deer. Instead of 75 cents worth of lead and gunpowder, it took $3,200 worth of steel and plastic.

It probably was about time. I've had a 37-year streak of not hitting deer, and that's pretty good, especially since I've learned I live in one of my nation's top 10 states for the likelihood of a collision with a deer.

I've had some close calls — close enough to leave a little deer hair on the bumper — but this is the first time I actually made full, plastic-cracking impact.

It happened in broad daylight, just before 9 a.m., heading to church on Sunday with my wife and offspring (really). I turned to my wife to engage in a little leisurely conversation and — bam! — the deer jumped out of the ditch and got us.

It was bound to happen. One insurance company's data says I have a one in 125 chance in North Dakota of bumping into some venison on our roadways. Not one in 57 like West Virginia, but good enough odds to put us in the top tier.

I'm in a pretty bountiful region. The adjoining states of Montana, South Dakota and Minnesota made top 10 status as well. Manitoba and Saskatchewan have plenty of deer in their headlights, too, I understand. We live in the venison basket.

Car repairs

Like a lot of folks, I carry insurance for just such a possibility. So, like a lot of folks, I only pay a modest amount of curious attention to what the repairs are going to cost. I know they're only going to get the $100 deductible out of my hide. That's why I buy insurance.

I'm close to average. The average cost of a deer wreck is $2,900; mine was just a few hundred more than that. Who'd have thought molded plastic would be so expensive?

If I didn't have insurance, you'd have heard some screaming when the body shop man told me a headlight for our van was $800. I wonder if the headlight really would cost that much if we all were paying cash for the repairs?

I'm guessing that if fender benders were paid for with cold car owner cash, you'd see a lot cheaper headlights going into them. You'd probably see some people driving around with two cell flashlights duct taped to their front fenders.

As it is, we shrug our shoulders, say, "well I guess we gotta fix it," and tell them to order the parts. And we wonder why our insurance premiums go up.

Deer season

Autumn is the high season for cars hitting deer. Something to do with deer migration and mating, they say. Too many really important things going on in their deer brains to worry about looking both ways before they cross the street. So look out.

I hope to harvest my next deer with a rifle instead of the car. Deer season just opened in my state, so the population should get thinned down enough to decrease the car collisions a bit.

I read in the newspaper that there's a place for those of us who live in fear of hitting a deer on the road. Hawaii. It was number 50 on the list of our 50 states with a one in 16,624 chance of a car/deer collision. That's a nice feather in their cap since the state has so little else going for it, except all that sunny beach and paradise stuff.

When I get our car fixed, I may try to drive over there and check it out.

The road home
Longer than it seems, but worth the drive   November 26, 2007

One of my all-time favorite songs is called "Same Road Home," by Great Plains folk-singing icon and genuinely nice guy Chuck Suchy. It brings tears to my eyes nearly every time I hear it.

It's about a father saying goodbye to a 17-year-old child who's graduating school and is about to embark on the world beyond their farm. He ponders the job he's done rearing this child and begins missing her before she's even gone because, "short is the road that takes you away, long is the same road home."

Most of us can relate to the metaphor. Every time we take a trip, we remark on how quickly we get somewhere and how incredibly long the drive home is. It's hard to figure because the odometer reads the same miles going each way.

My wife and I recently drove to Denver, supposedly an 823-mile drive each way. That's impossible, though, because I think it took about two hours to get there and it felt like a solid 39-hour drive home.

Every time we thought we were getting close to the next town on the line, we'd look at the map and find we were still 80 miles away. It was a long road home.

It was fitting to think about short roads away and long roads home because we

221

were in Denver to provide some rope-twirling family entertainment at an event to recruit former North Dakotans back to the state. There are jobs to fill here, and we're hoping our expatriates have a hankering to get back home next to family and familiar places.

It's Thanksgiving Day as I write this column, a day that brings folks home to be with family, partake in a feast and offer thanks for all they have.

It's been pretty easy for me to get home for Thanksgiving. Actually, I'm home every day, one mile from the house I was raised in and running the ranch that's been home to my family since 1903.

It's easy enough to get home to my wife's family, too. A mere 142 miles puts our family roadster in the yard where she grew up.

I wonder, though, how often we'd get back if we were 800 or 1,000 miles away. The road home might be longer than we were willing to tackle, especially with two small children, high gas prices and the cost of taking a couple days off.

I guess we assign a value to certain things in life and make our decisions accordingly. Some might consider it a little boring to live in the same area code you grew up in or a little less lucrative career-wise.

But what's the value of having our kids see their grandparents on a regular basis? What's the value of being firmly rooted with a sense of place that's generations deep? What's the value of driving two hours for Thanksgiving dinner with the relatives instead of 12 hours?

There're certainly good reasons and justification for being far from home. It might make sense to re-evaluate those reasons on a regular basis though. At some point, the excitement and the bright lights fade, the money might matter less, the family might matter more, and despite what some might say, you can go home again.

The road might be long, but it's well worth the drive.

Tall, skinny cowboys
Built right for tight spots   February 4, 2008

When I graduated from high school, someone told me I'd have to pick cowboy as my career of choice. I was 6 foot 2 with a 28-inch waist, and they said anyone that tall and skinny just had to be a cowboy.

They were typecasting me for a career, of course. If a cowboy crook was on the loose, police profilers would start by looking for tall, skinny guys.

Not every cowboy is tall and skinny. Even my waist has expanded to a hearty 32 inches in the last 20 years. But, for some reason, a lot of cowboys are tall, skinny fellas.

Cowboy poet Baxter Black lays out the small-waisted phenomona in his poem, "The cowboy and his tapeworm."

In my case, it's purely genetic, not parasitic. I have two tall, skinny parents and the genetic process worked. A rancher's diet and exercise doesn't hurt, but I have to give the lion's share of the credit for my twig-like, slivery physique to my folks.

I suppose the iconic image of the lanky cowboy is in jeopardy, though, as everyone's waistlines grow and grow.

Modern diets, modern conveniences and modern lifestyles have everyone in expansion mode, it seems. In the last 20 years, U.S. obesity rates have grown 36 percent.

But we're doing our best to engineer an answer to the changing population. As we get bigger, we try to make everything we need bigger.

Old-time saddles for old-time skinny cowboys had a 14-inch seat. Today's saddles come with a 17-inch space between the horn and the cantle for the new-age cowboy's gut and the belt buckle hiding underneath.

Movie theaters are coming out with bigger seats to accommodate bigger movie watchers. Fewer seats in the same space means fewer ticket sales, but the theaters are making up the lost revenue in increased sales of candy, popcorn and jumbo sodas to the big seat sitters.

Even tractor manufacturers are bragging about having "the biggest cab on the market." I guess it ain't just the farms that are getting bigger these days.

Not much on our ranch has been super sized since my rate of gain has been so pitiful. Maybe I've consciously kept my boyish figure just to make sure I still fit in to the tight spots on the ranch.

Like every other year, when the weather got cold, I found myself with water trouble. A heater quit in my pump house, the water froze and when I thawed things out, the brass fittings burst.

My pump house obviously was built by a skinny cowboy. Why else would a ranch have a structure the size of a phone booth, but half as tall with an entry point the size of a pet door.

I squeezed through a door that was just a couple inches bigger than my 32-inch waist, popped in one shoulder, then the other and pulled in my plumbing tools.

The only thing comfortable about the situation was the temperature. The windchill was 50 below zero outside and 50 degrees on the right side of Fahrenheit inside the little hut.

Hunched over with a flashlight between my knees and a pipe wrench in each hand, I turned pipes, twisted my back and got the water flowing again.

I told my wife she was lucky to have such a skinny cowboy for a husband or she'd still be without water.

She assured me that if her husband weighed 350 pounds instead of 175 pounds, he'd have probably built a bigger pump house.

Probably.

Staying put
Pick your place and hole up   January 5, 2009

With record-breaking amounts of snowfall so far this winter, we've made some adjustments in our winter travel routines.

We've had to reconsider our choice of vehicles. Our mini-van may have won awards for family cruising comfort, but punching through 2-foot-deep, hard snowdrifts is not one of its four-star qualities.

You can leave a lot of plastic pieces on the trail behind you if you ask too much from a mini-van on heavy, two-track roads when it's 20 below zero.

So we're trying to think of a place in town where we can park the mini-van for the winter. That way if we want to go somewhere in fuel efficient comfort, we can load up the family in our four-wheel-drive pickup, ram it through 16 miles of blocked roads to town, then transfer into the van and drive down the highway that's usually passable to all manner and models of vehicles.

If we want to get any use out of the mini-van this winter, it might be best for it to be snowed out away from the ranch rather than snowed in on the ranch. That's the question of the season — state your preference, snowed out or snowed in/

There just isn't any free-wheeling middle ground this year.

Getting home

Last night, I was afraid I might be snowed out as I tried to get back home. Even with the pickup, it was drive, shovel, drive, shovel.

I called my wife once in a while to keep her posted of my progress. I got the feeling she'd have preferred being the one snowed out in the cold rather than snowed in with three cooped-up kids, albeit toasty and warm.

If I didn't make it through the next drift, I'd have cows that wouldn't get fed and a wife that would be fed up. I knew I could make the cows happy with a little hay. I'm still unsure how to make my wife happy, but I knew getting home would be a good start.

So I surveyed the drift ahead. It was long, it was deep, a 180-pound cowboy could walk across the top of it, a 9,000-pound pickup would just get stuck in it. I put my shovel away and called my neighbor. Luckily, he was snowed in, and he was willing to start his tractor and lend a hand.

It took a lot of work with his tractor and an 8 foot loader bucket to clear that spot in the road for me. I'm glad I didn't try to do it with my back and a 15 inch grain scoop.

Thanks to my neighbor, I made it home. I was packing plenty of milk and bread home from town so we can hunker down awhile and wait for the snow plows now.

Pretty soon, though, I might have to leave the pickup in town with the minivan and start shopping for a cheap, dependable snowmobile. Someone told me those three words don't go together. I guess I'll have to decide which word I'm willing to change, cheap or dependable.

Otherwise, we'll have to buy some big bags of flour and powdered milk, sit tight and wait for spring.

Mass transit
A long ride home   January 19, 2009

I don't live in mass transit country. This winter I'm not even sure if I live in transit country, of any kind. We're fast becoming a no-transit zone as the snow falls, blows and drifts across our roads.

Last week, I was at a rancher meeting in Boise, Idaho. Somehow we got there without having to drive through a blizzard. We had three people in our car driving straight through for 17 hours. We like to carpool when the weather gets hazardous. Harder to freeze with more people in a small space.

My fellow carpoolers were going on to California, though, and I had to get back to North Dakota. I was hoping to take the train. Passenger rail service is mighty scarce in America, but our ranch is lucky enough to be just 12 miles off the line. On a still night, we can hear the trains go by. That'll give you a little insight into the general lack of noise pollution around our place.

The train option was not to be, however. Flooding and mudslides in the wintry then warm west had knocked out rail service for two or three days.

I cobbled together another mode of travel. I needed a car for part of the trip. I couldn't afford to buy one and I didn't feel right about stealing one, so I decided to rent one.

It's one of the amazing benefits of capitalism that you can jump in a $20,000 or $30,000 vehicle and drive away leaving nothing but your name, address and, of course, an imprint of your credit card.

I could drive the rental car to Bozeman, Mont., drop it off there and make the next transportation transfer in my epic journey, going Greyhound.

I haven't ridden a cross-country bus since I was 20 years old when I went from Abilene, Texas, to Fargo, N.D. At the conclusion of that trip, I'd had my fill of bus travel. I think I even promised myself, "never again." As they say, never say never.

I found myself at the depot in Bozeman in the middle of the night waiting for a 3:10 a.m. east-bound bus. Of course, the depot was locked, so I stood outside and waited. And I waited and I waited. The 4:05 a.m. westbound came and went. I'm relatively weather tough, but this was Montana in January and I was starting to get cold.

I finally found out the bus would be there at 4:30 or so. A kind taxi driver let me sit in his car to warm up while he waited for the same bus and a possible fare.

When I finally crawled on the bus, I swear I saw some of the same people I rode the bus with 18 years ago. Let's just say bus travelers are a funny group. Funny, hmmm, not funny, ha ha. And I was one of them, so I can't pass much judgment on the rest of them.

Many hours later, we rolled into Bismarck, where my pickup grudgingly started and backed out of its snowy tomb. It seemed only fitting that I end my trip with a little more travel excitement, so I gave my new friend and busmate, Jose, a 100-mile ride north to Minot.

He didn't speak much English, I speak just a bit of espanol. We taught each other a few key phrases as we finished my journey.

One author, years ago, said you can't go home again. I know we can go home again. But in some places and some winters, it just takes a little extra effort.

Let them eat steak
Eating well in a recession   April 27, 2009

The phrase, "Let them eat cake," may have symbolized royal ignorance of peasant famine in revolutionary France, but here in Gorman Township, we're in the middle of an economic recession and I'm saying to my family, "let them eat steak."

We actually have the steak in our freezer, too, so the statement shouldn't send me to the guillotine like Queen Marie Antoinette.

My father always was proud to tell us that, although we never were wealthy, we always had plenty to eat. It was one of those comments that we probably only hear from Depression-era parents and family members. Most of us younger than the Depression just take food for granted.

Personal food security is one of those things folks in agriculture keep in the back of their mind as a fallback position in hard times. We have the capacity to raise livestock, grow food crops, plant a big garden. If things go to heck, we shouldn't starve.

I grew up thinking that everyone had two big chest freezers and an extra refrigerator in their shop to store a year's supply of food. As it turns out, there're people who go to the grocery store nearly every day to buy food as they need it.

We are a little dependent on electricity to keep the meat and other provisions frozen, but as long as the rural electric lines are up, our grub won't spoil and we won't die for lack of burgers.

Tender and juicy

On our ranch, we've always had plenty of meat in the freezer, but I can't say we always put the very best meat we ever raised in there.

It always was good, but it didn't often include a lot of juicy steaks and tender roasts. Many times it was just a whole lot of hamburger from an old retired cull cow, a bull with a bad shoulder or an aged roping steer of questionable genetics. Most times they came off a diet of dry hay or dormant grass.

We ate that second-tier beef when the economy was strong and the Dow was climbing.

Now that times are tough, I decided my family should have nothing but the finest beef the herd has to offer.

This winter, we had a pen of yearlings being fed to finish. High-quality, young cattle standing around eating the finest of feedstuffs. These were the kind of valuable cattle we always sold and never could afford to eat ourselves. This year, we decided to hold one back from the market for our own eating pleasure.

By denying the market one of my harvest-ready heifers, it probably created a little supply shortage and resulted in a significant market spike. My own little stimulus plan.

My wife didn't know what to think when I came home from the butcher and stocked our freezer. Instead of rows and rows of 99 percent lean cull cow hamburger filling the freezer, there were T-bones, rib-eyes, tenderloin filets, sirloins, chuck roasts, round roasts, a couple big briskets and hamburger that wasn't quite so lean.

Like most ranchers with a newly filled freezer, we started in on the steaks. They were absolutely wonderful, perfect in every way.

I'm not sure how long it'll take us to eat our way to the bottom of our freezer, but

I'm looking forward to every pound of it.

Times may be tough, but our beef is tender—and plentiful. I'm sure glad I'm a rancher and not a stockbroker.

Mail time
Back on the route
May 25, 2009

Earlier this spring, I drove into the ranch and I couldn't believe my eyes. There, atop a post by the shop, was our mailbox!

After more than 50 years of driving 3 1/2 to four miles to retrieve the ranch mail, I thought we were going to have door stop mail delivery. I was impressed, the U.S. Postal Service not only decided to finally bring the mail all the way to the ranch, they even delivered our mailbox to start this new expanded service.

Upon closer inspection, I began to realize it wasn't the postman that brought the mailbox. The box had some new dents and instead of its usual upside-down, symmetrical "U" shape, it more closely resembled an upside down, flattened "V."

It was the road grader operator who delivered our mailbox after enough snow melted to see it lying in the ditch. It was a tough winter for everybody, including mailboxes.

The fate of our mailbox was the least of our worries as we tried to keep a road open after receiving 9 or 10 feet of snow and the wind necessary to pile it all on the roads.

Our mailbox came off its post early in the winter. For awhile, we just balanced it on top of the snowbank and kept getting delivery. Eventually, when the roads got so bad the mailman couldn't even get to our appointed snowbank, we just told him to keep the mail in town and we'd gather it up once a week.

Mailbox repair

Once I realized we weren't getting curbside delivery, it was time to think about straightening our mailbox, pounding out the dents and putting a new post under it in its usual spot 3 1/2 miles up the road.

I thought I was going to have to spring for a brand new box but after a little fine tuning with a sledge hammer I had the old one back in operating condition. I thought about plugging the bullet holes that have been there for 30 years, but decided to leave them for ventilation.

I did talk to our local postmaster about letting me plant my reconditioned mailbox a mile or two closer to home. Of course, there's a set of rules written for how to extend an "established route," and we'd have to establish a small compound of several families wanting mail delivery to get that done.

I decided to let it be and put the box back where it was. It was still 13 miles closer than going all the way to town, and I considered it my own small contribution to not further stress a postal service already fighting a potential $6 billion deficit.

Having us pick up our mail in town for a few months this winter must have saved them some money, too. Once that's realized, they ought to be in the black.

I'll even pay the extra 2 cents in postage they're asking to mail a letter these days. I'm sure I'm one of the folks who gets their money's worth and then some on the 44-cent letter.

Even if I do have to drive a few miles to retrieve them from our well-worn mailbox.

Repainting the prairie
Beyond black and white, and brown   April 26, 2010

I remember the first color television we got. Seems like Dad plugged it in on a Friday night and come Saturday morning, I was watching full-color cartoons in my footed pajamas. Color made for better cartoons than my black-and-white past, even with those dynamic shades of gray.

That's kind of how spring is on the prairie. You go through a winter of white snow and gray skies. The snow melts off and you're surrounded by 100 shades of brown.

Then, one fine spring day, it's like turning on that color television on Saturday morning. The world goes from black and white and brown to green and purple and blue.

Expanding spectrum

I wait for the green. Every shade of it.

My favorite green comes from the poplar trees that riddle our ranch. If we were better marketers, we'd call them aspen trees, or better yet, quaking aspens. But we're not marketers, we're ranchers, so we call those stands of trees plain ol' popple thickets.

When those poplars pop their leaves in the spring, it's the brightest limiest green you ever saw. They come just in time to let your eyes know they aren't color blind after all.

The grazing members of the ranch prefer the green sprouts of grass to the green of the poplar leaves. I know the grass is more valuable than the poplar leaves, but I still go for the leaves.

The first flower in our neighborhood is the prairie crocus. Just a couple inches tall, it keeps a low profile, but its pale purple petals never go unnoticed. A cupful of crocuses on the table will get you through some rough spots with the woman of the house. I guess their eyes need a little spring color too.

Our 3-year-old picked every crocus he could find this spring to give to his mom. I think he was trying to bank some good will with her to help get him through another week of being a 3-year-old boy.

My favorite blue in the spring comes with feathers instead of leaves and petals. When I see the male bluebird flit across my path, I know we've left the gray season. This is a fella who isn't afraid of having some color in his wardrobe.

The species we have is called a mountain bluebird even though we don't have any mountains, but I am glad we get the bluebirds.

Some birdwatching friends of our family hung up a bunch of bluebird houses in our pastures years ago. Don't ask me how a bluebird knows the houses were meant for them. I think it has something to do with the size of the front door. Anyway, they work and it's added a splash of vibrant blue to our pastures when they return each spring.

Spring fever

There are plenty of reasons to appreciate spring when you're a northerner. Some of the reasons come color coded in poplar green and crocus purple and bluebird blue. And they keep coming into the summer with tiger lily red and coneflower yellow.

Even the blacks and grays and browns look better when they get the color accents that they lack in the winter.

Springtime on the prairie is even better than the Saturday morning I woke up to color cartoons on the new television set. They just can't make a TV big enough to match the view nature gives us in the country.

I wouldn't mind still having those footed pajamas I had in my color cartoon-watching days, though, for my morning nature viewing.

Yard pets
Life in our wild kingdom   June 21, 2010

We don't live on the African savanna, but we have our share of wildlife here on the ranch. Some of it's pretty wild, but some of it is getting downright domestic.

The idyllic morning critter on Old MacDonald's farm was a rooster, ready to crow at the crack of dawn and get everybody out of bed and off to work.

I was up making coffee the other day, pretty close to the crack of dawn, and heard the shrillest, most blood-curdling racket I'd ever heard come from an animal outside. I looked out the window, but it was no rooster. It was a crowing coyote that stopped by to make sure we were up for the day, standing about 50 feet from the door.

I looked around for my trusty guard dogs, a hapless hybrid Labrador and a cowardly collie of the border variety. The black Lab turned yeller, the border collie retreated from her border. I think the Lab actually put his paws over his ears and tried to keep sleeping, sort of a low-tech canine snooze button.

The dogs weren't about to stand up to this invasive coyote. Even our sometimes-protectant tom cat was gone, probably on the long walk home after trying to locate a neighboring mate within five miles.

It was up to me to protect the family. I'd been working so hard to try and keep the wolf from the door that I somehow let the wolf's sneaky cousin, the coyote, come a knocking and yipping.

I went and got a rifle, loaded it and stepped out the back door to try and get the sneak on the visitor. As quick as he came, he left and ran back into the trees. I guess coyotes haven't survived this long by being dumb around humans who are carrying the long, black stick.

Maybe next time.

Predator's prey

It wasn't long after the coyote left that our regular morning visitors came traipsing through the yard. The local herd of wild turkeys that are anything but wild came through for their usual breakfast of dog food and a morning stroll through my wife's garden.

It is disappointing that our guard dogs won't even guard their dog food from these fowl invaders. If they were a little sharper, they could have a Thanksgiving turkey dinner every morning. You'd think the collie would at least try to herd them around a little. If she'd herd them into the horse trailer, I could shut the door and haul them to a place where they'd be a little more appreciated. Like a processing plant.

But the dogs aren't into fighting coyotes, and they aren't into eating turkeys. I thought for sure, though, that the coyote would be into eating a turkey.

The path he took away from the house had to take him right by the turkeys. I didn't hear any sound of a ruckus. No feathers flew and no turkey drumsticks got eaten near as I could tell.

Maybe I just need to buy more dog food. A trough full for the turkeys by the garden, a dish for the coyote by the front step and a little for the worthless guard dogs if they can wake up long enough to eat.

Vacation weather
Trying to enjoy myself away from the ranch — July 19, 2010

There's always something you should be doing when you farm or ranch. Makes it kind of tough to get away with the family and take a little vacation. Or, if you do get away, it's hard to enjoy yourself when you think you should be back home.

Some people are great at vacationing, but terrible at working, which makes it hard to afford vacationing. Others are great at working, but awful at vacationing, which eventually is going to affect their working. I don't know if I'm real good at working or vacationing, but I am good at thinking about work while I'm vacationing and thinking about vacations while I'm working.

Ranch work is relaxing to me — moving cattle, fixing fence, making hay — ahhh, it makes me breathe easy, especially if I'm getting things done in a relatively timely manner. Vacationing with a 6-, 4- and 2-year-old? Kind of fun, but not so high on the relaxation scale. Vacationing with my wife is nice, especially if I'm caught up with important tasks back at the ranch.

But I'm not usually caught up. I'm just now catching up on the things I meant to get done last fall. If you get far enough behind, like a whole annual cycle, it tricks your neighbors into thinking you're ahead of schedule.

So leaving the place when you're this far behind is a tall order. I decided it helps to have the right weather.

A lot of travelers hope for nice weather when they're taking a little time off. They like sunny skies, calm breezes, warm temperatures.

Not me. To really enjoy my time away from the ranch in the summer, I need some pretty awful weather.

Cloudy and rainy is nice. That means it's too wet to hay at home anyway so I just as well enjoy myself. A good steady drizzle is best to keep the mind off work and on the vacation.

Winds blowing 30 or 40 miles per hour really reduce the guilt of being gone. Too windy to spray or cut hay or stand in some dusty corral sorting cattle. The bonus of vacationing in the wind is you know the windmills are pumping to beat the band and your cattle shouldn't run out of water while you're gone. Now that's good vacation weather.

I'm not sure my wife understands my reasoning on wishing for cloudy, rainy, windy weather while we're vacationing. But she's seen me on what she calls "nice" days away from the ranch. I wake up, see the sun shining bright and feel a light breeze. There's not a cloud in the sky and I begin to grumble and complain. "Grrrr, another sunshiny day," and I lament about not being home to lay down the alfalfa to cure in the sun.

There could be a happy compromise for us on vacation weather. First, go far enough away so the vacation weather doesn't necessarily match the ranch weather. It could just happen that the ranch will get rain and wind, while the vacation area pulls in sun and calm.

Or, she could limit my exposure to weather forecasts for the ranch. Like a prisoner I could be allowed one phone call and it'd be to a predetermined neighbor instructed to report, "it's just awful here, Ryan, you couldn't do a thing. Just as well enjoy yourself there."

Pairing wine and beef
Or pairing wine and cattle to make the beef   September 13, 2010

Nothing surprises me anymore. When I read about some folks in British Columbia feeding wine to their cattle and specially marketing the wine-fed beef, I just shrugged and said, "I suppose that makes sense."

Cattle are pretty adaptable ruminants and it seems like they can eat most anything. No reason they shouldn't have a nice cabernet sauvignon or merlot to help wash down their ration.

I've always heard the story that some of the Wagyu cattle in Japan are fed beer as part of their diet to help create the highly marbled, tender Kobe beef. Supposedly, they even get a little bovine massage and some soft music with their bucket of brew.

I've known people who've used the potato slurry given away by local potato processors to feed their cows. That's another bunch of really happy cows because as that slurry starts to ferment, the cows are getting a good stiff belt of potato vodka.

I stuck my arm into one of my second cutting-alfalfa bales put up here in the new North Dakota monsoon season, and from what I know of fermentation, it looks like even my cows will start boozing this winter with a little alfalfa schnapps. Or maybe it'll be an alfalfa liqueur, or a cordial. I don't know the difference, but I doubt the cows do either.

The folks doing the wine fed beef claim the meat is distinct and delectable, and, of course, worth a fair bit more per pound than your run of the mill calf fed hay, grain and (gasp) plain old well water.

Good for them, I say. If you can do something a little different to separate your product from the commodity world and develop relationships with a particular set of customers, more power to you.

They use local cattle and give them local Okanagan wine. I suppose the French would say the beef has a double dose of "terroir" with unique flavors relating back to the geography of the area.

One of the local chefs figures the premium for the meat is well worth it because it's local to his restaurant and, conveniently, he says, it comes pre-marinated. A good trait when the kitchen is busy.

AA for cows?

In Canadian beef grades, I suppose the wine fed beef has to be at least Grade AA, or Select in U.S. terms, but I wonder if the cattle end up in another AA, Alcoholics Anonymous?

Thanks to controlled rationing, it's fair to say the cattle probably would be termed social drinkers. A liter a day for the size of the cattle is like a glass a day for a person. Enough to take the edge off and relax a little, but not enough for them to do anything stupid in the corral that they'd regret in the morning.

The owner does say they come to the feed bunk at a faster-than-normal clip. They moo a little more, probably chatting about the day's vintage and smartly discussing its soft, round tannins, its dark cherry undertones and the long, smooth finish they got with their pail of pinot.

If I'm ever in B.C., I might give the beef a try, but for now, I'll have my steak and wine the old-fashioned way — medium rare with a glass on the side.

Lanky Labrador
A (ranch) dog's life   November 8, 2010

I don't think anyone would label me a dog lover, but we've always had a dog or two or three here on the ranch. The majority of them were pretty worthless, but all were likable mutts. So call me a dog liker.

Dogs don't have much to complain about here on the Taylor Ranch. Free to roam for miles around without so much as a collar on their neck. Plenty to eat in their dog dish and plenty to scavenge out in the pasture because, to be honest, not every critter here gets to meet their demise away from the ranch.

It's hard to believe there're dogs in town that never get out of a fenced yard, get to drag a little carrion back home or go out and about without a collar and a leash attached. For some pups, a people house and a bathroom break in the city park is the extent of their freedom.

So if you say "it's a dog's life," there's some variation. If you say someone "works like a dog," it all depends on what dog you're referencing. We have a border collie that used to work cattle a little, but she's pretty much retired now. Her life revolves around going from the dog house to the dog dish to the trees and back to the dog house. Once in awhile, she'll join me if I take a horse out to the pasture. Pretty easy life.

Then we have a hyperactive hybrid black Labrador/border collie cross. He ranges out quite a little farther. He runs with the pickup on every trip between our house and the ranch homestead where the shop and corrals are, a little more than a mile. Back and forth, back and forth.

He especially loves hay hauling season. Our hay is fairly close to our wintering pastures, but it's still anywhere from a mile to six miles when we drive the high-and-dry route where we won't get stuck with the mover. The loping Labrador will make most every trip with me. Sometimes he waits in the field by the loader tractor until I return for another load. He logs an easy 20-plus miles a day though.

It's especially nice that he replaces a lot of the calories he's burning while he's running back and forth. He's on point every time I pick up a bale with the loader. He darts under the loader bucket as soon as it's clear for him, snatches a nice plump mouse and sends it down the hatch. Sometimes he can get two.

He's a better mouser than most cats I know. Saves on the dog food and we're picky on the dog food brands we buy. Nothing but the cheapest for our dogs. Maybe the option of eating that cheap dog food back at the house stimulates his appetite for fresh rodent protein.

When we first got this black dog as a puppy, we named him "Pudgy," you know like plump, chubby, slightly overweight. We still call him Pudgy, but diet and exercise has made him plainly lanky and rather svelte in his maturity.

So if anyone would ask me what they should do to lose some extra weight, I have to look no farther than my loyal Lab and say, "have you tried running 20 miles a day, eating mice and cheap dog food and drinking slough water?"

Worked for Pudgy, should work for anyone on four legs or two.

Hot sales incentives
All-expense-paid trip to Fargo   December 20, 2010

I spent a few years in the sales business. I've been to a few national sales meetings. No where too exotic, mostly Kansas City or Denver. I was just happy to have a hotel room with the little coffee pot in it and the two free coffee packets.

But sales meetings are a real motivator for some company sales forces. Where the annual sales meeting is held tells something about the kind of year the company is having. If sales were good, it could mean a fancy resort. If sales were bad, well, the meeting place might be a little less than four star.

My home state was in the news this week as the location for the sales meeting of a Pennsylvania based candy company. I guess coming to Fargo, N.D., for their sales meeting was pitched as punishment, not reward.

Sales isn't just about selling stuff, it's really about selling more stuff than last year.

You gotta hit your number, grow your territory, reach the goal, bring in the year end. Sell, sell, sell!

The folks at Just Born candy company told their team if they grew sales by 4 percent, the meeting would be in Hawaii. Miss that mark and the meeting will be in Fargo, N.D.

They came to Fargo last week. I'm not sure if the 2 percent growth they achieved was an actual failure to reach 4 percent, or just a sales force that knew what a great city Fargo is and purposely kept sales under 4 percent to avoid the tourist trap of Hawaii.

OK, they probably would have liked to hit their goal and the sandy beaches of the Aloha state. But they may have learned a thing or two on their northern sojourn.

Cold is OK

Like any kid raised in the North, they learned how to have fun when the temperature is cold and there's snow on the ground.

First, you have to dress for the elements. I saw pictures of the candy sellers in furry winter bomber hats. Good move. As our folks have all told us from an early age, "Cover your head! You lose 87.34 percent of your body heat from your head you know!" or some other oft quoted number of cranial thermal escape.

Once you're buttoned up, go outside and do something. They took a sleigh ride and went tobogganing. You've got the snow and it's pretty slick, so why not do some sliding on it?

If I had a nickel for every sled run I made down the hill behind our house when I was growing up, well, I'd have a lot of nickels. And I could've bought enough Mike & Ike's and Peeps to send these guys to Hawaii.

The last lesson — after you've had your fun outside, get indoors, pull off that furry hat and warm up. Reports are that these people learned the comfort of a hot toddy next to the fireplace, the social benefits of eating with large groups of people at a neighborhood spaghetti feed in the local veteran's hall and the heightened joy of popcorn and a movie because you're inside and it's warm.

So, it wasn't Hawaii, but I doubt it was as bad as they thought. It's fair to say Fargo far exceeded their expectations because they probably didn't have any. And they created enough quirky buzz to make the national news and get their company and their candy mentioned in countless stories. A good free media start to help propel them toward next year's sales goal like a speeding toboggan.

These folks in the furry hats are better sales people than they made themselves out to be.

Behold the biathlon
My kind of sport   March 14, 2011

No one's ever accused me of being a jock. Sure I played plenty of red barn basketball and backyard baseball, but I didn't do a lot of organized athletic school sports.

I never played football. I ran a little track because I could train on the gravel roads around home without having to drive 32 miles round trip each day for practice. My basketball was strictly neighborhood league; we called ourselves the Smokey Lake Lakers. I wasn't very good, but I was tall.

We didn't have wrestling in my school when I went. We didn't have a baseball team. But I was plenty active. There's always plenty of exercise for a kid growing up on a ranch. We didn't call it exercise though. We called it work. It was physical and it was part of my education, but it wasn't what you'd think of as physical education.

I did get time for recreation though. I did a lot of hunting. Walked a lot of fields for grouse, hiked plenty of pastures looking for deer. Carried a shotgun or a rifle like it was an extension of myself.

I did a lot of fur trapping for coyotes, muskrats, beaver, mink. Much of that meant strapping on my cross-country skis, swinging a pack basket of gear onto my back and heading out across the snow a mile or so to the frozen lakes and sloughs on our meadow.

So I suppose if I had to pick a sport where I'd have a little experience and a remote chance of being competitive, it wouldn't be something normal like football, basketball or baseball. I'd have to pick the biathlon.

Yes, the much celebrated biathlon — watched by millions of adoring fans, televised worldwide on network and cable broadcasts, kids trading cards and buying posters of their favorite biathletes, stadiums selling out their entire venue for people wanting to see a little of the excitement as participants race on cross-country skis, stop and shoot their rifles at targets and ski some more. Or maybe not.

But not every sport has to be about attracting fans. I'm fine with the satisfaction of individual achievement, personal records, the camaraderie of a small team of skiers and shooters excelling at something that few people even understand.

I really like cross-country skiing, and I like shooting guns, and I like people who are a little out of the mainstream of sports. I need to find me a biathlon team to join up with.

I might just have to join the National Guard. I'm very proud to say my home state North Dakota National Guard holds the national title in the biathlon amongst their fellow Guard competitors. They're defending that title now out in Vermont.

I like that there's still military training for winter combat situations where you might end up skiing and shooting a gun in the defense of your country. There's plenty of high tech in the armed forces, I like to see a little old-style training and competition.

I may not be cut out for Army life, but I will cheer from the homefront for my fellow North Dakotans in their biathletic endeavors. I doubt that I'll be able to see the competition on the Sunday sports shows. It may be a little like golf — more fun to play than to try and watch on television.

The biathlon is a winter Olympic sport, though, so at least once every four years we can all become fans of the athletes that ski and shoot and ski and shoot. So get ready, biathlon fans, for the 2014 winter games in Sochi, Russia.

And if you go to the games to cheer for your favorite biathlon team, be respectful of all those competing. Remember, these athletes are armed.

Puddle problems
Looking for some sunshine

As they say, timing has a lot to do with the success of a rain dance. Around here, you so much as tap your toe to the beat of the music and it will rain. And, if you don't dance, it'll still rain.

In Texas, they can't even find a cloud to wring a raindrop from. Here we're looking for the sun to try and dry off from the rain last fall, the snow last winter and the big spring rains that have kept coming into August.

Texas is as dry as it's been since records have been kept. Meanwhile, we have lakes and rivers and rainfall breaking all the old records in North Dakota. I wish it was a little easier for us to share our excess.

Our ranch is about as wet as it's ever been. I only have 41 years to work with and don't remember too much from the first few years, but I'm sure if my dad still were here, he'd agree.

Our water wells are starting to flow artesian style if their cap is so much as a foot or two below the surface, and the ponds that used to dry up in the summer have taken on a new life in every pasture and hayfield.

Woe is us

It's hard to complain about rain on the prairie, but here goes.

We used to just get puddles in the yard in the spring; now they're here most all the time and recharge with every shower. Puddles are popular with our splashing kids, the tadpoles and egg laying mosquitoes.

Good roads are hard to find in some areas. We often can't find a bad road to get us from one point to another with a relatively straight line.

Section lines and prairie trails that lead us to fields and pastures used to be pretty dry and passable. Now, there's no chance of getting through the mud and water with a 4-wheel-drive pickup and sometimes they're too deep for the not-quite-all terrain vehicles. You really can mess it up after a few trips with a 4-wheel-drive tractor and then we're left with four-footed horse travel.

We have to walk some of these puddles to fix up the fence because the cows still will find where it's down even if they have to walk through mud up to their bellies to get to the gap. It's amazing, the grass is green on all sides of every fence this year, but the cows still like the other side better.

Cows are the only way to harvest the grass though since 80 percent of our hay ground is either sitting in water or won't support the machinery it takes to turn it into hay bales for winter. Unfortunately, if the moisture continues this winter, the snow will be about 5 feet too deep for winter grazing.

Chin up

Enough grumbling. I bet every Texas farmer or rancher would trade me for the problems I have. I've never seen so much grass in our pastures, and every time I drive by a patch of 5-foot-tall big blue stem, it makes my prairie heart sing.

I've never seen the country this green in August and I'm still holding out hope that we can make some hay this fall if it dries up a little.

If my windmills don't pump or the power goes out for the electric water pumps, I don't have to worry about the cows going thirsty. They can just walk to the nearest puddle and take a pretty clean drink.

It's hard to remember sometimes, but I'd still rather be waiting for a dry spell than waiting for a rain.

Historical weather
Wondering the price we'll pay   January 16, 2012

After a few years of having winters we'd like to forget, we've gotten a winter we want to remember this year ... so far. Yesterday was Jan. 10, and I did chores wearing a vest instead of a jacket and there wasn't a speck of snow on the ground. It was so nice I even had my earflaps tucked up inside of my cap, and that doesn't often happen in January in North Dakota.

These are the little things that memories are made of, and good memories at that. Now, today, as I write this, the weather is more like old times. The temperature has dropped, the wind is blowing, and snow is coming down, not a lot, but the ground is white again.

When we started having these record-breaking warm temperatures, I was struck by how many people dug back in their memory banks and remembered winters past for the sake of comparison.

My uncle told me back in December, "this is the kind of fall we had in 1936. But we caught heck in the new year after." A friend told me we were having another 1941, and it stayed nice all winter. I heard another farmer on the radio say it was just like 1979. He remembered because he was building a shop that winter and they worked on it until the middle of January without any cold weather or snow to slow them down. He didn't say what it was like after that.

I suppose those of us who spend a lot of time outside have reason to remember the easy winters and the hard winters.

Dad would tell me pretty vivid stories about the winter of 1948 and '49, feeding cows with a team of horses and a hay sled and making the 16-mile trip to town with the same team and sled when the snow was deep and the temperatures were frigid to get supplies. I don't suppose the memory would be so indelibly marked if you go from a warm house into a warm garage to get into a heated car to drive to a heated office to do your day's work before auto starting your car for the warm commute back.

So I wonder if we've gotten out and enjoyed enough of this nice weather to mark our memory of it for the future. Remember that winter it was so nice in January that we stayed inside and watched television? No, that won't cut it. Remember that winter it was so nice in January that we rode our bikes down the road and it felt just like spring? That might make for a longer-lasting memory.

The other common denominator I hear, along with the comparisons and reminiscing about winters past, is the fear of the price we'll pay for having it so nice this long. That's the kind of people we are, I guess. We believe in retribution.

We're really going to get it now, people say, as they imagine torrential snowfall, a plummeting mercury and general misery as we pay for the good times and nice weather we had in November, December and January.

It's a little twisted, I know, to think you can't have something positive without a negative payback to even the score. Kind of a northern climate ying and yang universe with a commitment to vengeance.

Whether the weather is fair or foul from here on out, there ain't much we can do about it. If nothing else, I'll be warmed by the memories of the way the winter of 2011/2012 started out. We've already made that deposit to our memory bank.

Christmastime thoughts
Taking stock and giving thanks   December 19, 2011

Sorry, Bing, but I'm not dreaming of a white Christmas this year. I enjoy a little snow as much as any kid who likes to do some sledding and skiing to help pass the winter months, but after our last few winters, I'm fine with the mere dusting of snow we've had up to this point and the chance for a slightly brown Christmas.

A whole lot of snow can turn into a whole lot of water in the spring and North Dakota had more overflowing rivers and lakes than it needed this year. So starting the first couple months of winter without much snow puts us two months closer to spring without the work and worries of the deep stuff.

Like a lot of my ranching neighbors say, if you're going to have a little drought, winter's the time to have it. The cows are out grazing the extra grass we grew last summer, the hay pile is melting away a little slower, and ranchers are saving a little chore time to stay inside and admire the market reports.

Snow likely will come, and it might be a lot if you believe some of the predictions, but at least we're on our way to spring and longer days once we cross the winter solstice. So it seems right to take the time we might have been spending shoveling snow to take stock in the blessings of the year.

Our family has had good health this year, and any year you can't recall any bad turns of health worse than a short flu bug or a nasty cold can be labeled a good year. No trips to the emergency room this year, and when you have a couple of boys who like to butt heads and play a little rough, that's worth noting. And they're old enough to know not to shove peas up their nose, so that cuts back on the doctor visits, too.

Good health has allowed us to get up each day and get our work done, and that's something to be thankful for. There was plenty of extra work to be done because of excess rain and moisture in our part of the world, so a strong body and a clear mind was much needed.

We're thankful for all the people we're glad to call our friends and neighbors. My favorite part of the year is still the days of early summer when we work all the calves in the neighborhood and watch the pickups and horse trailers descend on a ranchyard, the horses get saddled, the calves get roped and the stories get shared at the end of the day as neighbors practice the old art of being neighborly. We remind ourselves to be just as neighborly the whole year through.

We're thankful for the promise of Christmas, the start of a new year, turning the page as our days grow a little longer and the sun shines a little farther into the evening. A lot like when our three youngsters open the next drawer on our Advent calendar to see what it holds, I'm anxious to see what the next year holds.

This time of year's a little like bedtime. We tuck the kids into bed at night with hugs and kisses and bedtime stories, and any of the rough spots of the day are forgiven. We give thanks for the day and for each other, and we look forward to tomorrow.

And the funny thing is, none of this stuff that really matters can be bought at the shopping mall.

Merry Christmas and Happy New Year, friends.

Running
For the health of it
February 13, 2012

After a long hiatus from my old running days and marathon training, I've decided to lace up the sneakers and start pounding the gravel roads and trails around the ranch again. Why on earth would a guy run when there are so many other perfectly good modes of transportation available out there?

That's a good question, but it's not the easiest one to answer. At 6 foot 2 and 180 pounds (soaking wet, after Thanksgiving dinner), I wouldn't say I'm doing it to lose weight. It's not that I don't have perfectly good horses to ride or vehicles to drive that could get me from point A to point B. It's not done with the thought that I might win the next marathon I enter and bathe in the fame and winnings as a world class athlete.

Like other painful, physical challenges, I suppose I run because it feels so good when I stop. Kind of like beating your head against the wall, but different. There's actually some science to the phenomena of feeling good after you run. Something about endorphins, the name of an opiate protein in the brain that is short for endogenous morphine. This is not a street-purchased illegal opiate, but one we produce ourselves when we run.

When I was running marathons and shorter road races, I met more than a few runners who were recovering alcoholics. I thought to myself that running and its beta-endorphins were certainly a healthier addiction than alcohol or tobacco or drugs. And if a person knows they're prone to addiction, better to have an addiction that makes your heart and lungs stronger than one that makes your body weaker.

So I'm brave enough to go out running on our lonely country roads. I say brave because my only fear is that a neighbor will drive by while I'm running and they'll slow down and razz me about being a "jogger," especially for being a winter "jogger."

But on those rare occasions that they do catch me out running, they usually just smile and wave, or laugh hysterically and wave, or, if they do slow down, they might drive alongside and visit with me. That's a good thing because we seldom take enough time to visit with our neighbors these days, and it's good to maintain conversation when you run because they say if you can talk conversationally and run, you're maintaining the nearly perfect pace and heart rate for your run.

I like running. I feel better when I run. I burn off some stress and I think my clearest thoughts while I'm out there listening to my feet strike the dirt road. There's little traffic where I run and few people. I suppose that's why I am bound to run home when I turn around — there's no one to pick me up and give me a ride even if I wanted one.

A fellow runner, a woman named Sherry Arnold, did not return from her run several weeks ago on a road a couple hundred miles west of where I live. Kidnapping, murder — the law still is learning what happened and they have two men in jail to learn from.

What I know is that in a couple days I'll be running with hundreds or thousands of others to remember Sherry and the positive impact she had on her community as a mother, daughter, sister, wife, math teacher and friend. And she was a runner.

We'll all be looking for some endorphins to help us with the sadness of this senseless crime.

The will to endure
Ponying up to the Iceman challenge   March 12, 2012

I've done a few things in life that might seem a little out of the ordinary for a cowboy and a rancher. I ran a marathon in Chicago, I went to a Black Eyed Peas concert, I heard a symphony perform in Carnegie Hall in New York, and I once ordered a fish sandwich at McDonalds. Not typical cowboy stuff.

But when I entered the Iceman Triathlon in Grand Forks, N.D., for a frigid three-event competition in the height of winter, it seemed to fit right in with my ranching lifestyle. Physical activity, endurance and exhaustion outside in the winter? Perfect.

It's done all the time on the ranch. I roped a cow the other day to try and convince her to come into a corral, and when I decided my horse wasn't up to the task, I had to get the rope that had tightened up around her neck off of her. The skills required for that task with a little ice and snow was more of a winter decathlon, so I figured the Iceman Triathlon would be a piece of cake.

Now saying something like "the height of winter" this year isn't much to brag about. We've been mostly mild and snow-free this year, but, fortunately, Grand Forks got a nice dump of snow just in time for their triathlon. The temperature on race day was a balmy 20 degrees Fahrenheit, winds were calm and the sun was shining.

Ironman or Iceman

I've watched bits of the Ironman triathlon in Hawaii when it's been on television. I could envision myself doing the running leg of the triathlon, but bicycling would be a bit of a stretch for my skill set, and swimming next to a bunch of other people in the ocean with flailing arms and legs seemed downright terrifying.

The distances for an Ironman are pretty intimidating, too. Swim 2.4 miles, bike 112 miles, then run 26.2 miles. All in a row, no rest or recuperation. That's why they call it Ironman. If it were easy, I suppose they'd call it a tinman or an aluminuman triathlon.

The selling point for the Iceman triathlon in Grand Forks was that they swapped

240

out the swimming and replaced it with cross-country skiing. Now they were talking something this Norwegian cowboy could understand. Aside from my English Taylor heritage, I'm mostly descended from Dokkens, Oiums and Larsons, from places in Norway like Hallingdal and Gudbrandsdal.

They say Norwegians are born with skis on their feet. My mother wouldn't have put up with that, but she did put me on cross-country skis at a pretty young age. So I entered the Iceman race and figured my skiing prowess would make me a contender.

The distances in the Iceman were manageable. Ski for 3.5 miles, bike for seven miles, run for three miles and wrap it up by running up a hill three times carrying a sandbag and riding a sled down with your cap pulled over your eyes. Creative competition.

Ski strong, finish strong

The skiing was my best leg as I did my best Norsk kick, stride and glide. It almost made up for the ground I lost in the snow biking. Race day was my first day on skis this season because of our lack of snow on the ranch, but, just like riding a bike, you never forget. Hmmm, that saying makes me think my biking should have gone better.

I finished the race pretty strong, made the top half, and I think most of the guys ahead of me in the solo men's division were 10 years younger than me. Makes no difference though. We're all Icemen now. Some of us have just been melting a little longer.

Post Script Tributes

Meanwhile, back at the ranch
My eulogy to Mom   Given at her funeral on January 21, 2009

Meanwhile, back at the ranch, the stories of the legendary Liz Taylor live on. She wouldn't approve of the term legendary, but it's not that much of an understatement in describing this striking, 6-foot-tall Norwegian with the wide smile and piercing wit.

Everyone who met our Liz Taylor probably didn't feel much like they needed to meet the other Liz Taylor out in Hollywood. Mom had enough star qualities of her own to satisfy most of us around these parts. She'd probably have been just as memorable as Liz Dokken, but when she married Dad, it didn't hurt for her to have a name like Liz Taylor.

When someone would say something about her name, she'd say something like, "It's a catchy name, but the checkout ladies sure look at me funny when I try to write a check at Kmart!" If those checkout ladies did mention it, she'd say, "I look a lot different without my makeup on, don't I!"

Most everything Mom said was accompanied by a big radiant smile. Even her wide grin had a story. "When I was born," she said, "I didn't have a mouth. So Mama just told the doctor to cut me one from here to here, and he thought she said cut one from ear to ear!" So her grin went from ear to ear the rest of her life.

Her mama did give her the doughnut recipe that many people remember her for. I still can taste those doughnuts fresh from the fryer. And I can remember the coffee that accompanied those doughnuts. I even told the church ladies here that if we're having coffee for Mom's afternoon funeral, they ought to start it at 4 a.m., let it boil, drink it down, add a little water, add a lot more coffee and repeat that several times until we all sit down for a cup at 3 p.m. It'd be a shame if we could look through the coffee and see the bottom of the cup today.

She used to tell the story about serving some of that famous coffee to our bachelor friend and neighbor, Carl Eidmann. Carl could be a little blunt at times, and when Mom asked him if he wanted another cup of that fine boiled brew, he said, "No, I don't want anymore more of that sh--!" Mom just smiled, touched him on the shoulder and said, "Now, Carl, I'm sure what you mean to say is, 'Why no thank you Liz, I've had quite enough,'" to which Carl had to smile and say, "Yeah, Liz, I guess that's right!"

She could pick a gallon of Juneberries and bake them into a pie. She could fix a hearty meal for a branding crew. She could catch any horse on the place. Horses that would run circles around Dad or I let her walk right up to them and put her arm around them. Todd Nelson and I went riding and camping in our hills one time, and when we woke up, there our horses were ... gone. But just a little later Mom comes walking up to our camp leading those two horses, chastised us a little and joined us for our best stab at boiled coffee.

She taught me how to set a coyote trap and even catch a couple when I was 12 years old. Before that, she taught me how to shoot a gun. I remember she took me on my first grouse hunt. We were going out to the hayfield with lunch when we spied a few sharptails. I think we shot two or three. We showed 'em to Dad in the field and he asked if they flew very far. Mom said, "Heck, I didn't know they could fly." I guess we did groundball one or two of those birds, but I was only 8 or 9 years old and it was a good confidence builder. Not ordinary things for a mother to do, but she was no ordinary mother.

She was truly excited every time I came home from a deer hunt and the dogs would jump up on the pickup signaling to her that I had one in the back. "Did you save the heart and liver?" she'd always ask. She hunted deer when she was young, even fulfilling her dying mother's wish for venison when Clara's appetite was soured by her own cancer. I'm not admitting anything, although there is a statute of limitation, but that deer may have been shot out of season. And her sister, Sigrid, let her haul that deer home in the trunk of her brand-new car. The last deer she shot wasn't that many years ago, hunting on our Belle Quarter with Alice Rosencrans. Mom claimed she shot it out of self-defense -- it was headed right toward her. And the two older-than-average outdoorswomen then had to figure out how to drag it out of the hills without the advantage of lightening the load by field dressing it. I guess it's hard to drag a deer when you're busy laughing with a friend.

She and Dad gave me lessons on marriage and standup comedy. The two would start with Dad telling someone that when he got married, the first year was the hardest. Then Mom would say, "If I'd have had the money, I'd of left him that first year." To which Dad would reply, "If I'd have known that, I'd have give you the money!"

She encouraged Justin's music. She became Tara's best friend, talking on the phone at least three times a day, so it was especially nice when Minot ceased being a long-distance call in the SRT exchange. She became my biggest fan when I began writing a column. She spawned in me an interest in politics and public policy, and she instilled in me a belief in the power of government to do good things for people. You may have heard that her surgery was on Election Day, and when she came out of her grueling six-hour surgery at Mayo, and another day or so of sedation, she didn't ask the common questions like "where am I" or "what happened," she picked up her pen and wrote on her white board, "who won the election?"

I had coffee with this woman most every day since I was 14 and started drinking that thick, black brew. A few years off for college, a few months for legislative sessions, a few mornings away when I was doing over-the-road sales, but otherwise, every day I was on the ranch, at some time of the day, I was sitting across that old oak table with one of my very favorite people in this world. I'm going to miss her so much. But now she can share a cup with her mama and papa, she can watch "Meet the Press" with Hjordis, she'll probably share a story and a cold one with Reinhart and Ernie. God bless you Mom and Godspeed on your journey to the "green, green grass of home."

Everybody's Bud
My eulogy to Dad
Given at his funeral on June 1, 2010

Here's a futile exercise, try to think of anyone who didn't like Bud. I couldn't come up with a single name of anyone who knew Dad who could say that they didn't like him. Everyone liked Bud. What a good name for someone so likable, Bud. He got his nickname as a little boy because his baby sister, Betty, had trouble saying Marshall. The name stuck. He was a likable little boy, others have told me, and he was never a complainer. Even at the end, when he had a lot he could complain about, he didn't. And like everyone else in his life, soon the nurses in Rugby all liked Bud.

Everyone liked Bud and I always wanted to be like Bud. Easier said than done. There're a few things you need to be like Dad. To be like Dad, you have to like horses and cattle. They weren't just livestock; he took real pleasure in watching the baby calves stick their tail in the air and run for all they're worth. He spoke to little colts like you'd speak to baby grandchildren, scratch them where they couldn't reach to make them feel good. He liked good horses and cattle enough to drive all the way to Belgrade, Mont., to buy a good Hereford bull in days when a lot of ranchers wouldn't drive past Minot for seedstock. He drove 550 miles to Gillette, Wyo., with his pickup and stock rack to buy a registered quarter horse stud in 1956. It took 50 years for him to fess up and tell Mom what he paid for that stud — it was plenty for those days and maybe best he waited 50 years to tell her.

He started his serious learning about horses when he was 11 years old and started spending his summers with Gordon Taylor, his father's cousin, along the Missouri River near Culbertson, Mont. Gordon ran about 500 horses and mules on his place so there were plenty to study. Dad said the first horse he got to ride at Gordon's was a big brown horse named Dick. There wasn't a lot of entertainment on a remote ranch for a kid in those days, so he spent most of his days riding and exploring the ranch. Lots of riding. That Dick horse headed east that fall and swam across the Missouri River, not an easy feat for a horse. Gordon told Dad that "Dick swum the river just to get away from you!" Maybe.

To be like Bud, you have to enjoy your work. Dad liked every job on the ranch, at least every outdoor job. He liked to share his enthusiasm for ranch work with his family. He knew a compliment would propel a kid a long way in getting them to work. He bragged about my post hole digging and called me "Badger" for a while to compliment my prolific digging abilities. No wonder he bought those little oak posts from the Turtle Mountains longer than anyone else. He truly liked to make hay and he loved his days out on the hay meadow. He never bawled us out if we made a mistake, and we made plenty. He'd wave at me every time we passed each other in the field. Him stacking and me bullraking, or each of us pulling a 9-foot mower. Every round or pass we made close to each other, a goofy expression and a wave. Some waves were signals, not greetings. He once waved like heck at Mom to try and keep her out of a boggy spot and getting stuck as she came out with lunch. She got stuck and Dad asked, "didn't you see me waving?" "Yeah, I saw you," Mom said smartly, "I couldn't tell what it meant so I figured you were just drying your fingernail polish!" He waved Justin over to the side of the field while he was mowing once in the summer between college semesters at Concordia. Dad heard something that didn't sound right, flagged him over and asked Justin what that sound was. "I was singing one of my choir pieces," Justin said. "Oh good," Dad said, "I thought there was a bearing going out!" Justin eventually would perform with a symphony choir in Carnegie Hall in New York. No one there thought they heard a bearing going out.

To be like Bud, you have to put more stock in people and relationships than in material things. He always provided well for his family, but he didn't chase a dollar like it was the be all and end all in life. He took time for people, for a visit or a good story, for afternoon lunch in the hay field. You'd never catch him eating on the go like we do today. One of Dad's more famous stories is about the day he pulled his hay crew over for lunch, most surely summer sausage sandwiches and hot, boiled coffee. A neighboring outfit was on the next piece over, lots of equipment, busy as beavers -- they kept on going while the Taylor crew was having lunch, I think they even had the audacity to put up a stack while Dad's crew was drinking coffee. As the story goes, Dad told the crew to "pack 'er up fellas, we're going home." They'd finish their piece after the overzealous crew bordering them finished up and moved out. "We don't have to sit here and put up with that!" A true story, as far as I know.

Another time, a cattle buyer had stopped to look at the yearlings and Dad and him sat down in the yard under the shade of that big cottonwood tree for a cold drink. We had a new puppy playing in the yard, us kids were little and nearly as cute as the puppy, a few horses were grazing across the road. The cattle buyer commented on how nice it was to sit there, like he was surprised. It was no surprise to Dad, "Well, what's not to like?" he smiled. Little kids playing with a puppy, conversation, a cool drink and a shady spot. Nobody even noticed that the house was old, the barn was leaning or that the shop was tiny and spilling out around the edges. I think he'd like us to sit and do some visiting today as well when we get done with this business.

He always was happy with what he had. Once he'd gotten his John Deere 60 with its power steering, he wasn't in need of much else for machinery no matter what everyone else was haying and feeding with. He pretty much completed his ranching career into the 1990s without ever having owned a tractor that fired on more than two cylinders, a shop big enough to pull anything into, a four-wheel-drive pickup, a four-wheeler or a horse trailer. All necessities now, we think. He knew how to get by.

Family, friends and neighbors were important to Dad. He was good to us kids. He wasn't a musician himself, but he had great pride in Justin's music, even drove the family in the old Ford pickup with a load of feed on the back to get through the snow for a concert performance of Justin's one winter in Jamestown. He had that special connection that most daddies and daughters have. Mom said when Tara was little and would give Dad some love and a kiss, he'd tell her, "ohhh, that's worth more than money to me." With a daughter of my own now, I know what he meant. In the last almost 40 years, I had the pleasure of spending more time with Dad than probably anyone else but Mom. On the ranch, every day is "take your kid to work day."

Dad and I worked together a lot, and ranched together after I came home from college, and we did it without much disagreement. To say we were close would be an understatement. He was old enough to be my grandpa, but he was my dad. He was just shy of 49 years old when I was born, so I knew I'd have to watch him age well before my friends and their fathers. But none of us were probably ready for the speed of the decline after Mom died. Dad had his stroke one year and one day after Mom's burial last spring. The days following the stroke were heart-wrenching.

On the morning of the day Dad died, I called the hospital and told the nurse, "Tell Dad I'm saddling a horse to go check the cows and then I'll be in to see him." Although Dad hadn't been responsive for days, they were glad to have something to tell him. I went out and saddled the last horse Dad had gotten on. He was 84 and I helped boost him up on that bay gelding. He was as proud as could be. The saddle I put on that horse was the Fred Mueller saddle that Dad bought with money sent home while he was overseas in World War II. I hadn't ridden that saddle in years, but I wanted to that morning as I thought about Dad. I was riding along a hill that overlooks the ranch and I couldn't help but notice the beauty of the morning. The sky was clear blue, not a cloud in sight. The wind that was blowing 50 mph the day before was now a gentle breeze. The cows were grazing contently on spring's green grass. I said out loud, "it's a good day to die, Dad." And I prayed to God that if he was going to take Dad away from his pain and suffering, to do it then in the perfection of that moment. And God did, almost to the minute of when I asked Him, 25 miles away in Rugby. I wish we could've kept Dad here longer, in good health, but I know he has better days awaiting on the other side. Better days with the woman he's missed since Jan. 17, 2009.

Bud and Liz, you see, aren't two separate words. It's "Budnliz." Like, where you been, Randy? Budnliz's. Who'd you see, Jeff? Budnliz. The first time Dad had been away from Mom for more than a week in 49 years was when she was diagnosed with her cancer and spent 60 days in Rochester and a couple of weeks in Minot. I remember leaving Bismarck to go get Dad in Rugby so he could see Mom again. It was a pretty touching reunion. They held each other and sang together and left no doubts about their feelings for each other. One thing Mom told Dad was, "I'll miss you." She died that night. She won't have to miss him anymore. And Dad won't have to miss her. "Faded Love" is one of the songs Budnliz used to sing together, one of the lyrics say "it was in the springtime that you said goodbye." Dad said goodbye to Mom last spring on the day of her burial, we say goodbye to Dad this spring, but our goodbye is their hello. God bless their reunion.

Fathers, sons and North Dakota
Cultivating the ties that bind on the agrarian landscape
Written for On Second Thought magazine, Autumn 2011

One reality I've resigned myself to is that I'll never get every book read that ought to be read. That's one reason I appreciate book recommendations to help me sift through all that might interest me.

Several years ago, a friend recommended "Iron John," by poet Robert Bly to me. It's subtitled, "A book about men," and, even though I wasn't a father at the time I read it, I was a devoted son. Now that I am a father of two sons and a daughter and have lost my own father to age and Parkinson's, I find myself thinking often of the themes I discovered in "Iron John."

I read a little of everything, and although poetry and mythology aren't regular residents of my literary nightstand, I'm not afraid of them either. I hadn't had a lot of exposure to Robert Bly, and, if you Google him, you'll find a range of opinions on him and his work, but I thank this poet laureate of Minnesota for getting me to think about my father, fatherhood and male mentoring in a new light.

It's an interesting world we live in where a Harvard-educated poet can speak so directly to a North Dakota cattle rancher. We are all connected, though, no matter how we try to divide ourselves, so it shouldn't surprise me. "Mitakuye Oyasin," or "All my relations," as my Lakota friends would say.

Bly uses the story of Iron John, a Grimm fairytale, to voice some opinions on the way male relationships have changed as we've moved from an agrarian- and craft-based culture to an industrial age.

It is rare now for fathers and sons to work alongside each other. More often, a father is someone who leaves early in the morning to go and ply his trade and comes home at night for a few hours or less of family time.

Although North Dakota, by definition, is considered an urban state because the majority of our people live in incorporated cities and towns, most of us still consider it rural and agrarian. As a rancher's boy, I'm a bit of an anomaly to the typical Industrial Age son, and for that I am grateful.

Some of my earliest memories are being outside on the ranch with Dad — feeding cattle, making hay, riding horse, doing chores of one kind or another. Now that Dad is gone, I feel like the luckiest son in the world to have had that "quantity time" with him.

Bly says the father as a living force in the home disappeared when the demands of industry sent him away to work in the factories. The living father force always was present on our ranch.

Bly probably would say our ranching relationship was a little like tribal culture. "Fathers and sons in tribal cultures live in an amused tolerance of each other. The son has a lot to learn, and so the father and son spend hours trying and failing together to make arrowheads or to repair a spear or track a clever animal. When a father and son do spend long hours together, which some fathers and sons still do, we could say that a substance almost like food passes from the older body to the younger."

I certainly received that food, and the teaching, as Dad and I tried and failed in amused tolerance of each other while working cattle and completing all the regular, seasonal tasks on a ranch. Conversely, Bly says, "When a father, absent during the day, returns home at six, his children receive only his temperament, and not his teaching." The act of teaching, he says, sweetens our sometimes harsh and human temperaments.

I've lost track of all the things my father taught me. Some of the lessons are pretty common — how to shut a gate with a double half-hitch or tie a horse to the hitching rail with a bowline knot, how to prime the leathers of a well cylinder beneath a windmill, how to judge when the hay is ready to be stacked or baled. I continue to do these common things so often; they are constant reminders of him that have helped me handle the grief of his loss.

I always knew that my relationship with Dad was special, and different, from many of my friends whose fathers had to leave for work every morning. But Dad was different, too, because he was 48 years old when I was born. It was a little like being raised by a grandfather.

While my friend's fathers were baby boomers, my father was a World War II veteran of the South Pacific. He was a boy who grew up taking on odd jobs to help his family through the Great Depression. Those circumstances shaped him, and, in turn, helped to shape me.

One circumstance that shaped Dad was that he was raised without a father. When Dad was just a year and a half old, his father died from small pox; he was unvaccinated. What's more, in the short span of time between 1921 and 1923, his grandfather also died suddenly from a rupture and his young uncle was killed when he was rammed by a grown steer.

That meant every man on the ranch had been tragically taken within 16 months time, leaving two widows to care for two small boys and a soon-to-be-born baby girl. So my father never knew a father, or had the male presence of his uncle or grandfather in the immediate vicinity.

But he did have his father's cousin from Montana named Gordon, and he would become the father figure in Dad's life. I don't want to overstate the whole male mentoring influence on rearing boys because Dad, one of the truly wonderful people in this world, was first and foremost a product of his mother and grandmother's care and nurturing.

I always described him as a gentleman who was a gentle man, who was caring and thoughtful, who put stock in relationships and knew the importance of helping a neighbor. Those traits were surely influenced by the strong, independent women who raised him and brought the young family through the 1930s.

But there was a need for a man in the young boy's life, and that's where his elder cousin came in. Gordon was a cowboy's cowboy who ranched in the rugged breaks of the Missouri River near Culbertson, Mont. He grazed several hundred horses in the area and made his living trading horses at a time when horses were still a valuable tool on the northern plains.

When Dad was a young boy, he would get on the train and spend entire summers on Gordon's horse ranch, and I think that was his "Iron John" time when he left his mother and discovered the metaphorical wild man in the forest.

Gordon was plenty wild when it came to riding bucking horses and living in rough country, but pretty tame in social ways as Dad said he never saw his male mentor drink, smoke or gamble.

Bly speaks often of the importance of initiation in a boy's development when he leaves his mother, and his father, to be with the wild man. For Dad, I believe he accomplished that when he was 14 years old and he helped Gordon chase 40 horses from Towner to Jamestown, N.D.

It was 1935 and the overland horse chase took several days of camping and herding as one of the two rode horse and the other drove the 1927 Buick coupe with the camping gear. The food was pretty ordinary and Dad always remembered Gordon buying a pail of eggs at a farm along the way. When Dad asked how he was going to keep the eggs from rotting, Gordon built a fire and hard boiled the whole pail. Dad claimed he ate enough hard-boiled eggs for a lifetime on that trip.

Dad spoke often of this grand boyhood adventure, so I know it had a big impact on his development. He was just 14, but he was given a grown man's responsibilities to help chase and sell those horses. Gordon bought him his first hat, boots and saddle. He made him a cowboy and a man.

My male mentoring and initiation with Dad was more of a long and continual process. It was the hundreds of summer sausage sandwiches shared in the hayfield at lunch time. It was the conversations that I took part in, or just listened to, as Dad visited and shared stories with hired help and family friends who helped us put up the hay on our meadow.

It was the visits and the silent time together while we dug post holes and built fence or tamped in a railroad tie for a corner post. He'd be teaching while we were working. This is how you run the fence stretcher, this is how you measure the distance between the top wire and the ground (it is hip height on a tall Taylor), this is how you practice your stoicism when you rip your hand open on the barbed wire and watch the blood trickle onto the ground.

We harnessed teams, saddled horses and broke colts. We branded calves, doctored cattle, chased cows and learned the temperament of animals and the proper temperament for people who work with them.

This all took time, and Robert Bly validated that time for me. There was no shortage of stories for me to share in the eulogy I delivered at Dad's funeral because our time together allowed for the creation of so many. He had given me his time in abundance, and with that "substance almost like food passing from the older body to the younger," I knew that I had been well fed.

But ranches and farms are fewer on our landscape, and there are fewer families with careers that allow them to work side by side.

Yet I believe fathers and sons, male mentors and boys, can make the most of the time we are given. Society will reap the benefit of young men with a sense of direction and the grounding of their fathers and close male role models rather than the skewed male icons of popular culture.

I take a couple of clear messages from "Iron John" as I ponder good fatherhood, and it matters not if you work from a ranch, an office or a factory. First, it's about time and lots of it. If time is limited, don't shortchange the little there is.

I think the time ought to be invested in three areas — the outdoors, working together and teaching. In the fairytale, I believe Iron John is found in the forest, in the outdoors, for a reason. As we continue to move ourselves indoors, it's more and more important for all of us, but especially fathers and sons and male mentors, to get outdoors. The forest, the prairie, the green and living spaces are fertile ground for relationship building and initiation.

North Dakota has a lot to offer for outdoor experiences. Take advantage of it — camp, hunt, fish, hike, bike, learn our history, feel the sun, wind, rain or snow together.

Working together is easier for me as a rancher, but we can find chores and tasks in other settings as well. It could be in the garage or the backyard or at the workbench.

We should be on the lookout for tasks and jobs where we can have long hours of "amused tolerance of each other." I think it's nice to have something to point to at the end of the effort. Stand back and admire the yard fence, listen to the rebuilt motor, appreciate the woodcraft you completed together.

Finally, teaching. It's easy to be harsh after a long and stressful day. The act of teaching makes us think about the words we say and reminds us that there is something to learn, that skills are not automatic but take some coaching from an adult who is forced to keep their temper in check.

We're not teaching calculus here. We're showing how to tie a knot, build a campfire or explain some of the tasks we do when we are away at work.

Take the time to be a dad today, take the time to mentor a boy you know. Bly made me think and gave me some of the key ingredients in his book. It made me appreciate all that I have been given and inspires me to be more giving. All from a poet writing about a fairytale.